Disabling Ableism

Samantha Maxwell

First published in Great Britain in 2024
© Samantha Maxwell 2024

ISBN 9798884781924

Wordworx
Wrexham Enterprise Hub
11-13 Rhosddu Road Wrexham
LL11 1AT

Disabling Ableism

Samantha Maxwell

Prologue

"Disability is part of being human and is integral to the human experience." – [WHO (World Health Organization)]

Disability, in general terms, basically is something that's just a standard part of life, just like how race and awareness of gender stereotyping is today for example. We have come a long way since the Rosa Parks and Emmeline Pankhurst days where things such as, Apartheid and sexist culture unfortunately ruled with an iron fist, and so the 'Votes For Women' movement was introduced for example, to try and combat some of the difficulties women unfortunately faced in the past. Civil rights activist, Rosa Parks, (even though the struggle for race equality continued to be a difficult thing, to say the least at that time,) the important thing was she started the conversation. It was that championing, that pioneering attitude that ultimately made people sit up, listen and take action. Up until those points in time, it was just accepted that women

Prologue

were treated as second class citizens, and people who were from different ethnic backgrounds, didn't have the same rights as others in society.

It's confusing today because we wouldn't dream of excluding anyone regardless of gender or race. We learned the error of our ways with subjects such as these. We find it strange, (and rightly so) that we could have ever have believed in such nonsense. We tell ourselves that those were "different times", and that "people are more accepting of all demographics". Are we really though? Often, we say these things just to look as if times have changed and so have attitudes. We try, (as a society and as a majority,) to stand up against what we feel was wrong in the past. Do we really accept things though? Are we really that forward-thinking? Something tells me sadly that we are not fully, we're getting there, and acceptance has improved greatly since, but something tells me that we still have a fight on our hands to get other demographics in society highlighted. Of course, like with everything, you still get the negative side to the subjects, the backlash, the sexism, the racism, the homophobic language, but these subjects are highlighted so often, so if anything happens as abhorrent as these forms of discrimination, it's called out immediately, and it's almost as if you are shunned by society. So, as a whole, it's showing some amount of progress. However, is that progression genuine or is it just a case of following the crowd? If you are highlighting certain subjects and demographics, then obviously, others will stay in the dark as a consequence. The most 'pressing demographics' seem to have all of the attention, and others such as disability, seems to always be on another level of acceptance. Nothing else has a chance to be highlighted, as those 'pressing demographics' hog all of the attention. It's **always** a difficult thing to have to try and highlight, all of the focus is automatically turned to the 'main demographics', that there doesn't seem much room (if any at all) for any other demographic to be heard. Of course, keeping subjects such as gender and race equality highlighted constantly is vital, after all, if these demographics fall in conversation terms, then other demographics will ultimately be a casualty for inequality. It'll be like a Domino effect, once one demographic goes, they **all** go. Basically, all I'm trying to get across is that other demographics such as disability **could**, and **should** be a part of the conversation and highlighted the **exact** same way as others today. We would see a vast improvement in how the world operates, I feel, if topics such as disability are highlighted in a positive way. That's all we need to be rethought of. Disability generally has this negative undertone to it when you look it up, not only collectively, but separately too, if you are researching a specific disability. There is **very little** positivity on said subject I have personally found. It's a collective with absolutely no individuality whatsoever to any specific disability. I know this from researching for *CP Isn't Me*, and doing further research for this book. Individuality comes from the individuals themselves. A university research paper, dissertation or even a thesis is **never** going to teach you about the **person**. Only the person themselves can do that. University studies sound good and you may think that they are the best tool to obtain information on a 'disabled' person, but those studies really only give you the 'facts', the basics. Where does the person come into it? Their capabilities? Their wants and fears? Their sense of humour? Their personalities? They don't. The **only** way to get that kind of information is to ask the person yourself.Progression is a wonderful thing to have, it allows us to move on, better ourselves, challenge perceptions, it allows us to grow as a human race, physically, emotionally and mentally. Progression allows us to accept things that we found difficult for whatever reason to accept in the past.

Progression only happens though if we allow ourselves to progress, saying and doing are two completely different things. Actions speak louder than words. Even though things have changed for the better significantly since those days where sexism and racism ran rampant, there still seems to be a divide happening between another demographic in society, disability. I truly believe that disability has gone unnoticed for so long because simply, nobody is willing to have the conversation, as I think that people somehow find having a conversation on disability awkward. I can understand that trying to start a conversation on disability or having a conversation with a 'disabled' person maybe a little uncomfortable, especially if you don't know how to begin a

Prologue

conversation of this nature,   without fear of offending, but ignoring it will ultimately make social acceptance worse. We need to stop being scared of asking, we should embrace inquisitiveness. This would be so refreshing and modern to reflect this 'forward-thinking' culture we like to believe we've become.

Disability, for the most part is just an extension of the challenges we used to face, it has somehow managed to become the replacement target for the level of scrutiny, and the most frightening thing is, nobody sees a problem with how disability is treated. I feel that I have a perfect analogy for this, but I will cover this later. What I will say for now is that I feel that there seems to be this total ignorance of the discrimination, which is often at the hands of the general public. Again, nobody saw a problem with racism and sexism, but, a change did develop in attitudes when the activism for these demographics took place. Why shouldn't disability be allowed in that activist mix for change? Why are we **always** treated as second class citizens? After all, we are **supposed** to be living in a democracy, aren't we? We are human beings just like the rest of society. I think that it's now time for action, the discrimination against disability has gone on for far too long.

Something **desperately** needs to change.

Chapter 1

Introduction

I want you to imagine a 'disabled' person now in your mind. Close your eyes and just imagine that 'disabled' person. No seriously. How do they look?

Now, I want you to imagine you going up and interacting with that 'disabled' person. Again, seriously, this is to try and prove a point. How do you act?

It's a bit strange that I asked you to do that right? You weren't expecting something as interrogating as that when you opened this did you? The thing is, there are certain things that people associate with disability. A wheelchair, a cane, hearing aids, etc. These are the international, and socially acceptable symbols of disability. We can identify disability if those symbols are there. It's through no fault of our own. I mean the main symbol for disability is a person sitting in a wheelchair. It's been culturally ingrained and accepted that these symbols are what disability represents. What

Introduction

people often fail to realise is that these symbols are discriminatory in themselves, in so many ways. Not every 'disabled' person uses a wheelchair for example. By using these symbols, people are just spreading the false narrative that disability is just one thing. In reality, disability is many things, but people who happen to have a disability, should **never** be treated any differently from the next person. A **person** often tends to get lost amongst all of the obsession around their disability. We are 'things' that need to be 'looked after', our **human rights** are automatically taken from us because disability is seen and treated as it has this unfounded, unfair, yet infamous reputation for being reliant on others. These beliefs are so extremely outdated and offensive that it would be absolutely horrifying to another person on the receiving end of such abhorrent behaviour.

This is exactly what I intend to argue in this book. I now feel that it's necessary to look at disability in general society but in a more in-depth way than before. For those of you who have read the first book, CP Isn't Me, I want you to know that this isn't going to be CP Isn't Me Part Two, because even though I know the importance of it, and how much it's needed for today's world to read, learn and understand, I also know that writing more of the same is ultimately boring. CP Isn't Me is just one person's story, my story. Like I said, this is a good starting point, but not everyone has had the same experiences as me. Everyone is individual. CP Isn't Me is really a gateway, a gateway into a topic that people often find it so difficult to talk about. This is why, to really hammer it home, to hopefully make the desired impact, I need to go a little further. This is why with this book I intend to dig a bit deeper than before, and actually ask the public for their opinions on disability, along with asking the Government what they think about the treatment of disability as a whole and whether things need to improve. This is the next logical step in my opinion. We need to keep the conversation going if we want to see any **real** chance of change. As they say, "Rome wasn't built in a day". There are still undertones of problems with racism and sexism even today, even with this new found accepting attitude, so you can only imagine the level of discrimination that 'disabled' people face on a daily basis with very little awareness. It would be so easy for me to now say,

Introduction

right, I've written *CP Isn't Me*, job done, now the change will happen. Unfortunately, no. I'd be ignorant and naive to believe that, even though I'd so desperately like, need and want to, unless I continue to build up a case for better treatment of disability, then nothing will change. It's like anything, take a car for example, if you have just enough fuel to get somewhere, but don't have any for the journey back, and there's nowhere to go to buy more fuel, then what was the point of starting the journey in the first place if you didn't plan ahead and buy fuel to get you from point A to point B and back again?

Exactly the same reasoning behind this second book, unless I continue to campaign for disability rights, disability awareness will ultimately just fall off the radar and 'disabled' people won't be any better off.

Since writing, I've come across people who believe I've changed in personality, that I somehow think I'm better than everyone else in society, now I'm an author. I'm not better than anyone at all. I'm still me, Sam, or 'Sammy' as my friends call me. I haven't lost who I am, and I

never will. That's a promise. For people to think this of me, hurts me in a way, as I've gone through literal Hell before writing, and even during writing (especially the first book) as I'm having to relive absolutely everything from my past, but I'm doing it for a very specific reason, to try and raise awareness of disability discrimination for others in the same position as me. Yes, these books are also helping me to deal with the negativity that I have faced from my past admittedly, these books are just like my diary, but the only difference is that my 'diary' is published for everyone to see, but I'm personally proud of that, as the books hopefully will show how difficult it is to be accepted, if you just so happen to have a disability of some form, and hopefully do something, (however small) to try and put an end to disability discrimination fully. To counteract this though, other people have said that I seem so much better in myself now, compared to a few years ago. That I'm much more confident and outspoken, which admittedly I am, and I'm happy to know that others can see the positive change in me. It was writing 'CP Isn't Me' that changed me. It was as if a literal light bulb suddenly came on

Introduction

when I wrote the book, that book gave me a reason to live really, an understanding of myself, and because of that book, I'm now writing a second.

People can say what they want, I absolutely get it, not everyone is going to support you in your endeavours, but I hope that these books do something to start a long overdue, pressing discussion. Just a quick side note, to anyone and everyone who doubts my authenticity and focus and prefer to call me out on something that I'm not, I'd much rather be where I am today, living a life of purpose and determination, than to ever go back to my depressive, defeatist period, where everything just seemed too much to handle. Call me whatever you want, it really doesn't bother me anymore, there was a time that any negativity would affect me badly, not now though. If you wanted to cause me any depression, you're about three or four years too late. I'm happy, and I'm fighting for disability equality. That is all that matters.

I'm not claiming that my books are here to change the world, not at all. Nor am I claiming that I'm the next Rosa Parks or Emmeline Pankhurst, far from it. No, I'm just a 'disabled' woman in her early thirties who knows what it's like to be discriminated against and want to raise awareness of it. By keeping the conversation going on disability awareness, there is a small chance of making disability discrimination a thing of the past.

I'm tired of all of the setbacks that come with having a disability. Trying to justify your worth to someone who knows nothing about you. It's just wrong. This is why I'm writing this, not for the glory, but to try and do a little bit to help raise awareness of the issues 'disabled' people face constantly.

Every single thing out there written on the subject of disability is designed to be used in a negative sense. It's just sensationalism, designed to harbour further segregation. People with a disability are less able to do this or that, or they're more prone to disease or infection that can have a greater negative impact on a 'disabled' person's physical and/or mental health. It doesn't seem to matter if a 'disabled' person is capable or not, as long as

Introduction

it's out there saying that we cannot do something, that is sadly the overall majority vote. It's universally accepted without question. Nobody seems to realise or even care about how their treatment of disability can affect a person so greatly.

Likewise, it can also go to the other end of the spectrum, by acknowledging the 'normal' things a 'disabled' person can do, but over exaggerating it and building it up to be this wonderful and incredible thing. There's no happy medium. People either go one way or the other and never realise that their actions have an affect. There is a word for that, patronisation.

As I say in *'CP Isn't Me'*, I'm proud of who I am, but I don't dwell on the fact that I'm 'disabled', I don't need to, I have a mild physical disability, it's quite obvious that I am 'disabled' with my wheelchair, so why should everyone else in society feel the need to dwell, on not only mine, but other people's behalf? It's not anyone else's business how anyone lives their lives. It's solely the person who is considered 'disabled' to choose how to live **their** life. Nothing should ever be decided for us. If capable, we can choose to live how we want. At the end of the day, absolutely **everyone** has a right and the entitlement to a 'normal' life, whatever that means.

This time, this book is going to focus on disability in general society, so that means involving more public views on the subject of disability, to hopefully get a better understanding of how disability is seen by people. This isn't just going to be my own personal opinions this time around. No, to get a clearer picture of the situation, I have widened my research with the help of surveys that I personally wrote and advertised in preparation of writing this book, and I have even been lucky enough to have some people who were willing to help from both the Welsh and Scottish Governments alike, including Lesley Griffiths, Member of the Senedd for Wrexham, of which I am truly thankful for. I have articles from ex journalists turned politicians who wrote on the subject of disability, *Cerebral Palsy Cymru, The National Bobath Cerebral Palsy Centre*, companies who specialise specifically in disability and disability equipment from America and Australia alike, alongside *Scouts UK*, and I have

Introduction

been granted permission to use quotes from the articles as and when needed. I am truly honoured also to have been granted permission from the *House of Commons* to use their Library, which specifically is only to be used by MPs and staff of the *House of Commons* alike. I am also truly honoured and grateful to have been granted an interview with Kerry Evans, the Disability Liaison Officer at Wrexham AFC. She has given me permission to use the information she has provided in this book. For Kerry Evans' comments, I will paraphrase, as mum took down notes of what she said, that I then typed up for her approval. Everything paraphrased is exactly as she approved and edited herself, nothing has been reworked or adapted in anyway. She has given me permission to quote her at the end of every single paraphrase that I use. Disability trainer, speaker and author, Aideen Blackborough, of '*Does It Wet The Bed?*' has also agreed to take part and has kindly answered questions for the book. I'm so pleased to have her on board as she has a form of Cerebral Palsy too. I wanted both Kerry Evans and Aideen Blackborough to be involved as it will hopefully show the difference between all disabilities and hopefully give society a greater understanding of disabilities, and also both Kerry and Aideen have Cerebral Palsy, however their forms are **different**. It was important to me that this is purposely done, to make people realise the **difference** between all disabilities, so that disability won't fall under the same umbrella. Of course, any other quotes I use, I will credit and embolden them for emphasis. I also have people involved with autism, long COVID, fibromyalgia, Myalgic Encephalomyelitis (ME), Duchenne Muscular Dystrophy (DMD), barristers who specialise specifically in the field of disability. Downs Syndrome, an amputee who is a 'disabled' actor, and a young woman who has a form of Cerebral Palsy who is a sailor, to name but a few. The majority of participants are happy to provide their name, however they were given the choice to remain anonymous, if so desired. So I will quote others as anonymous who requested anonymity. I will define each condition as each participant's quote is used.

If you are willing to continue the fight for disability equality, turn the page. Change starts with you.

Chapter 2
What is Ableism?

You may have noticed that the title of this book is *'Disabling Ableism'*. To be honest, (and I'm ashamed to say this) but I have never come across the terms 'ableism' or 'ableist' in my life. I didn't know that there were actual terms for the discrimination of disability, but really, why wouldn't there be? I mean it's obvious when you think about it. If it's a form of discrimination towards a demographic, then yes, there would be a term. I guess I didn't know about the terms because simply, I honestly thought that people didn't really think that there was a problem with the treatment of disability. There must be an acknowledgement of it though for terms such as 'ableism' and 'ableist' to even exist.

"Ableism is discrimination in favour of non-disabled people." – [Scope]

It's basically a version of racism, sexism, or homophobia for the 'disabled' from what I have read. Today, we are very careful not to say the wrong thing in modern, socially acceptable culture. People get called out for having and expressing negative views on the above, but it seems to me that as long as the negativity goes under the radar, it's perfectly fine to treat 'disabled' people so disrespectfully. I can say this, because of my past experiences trying to fight for equality in my life, and constantly being knocked down by the people who think they had power over me, because they thought that I was 'vulnerable'. The reason for this drastic change in attitude towards these things is simple. All of them have movements, *'Black Lives Matter'*, *'Me Too'*, and *'Pride'* are the reasons why I think there has been a drastic change, actually I know that's why attitudes have changed. There are terms for these things. They are categorised. It's in media everyday, I mean black history is now being taught in schools as a direct result of the *'Black Lives Matter'* movement. We know what is right and wrong now with these things and we have automatically become somewhat more accepting of these things as a result. I say somewhat because of course, things like racism, sexism or homophobia for example does still happen, it's

What is Ableism?

not a perfect world unfortunately, but thanks to the coverage and movements, most parts of society seem to have distain for those who still have beliefs that are out of date. For disability however, people don't seem to think that there's a problem when someone unknowingly offends a 'disabled' person. Another thing to think about is if you identify yourself with one of tgese movements (if not all), and you have a disability, where's the representation? Only half of you is being recognised. You are you, not your movements, the movements were created in order to highlight different demographics, 'normalising' them in a way. My argument is that if you identify yourself with these movements, but disability isn't in that representation, what's the point? Only half of you is being recognised and accepted. Basically, and I'm not just saying this for effect, I truly and honestly believe that disability is so far removed from society. There's an invisible wall that has been built to exclude disability from 'normality'.

There's even another term, 'disablism', that I've discovered through research from *Scope*, that basically serves as another type of discrimination towards disability, but with a small difference, which focuses more on favouring discrimination towards disability.

"Disablism emphasises discrimination against disabled people." – [Scope]

There's a **slight** difference between the two terms, but whichever way you want to look at it, it's **all** a form of discrimination towards disability. That's the fact. Disablism is just an extension of ableism and ableist attitudes, it just puts greater focus on those attitudes, which of course, isn't right at all. There's absolutely no hiding from that, no matter how much society likes to distance themselves away from it and pretend or play the blame game by pointing the finger. I do understand that nobody in the entire world is going to be PC all of the time, that's impossible, but there does need to be an improvement in how disability is treated all across the world. Disability cannot continue to be this alien concept, where people are either scared of it, or intrigued by it. Disability is part of humanity, why do we still have these thoughts that disability equals vulnerability? Stupidity? Weakness? Inability? Those thoughts belong in

What is Ableism?

the past. As of writing, it is twenty-twenty-three, and we still   continue to see this unjustified and unfair assumption that disability means vulnerability and therefore disrespect? At the end of the day, that is all it is, disrespect and just utterly vile. Everything else is getting a fair hearing nowadays. It's **definitely** the best time for disability to take part in this revolution. We shouldn't have assumptions without any proper rhyme or reason to believe it.

Disability Pride and Disability Pride Month

I was recently told by *Cerebral Palsy Cymru,* (formally the *Bobath Centre* in Cardiff), who so very kindly stocked and publicised *CP Isn't Me*, as well as helping me with my skills as a child, to make sure that I had somewhat of an independent lifestyle as I grew up, said to me that July, is *Disability Pride Month*. Something sadly I never knew existed, neither did the overall majority of participants I asked on my social media platforms and surveys. Why is this? If *Disability Pride Month* is an annual event, shouldn't it have more exposure than it does? A lot of people are unaware of *Disability Pride* from my own research.

It doesn't get the coverage it so wholeheartedly deserves. It's a perfect way to introduce all forms of disability in one big event; and in a fun and positive atmosphere. How is this event supposed to make waves if it's still stuck in the shallow end of the 'disability pool'?

"The month-long celebration originated in America and is now celebrated in many countries. It is a way of celebrating diversity and difference among the disabled community and highlighting ways to better understand and support colleagues in our workplace." – [Local Government Association]

This description of the annual event sounds wonderful. Yes, *Disability Pride* exists, but the majority of people who I asked, (both able-bodied people and 'disabled' people) said that they had never heard of *Disability Pride Month* before. This is sad, and unacceptable in my own opinion. Only a handful of people who I asked on social media and surveys had heard of *Disability Pride.* This is absolutely shocking. For only a minority of 'disabled' people to have heard about the event, is heart-breaking. The barriers that society

29

What is Ableism?

inevitably places upon disability, I wholeheartedly believe, is the reason why *Disability Pride Month* doesn't have the same level of exposure as *Pride,* if any at all. It's that fear of offending that just puts a halt on any potential celebrations of disability in my opinion. Burying your head in the sand **won't** make the topic of disability go away. Disability will **never** leave. The sooner society accepts this, the better. People were uncomfortable with the idea of *Pride* years ago.

This is what makes me question the authenticity of the world, and where disability is categorised, if at all? How can a world claim to be more forward-thinking, yet be so backwards on certain areas of life? How can a world pick and choose what they want to highlight? That isn't a democracy. A democracy is every single person regardless of ability, sex, religion, race etc. having the chance to have the same rights and opportunities as everyone else. Do you know that there are days and months throughout the year that highlight specific disabilities, such as the sixth of October is *World Cerebral Palsy Awareness Day*? Or that, *World Cerebral Palsy Awareness Month* is in March?

This is **exactly** what society needs. **Proper** education on these extremely important topics. I do think that *Disability Pride*, isn't as well-known as the *Local Government Association* would have you believe. I personally feel it isn't as well publicised because of the 'Disability' label in front of it. *Pride* doesn't have a label in front, and yet, everybody is aware of *Pride*, and it is celebrated. Why shouldn't *Disability Pride* be treated exactly the same (popularity wise) as *Pride* itself? You are just swapping one demographic for another after all. It doesn't seem fair that just because something has a distinctive word in front of something that is already acceptable, that it doesn't have the same level of exposure as the original. It does make me wonder if whether *Pride* had the specific term added, whether it would remain as accepted as it currently is?

Something desperately needs to be done here to improve disability relations. By ignoring something such as *Disability Pride*, you are being offensive, and discriminative.

On the other hand, people can have a disability of some form **and** be attracted to the same sex. So

What is Ableism?

how is **this** fair that people are segregated and put into a certain 'group'? What happened to diversity? Why does a person **always** have to fit into **one** category? People should be allowed to express who they are **fully**, without any fear of further, potential discrimination. Nothing makes sense.

I have come across those who confused *Disability Pride* with *Pride*. You may ask why? The two events are different after all. One has the word 'Disability' in front of it and the other doesn't. This though, in my view, just goes to show that society needs to know more about *Disability Pride* to understand fully what it actually is, and what it actually **means**.

Disabled model and Co Support Leader, Kirsty Taylor said:

"...it's awesome! Gives us more of a platform to post about any issues about disability (accessibility, ableism, and general disability awareness). My 2 cents to start thinking of ideas now, you can post because it's a good opportunity to educate people on what we deal

with" – [Kirsty Taylor, disabled model and Co Support Leader]

There should be more knowledge of *Disability Pride Month* if Kirsty's description is anything to go by.

I can also testament to how absolutely incredible *Disability Pride Month* is, as since writing about it, I actually attended my first *Disability Pride* event in Chester. It was absolutely amazing to be apart of, there was absolutely no hostility or discrimination whatsoever. Able-bodied people celebrated **alongside** 'disabled' people, the diversities. It felt as if the barriers were **finally** broken down, that acceptance washed over the city. There was absolutely no judgment whatsoever, just love, support and pride! I just wish that the atmosphere then, lasted forever. That would be absolutely incredible! Cheers, applause, smiles, encouragement, that was the day! No discrimination. No labelling. Nothing. Just an abundance of love, respect and acceptance. I am ever so pleased to have been apart of it! It **needs more advertising and exposure**!

What is Ableism?

It is interesting though as to why it's not well-known, especially with able-bodied people, as my own personal research has unfortunately shown. Many able-bodied people I asked about *Disability Pride Month* sadly admitted that they didn't know about it, or if even such a thing existed. Why? Simply because it isn't as well publicised as movements such as *Pride*. *Pride* was scrutinised in the past yes, but with the help of campaigning and canvassing in favour of it, *Pride* became a culturally accepted event. *Disability Pride* hasn't sadly had that same level of exposure. It plays into the psychological aspect of the mind and how the world perceives different things, if a certain familiar word is inserted into a phrase we know so well, but becomes almost alien when two familiar words are put together. I'm not a psychologist. I just find it interesting. There was **a lot** of backlash from certain people on social media when I first posed the question of if anyone has ever heard of *Disability Pride Month* before. A lot of people just went straight to the *Pride* version, not about the actual question that I was originally asking.

"I think the thing I take away from the negativity, is how certain disabled community

members can't see how closely related ethnicity, gay, gender, and disabled people's rights are interlinked. I class myself as an intersectional activist, so that means any marginalised group gets my support for equality and access. I think some people can't see that people don't choose their sexuality and of course think it's a lifestyle, but when you suggest they choose to be disabled it's a head scratcher, or outburst of anger at the accusation because of course, non of us choose to be disabled. I could go on for ages." – *[Elle Williams, social media participant]*

This is an extremely good point. I think people get defensive and protective when conversations that affect people are brought to light. It's human nature really.

According to the *Citizens Advice* website:

"It is against the law to discriminate against disabled people in various areas of their lives." – *[Citizens Advice]*

However, the ironic thing is, the same website says that it isn't against the law to discriminate

What is Ableism?

against disability in some areas including having the right to public transport services. It's funny to me that it's illegal to discriminate disability in general society with work etc. but it isn't illegal in other areas? That **is** counterintuitive and an awful fact to accept for me personally. Having a rule for a specific area of life, and not for the other, what is the point? I'll tell you, there's absolutely no point at all. It's like checking everything is safe before you go away on holiday and just leaving the door open anyway. Accessibility must be a part of everyday life in **all areas**, and this includes, (but not limited to) public transportation for wheelchair users, and other disability demographics. Public transportation should be accessible to all, regardless of ability.

"We need to make every single thing accessible to every single person with a disability." – *[Stevie Wonder]*

It is utterly ridiculous to say this in the twenty-first century, with all of the acceptance society likes to promote today. Really, discrimination has never really been eradicated, it's just been covered with this sickly-sweet false idea of acceptance. I do wonder why this is? Why people have adopted this offended attitude, when it is worse than ever deep down?

I asked Deborah Bayley, the mother of a 'severely disabled' person, whether she feels her son, Ashley, who has a severe learning disability, Hydrocephalus, Flaccid Cerebral Palsy with Autistic tendencies, alongside Ashley being sight and hearing impaired, has ever been discriminated against?

"It greatly depends on the environment at the time. When allowances need to be considered due to a situation, they're not. But on the flip side, when there is no need to treat him differently, he is...Occasionally he has, [been discriminated against]. Thankfully Ashley doesn't realise when this has happened. It makes me feel that he isn't as important as everyone else, isn't relevant so shouldn't be given a second thought." – [Deborah Bayley, social media participant, mum and daughter]

This right here is the issue why I felt the need to write, encapsulated in this one sentence. There needs to be a dialogue open that teaches society

What is Ableism?

how to treat disability properly. When to assist, and when not. Yes, all disabilities are different, but the way the person behind the disability is treated **shouldn't be any different**. This is sadly the treatment 'disabled' people expect constantly, day in, day out. There's no respite from the ridiculous treatment. You wouldn't like to have your every move closely monitored, in case you may need help, but because of the disability label forced upon those who have some form of disability, mild, moderate or severe, it doesn't matter, as long as that label is there, people with a disability have no hope to live a life. We're just really slaves to that term, we have to act and match up to expectations of what disability represents online, instead of what it actually represents and means.

Accepting modern culture today just seems to be a popular thing, nobody actually believes in equality in my opinion, they are just going with the crowd. There isn't actually any substance to the acceptance. That, in my view, is worse than having no equality at all. Pretending to accept equality just gives people permission to act as if they're moral, with no actual attempt to do so.

"Part of the problem is that we tend to think that equality is about treating everyone the same, when it's not. It's about fairness. It's about equity of access." – [Judith Heumann]

I do think this is why society seems just to entertain the idea of equality. It is wrongly believed that equality is basically just treating everyone the same, like carbon copies of each other, and although part of this is true, opportunity, accessibility and acceptance wise, but equality is so much more than that. Everyone in life is different, equality actually means providing the same level of opportunities, accessibility for all, despite differences.

"...I have especially faced discrimination around employment. For a long time I really struggled to find a job that was right for me and get the right support. For example, on my very first day at my job in a leisure centre, I was left on my own to deal with lots of customers trying to buy tickets. I was rushed and faced with a lot of jargon and big words, and when I raised this with my management I was told to leave. This made me really angry because they could have

at least tried to give me support. Another example was when I worked in a library. Again, I was faced with a situation where I was out in a role with no support and had to figure out what to do on my own. My spelling isn't great, so when I had to go and do some shelving I found putting things in alphabetical order very difficult. Working on the counter with customers and using a till was really hard as well, just as it was in the leisure centre. Once again, I was let go rather than accommodated."
– [Ciara Lawrence, ambassador, MENCAP]

I don't think that I have to explain my own experiences with disability and employment again, as I've already explained almost everything in *CP Isn't Me.* I have also explained in this book, my last negative employment experience during the COVID-19 pandemic. It just proves though that disability isn't treated fairly, yes in the broad sense of the word, but also specifically in terms of employment. In my case, it was due to being uncomfortable with the idea of disability, and not truly understanding disability and automatically dismissing me outright. Ciara Lawrence seems to have experienced the same level of negativity in employment, albeit, different circumstances, but the outcome was ultimately the same as mine, and I suspect that it's the case for many other people with disabilities. I like to think not, but it's highly likely to assume that this lack of understanding of disability is experienced unfortunately across the UK, if not the globe.

Giving people a lot of responsibility on your first day of a job can be daunting at the best of times, regardless of ability. Why would **anyone** give a new 'disabled' employee that amount of responsibility, especially if they have a disability as Ciara's employers did? There's absolutely no acceptable reason why Ciara was let go from her job, just because she raised the matter. You maybe thinking to yourself that giving a new employee a lot of responsibility on their first day, especially if said employee has a disability of some form, shows trust by the employer, but what you, and society in general must take into consideration is that someone's disability may make it a bit more difficult to do a copious amount of work. Nerves get the better of everyone in that type of situation anyway, so adding a disability into that mix, is just plain cruel.

41

What is Ableism?

I can't speak for everyone, I'm just going by my experience when I say this, but why I don't think 'disabled' employees don't raise this issue with the management of their employment, is simply because of the potential outcome of being let go if we do, as was the case of Ciara **twice**. It is a terrifying prospect to lose a job if you're lucky enough to get one, especially if you have a disability of some form. I can imagine that 'disabled' employees are just trying to cope in their job, just to potentially stop any unfair dismissal. It's sad and frustrating that we have to really, 'put up or shut up' in every single aspect of life, in case we are then dropped like flies with the lame excuse of our disability overshadowing our work performance, and destined to just exist rather than live.

When you have a disability of some form, it does seem that employers are so quick to blame a disability as to why the employee cannot do their job, nothing to do with any lack of training for the job in question. Employers just search for excuses and reasons to fire 'disabled' employees it seems, without publicly saying the disability is the barrier. It's absolutely fine if a person's work ethic isn't to the standard of a company, you can justify being fired if it's that reason alone, but when disability is in the mix, unfortunately there does seem to be a hidden agenda with employers to blacklist 'disabled' employees.

"Recognizing and respecting differences in others, and treating everyone like you want them to treat you, will help make our world a better place for everyone. Care... be your best. You don't have to be handicapped to be different. Everyone is different!" – [Kim Peek]

This is my argument, equality shouldn't just be segregated to one demographic in society, equality should be available for everyone. The differences don't make the person, it's the **person** that makes the person. The little differences people have, should never be an issue to debate on who deserves equality more. Equality is a basic human right. It's the barriers that ultimately stop any potential equality progression from happening. No more so than if you have a disability of some form.

"...people are disabled by barriers in society, not by their impairment or difference. Barriers

What is Ableism?

can be physical, like buildings not having accessible toilets. Or they can be caused by people's attitudes to difference, like assuming disabled people can't do certain things." – [Scope]

This is **exactly** what I mean, society seems to think it's acceptable to build barriers, either physical by creating inaccessible buildings, or metaphorical, by attitudes.

In an ideal world, no discrimination would exist towards anything or anyone, it sounds like a very naive way to think, but I personally feel that the world would be better off that way.

"Imagine all the people, Livin' life in peace" – [John Lennon 'Imagine' (1971)]

The amount of hatred and misunderstanding in the world, especially today, is unbelievable. Religion, gender equality, sexual orientation and race, still all come under fire, but at least there are conversations happening on these topics, years too late in my own opinion, but at least something is happening to try and combat the attitudes and break the stigma with these subjects that were scrutinised in the past. Disability still doesn't get any respect it seems.

Recently, one of my social media participants and Specialist Information Officer and Programme Lead at *Scope*, Richard Luke, posted an article from a certain media outlet who was reviewing a certain movie. Richard rightly called out the despicable ableist language within the review. I'm assuming, (possibly naively), that the media outlet in question never realised their mistake, that it was written unintentionally. This **is** the problem though, unless we call out ableism when we see it, the issue will ultimately snowball, until it becomes sadly uncontrollable.

In case you were wondering, the ableist language in question was the devastating term, 'spastic'. I refuse to use this abhorrent word again in this book, as I don't want to showcase any ableist language. I've used it once for context.

"Huge thanks to [online movie reviewer] and [newspaper] for this totally unnecessary use of an ableist slur. Great work! By the way, the 1970s want its journalists back." – [Tweet by

What is Ableism?

Richard Luke, Specialist Information Officer and Programme Lead, Scope]

Definition of the Specific Ableist Word

"A word, which was used by doctors in the past but which is now extremely offensive, used to describe a person who has cerebral palsy (= a condition of the body that makes it difficult to control the muscles), or to describe things related to or typical of the condition. – [Cambridge Dictionary]

To describe a **movie** using this offensive term, is absolutely abhorrent. I personally do take offence at this, having a mild form of Cerebral Palsy myself.

The term is outdated, irrelevant and unjustified. This **is** the problem though, society recognises racial, homophobic and sexist terms and slurs, but ableist? Not so much, if at all.

I mean, we have come a long way since the eighteen hundreds where if you had a disability of some form, (especially mentally), you were automatically, and wrongly labelled as "insane" and committed to asylums, more often than not:

"Due to financial constraints or the inability to provide for their relatives properly, families often struggled to care privately for their relatives deemed "insane" or with physical disabilities. When families could not cope with care, these individuals became wards of the state. By the 1800s, inmate numbers swelled." – [Disability History: Early and Shifting Attitudes of Treatment, NPS.org]

Given the lack of knowledge at that time of disabilities, financial constraints and just maybe being unable to care for their loved one, I can somewhat understand why, but that **isn't** to say that I agree with the methods, not at all. There is no excuse whatsoever in my mind for the mistreatment of disability, even if it was the eighteen hundreds, having asylums overcrowded by a number of 'disabled' people is still inhumane. Yes, lack of education **definitely** played a part in this mistreatment, nobody knew how to approach disability. Disability was treated by society back then as this alien concept. Sound familiar?

Today though, we know so much about disabilities and diversities, the information is out there,

What is Ableism?

however, we do tend to still reinforce the notion of disability being this 'alien concept'. Why? We don't know how to handle the topic. We are scared to interact with 'disabled' people, for a perpetuating fear of offending just like a certain movie that I just mentioned.

The difference is, the movie review was deliberate, maybe not deliberate in the sense to cause discrimination, but deliberate in the sense of using an outdated, offensive term, to review something as insignificant as a movie. Basically I think just to capture attention.

The majority of society don't actually intend to offend. This is what needs to be realised. As long as there isn't any malice, or intension behind a comment, just a genuine unintentional term, of which they are willing to rectify, if and when called out on, then it isn't as bad as someone **intentionally** using a term to either cause malice, describe someone or something, (in this case, a movie). I guess this runs a bit deeper as an offensive term/slur was used to describe something as irrelevant as a **movie** of all things, and that review is out there for **all to see**. This for me, just goes to prove that ableism does exist, whether we like to believe it or not, as long as there are people out there who are prepared to write outdated and offensive terms and slurs, then society will continue to be outdated and offensive, however much society likes to promote inclusion, as long as these terms and slurs are still in circulation, society **will never** change.

What we need now is to break the stigma and discuss the problem with disability, not shy away from it, but face it head on. I really do want and need to ask, what is the problem with disability? Even though *Citizens Advice* claims that it's illegal to discriminate against disability, people don't seem to be getting that message. Every other subject is being highlighted, so why can't disability have the same level of exposure? It's only right and fair.

What I'm having trouble understanding is the amount of able-bodied people who said they know the term 'ableism' from my own survey research, but somehow still use discriminative language and actions towards 'disabled' people on a daily basis, almost without realising it

49

What is Ableism?

themselves. It's bewildering to me to be honest, people are either unaware of the treatment they thrust upon others, or they know, but don't care. I don't know which is worse. Both ways are ignorant, but if it is the former, I can somewhat understand it, I don't agree with it, but I maybe can accept that there's no realisation there, it's a better theory in my mind than just being ignorant, and knowing full well the issues their attitudes and actions cause.

I recently had the honour of speaking to Jennifer Bergmann, actor, writer and aspiring director. She kindly told me a little about herself which she has allowed me to quote:

"I am an actor, writer, and aspiring director. In 2009, when I was 38 years old, I developed a neurological autoimmune illness called Bickerstaff Brainstem Encephalitis (a variant of GBS) after a series of vaccines. I was placed in a medically induced coma for 6 weeks and hospitalized for 18 months, then spent 2 years in rehab. As a result of the illness and long-term hospitalization, I have an Acquired Brain Injury, limited range of motion in my joints, and I am

an ambulatory power wheelchair user. 50% of what makes me disabled is the physical impairments that prevent me from fully functioning as the human body is designed, as well as my own residual internalized ableism. The other 50% is the external world, where lack of accessibility and ableist systems and perspectives prevent me from fully functioning as an average citizen." – [Jennifer Bergmann, actor, writer and aspiring director]

Jennifer speaks the truth here. Truth which society either likes to hide, or cannot understand the signs of ableism. Jennifer talks about her own internalised ableism, for a **long** time, I can now say that I developed my own version of internalised ableism. Of course I didn't know about the terms ableism and ableist when it was happening, I just continued down this very dark path of loathing and self-destruction and I started to despise myself, and my disability. I often would look in the mirror at this person staring back, and begin to verbally abuse myself (and admittedly, sometimes physically). I helped to pick apart what little confidence I had. I was my own worst enemy. Am I proud of that behaviour? No, absolutely not,

What is Ableism?

it was incredibly dangerous, both on a mental, **and** a physical level, and all that I am just going to say is, if you are doing this, or even for some reason thinking about harming yourself in some way, be it mentally or physically, **please don't**. There are better, more practical ways to deal with your issues, people love you, please don't go down that dark path, it is dangerous in more ways than one. You are only mirroring what society says. They don't know you, the real you, the you, that despite everything, there are those moments of laughter, your sense of humour, your kindness, your selflessness, your dreams. People can say what they want, but you are you. Try as they might, either intentionally or unintentionally, they cannot destroy you really. You know why? You **won't** let them. Words are just that, words. Yes, they may hurt in the moment, but they have absolutely no bearing on who you are as a **person**. You have that power to turn that hurt into determination and defiance. If I can do it, believe me, so can you.

Jennifer's experience is fifty-fifty. You may be thinking, what's the problem? People expect issues when it comes to disability. The word alone has negative connotations to it, regardless of what it actually means to be 'disabled'. After all, it's just how we've been programmed.

Actor, Paul Wild said:

"I was invisibly disabled with leg issues until my amputation in 2018, the difference in people's perception is stark. I was more crippled with the gammy leg than I am now without it, but people do not get that. I am an actor currently employed in a tour of the UK...and have a couple of film and voice over projects being released soon. My experience as a disabled person is vast and sometimes funny and sometimes sad." – [Paul Wild, actor]

People put so much emphasis on what they see, they more often than not tend to forget about the **person** behind the disability. Nobody it seems, can make that disassociation.

In Paul Wild's case, it is misunderstanding. Society misunderstands so much when it comes to disability. If it's a physical change, society focuses on that one change, and like the case with Paul, cannot comprehend that removing something

What is Ableism?

such as a limb, can actually enhance a person's independence. People often believe that if something so commonplace is removed, that it can only be a bad thing. That's not always the case.

Removal of a limb, can be a bit of a shock, and that does lend itself to the misconceptions of vulnerability, **but**, removing a limb when it's in the best interests of a person can only be a good thing. Yes, the limb has gone, but the **person** is still there.

That limb probably would only cause more harm than good if it wasn't removed.

Surgeons do have pretty good reasoning behind their decisions and methods, and a limb, for example, is only removed if the prognosis of a patient isn't deemed beneficial in the long run, unless an amputation is performed.

What is a missing limb when you compare it to living a life? You have to weigh up the pros and cons here.

Amputations are performed for a whole range of different reasons. Illnesses, accidents, disabilities, infections. Amputation isn't designed for you to feel sympathy. Amputations are done in order to give a person their life back in many ways. It's just a shame that society is so superficial and shallow, and cannot see past the differences in order to see the positives. People cannot understand how missing a limb for example is actually a positive. If that limb is constantly causing pain and issues, then having it removed, again just like in the case of Paul Wild, can only be a good thing.

Imagine being in constant pain, and medication just doesn't work. You've tried everything. You are then offered hope. Hope to live again, pain free, by having an amputation, and this was the only option available. Be honest, wouldn't you take it? Now imagine though, you've had your amputation, and you go out into the world which is now absolutely filled with sympathy, empathy, judgement, discrimination, labelling, segregation. Your independence is taken away in one almighty swoop, you only want to live your life, a life that the surgeons gave you back, but you can't as with every person you meet now, that one large amount of respect people once had for you, has,just gone in a click of a finger. You **look** more

What is Ableism?

'vulnerable', that doesn't mean to say you are, but with your missing piece that made you 'normal', you will be forever patronised amongst other things.

Welcome to disability!

Unless 'disabled' people try to change the narrative from what is believed to be 'fact', into what it **actually means** to have a disability, there is absolutely no hope.

Jennifer Bergmann, Paul Wild, Aideen Blackborough, and Kerry Evans, actually have jobs that are considered to be of high standing. Actors, directors, authors, DLO's at football clubs. Granted, maybe not so much Kerry Evans thankfully, but others that otherwise may **seem** different, actually have jobs which years ago, would somehow feel impossible for whatever reason.

This is the problem though, I feel people are unaware of ableism or even if they are being ableist in the first place. Both terms are hidden away, whereas the other negative terms have widely been in the mainstream for years. People have spoken out for the negative terms associated with racism, sexism and homophobia, but ableism hasn't had the same level of exposure and there lies the issue. Ableism goes under the radar, so much that people don't even know that they are being ableist. How is this possible? 'Disabled' people are judged constantly on how they look and their ability, or indeed, lack of ability. Nobody fully understands the impact that their behaviours are having on those who just want and needs to be treated as 'normal'. Jennifer, or anyone else who just happens to have some form of disability, should never be made to feel limited. This is where we currently are though unfortunately.

You may also be thinking that Jennifer has been through the mill, like so many other 'disabled' people, so a bit of empathy seems appropriate. People don't empathise though, they **sympathise**. Massive difference. The thing is though, empathy and sympathy do come under the same category. Why do we need to be sympathised or indeed empathised? We really don't, and what's the point of empathising or sympathising if nothing will change anyway? It's a bit redundant if I'm completely honest. Please do not waste your time

What is Ableism?

or energy with your misplaced attitudes towards disability. We don't want, or need it. You don't live our lives, so you really cannot understand or even begin to imagine our actual lifestyle. People only see a small percentage of our lives. What is the point of empathising and/or sympathising if you cannot see what it's actually like to have a disability of some form? The constant negativity. The judgement . The discrimination. The patronisation. Not even taking into account the personal aspect of disabilities, pain, medication, hospital appointments, physiotherapy sessions, equipment, accessibility issues. Everything that comes with having a disability. People only see a small minority of us, and that gives society the right to publicly empathise and/or sympathise? No. We deserve respect.

Your reaction to disability won't change anything for the better. Action will. Hence my attempts with my books, alongside **a lot** of 'disabled' activists trying their hardest to change the idea of disability for good. It is annoying that 'disabled' people have to constantly fight for a positive change, whereas really, it should already be in place. The world isn't perfect though. I wish it was, but sadly it isn't. Where there's disability, there will be misplaced judgement, empathy, sympathy, patronisation, you name it, it will be there whenever and where ever disability is involved. That's the truth. I do believe that it's genuinely because of the social acceptable way of life, which everyone has to conform to. In this case, 'disabled' people don't stand a chance to be seen as the socially acceptable idea of 'normal', as long as the current public way of life exists. It shouldn't be up to 'disabled' people to try and change perceptions, really, it's the twenty-first century, perceptions of any kind should **never** be a thing, but this is unfortunately where we are, and the general public should be taught properly and fighting for justice for 'disabled' people either alongside us, or even better, instead of us.

The most common, and offensive thing to do to a 'disabled' person is to patronise. Being patronised is so humiliating. Personally, even though I have a degree in graphic design, have a graphic design job in the motorsport industry, own my own small part-time business designing and selling posters online, and now a published author, my wheelchair almost wrongly announces to the

What is Ableism?

public that i should be patronised and therefore belittled. It doesn't matter how hard I work to try and eliminate this misconception in the minds of society, as long as there is a wheelchair, the negative perceptions will undoubtedly **always** be there. It's sad, but it is the truth.

To give some backup to this, Aideen Blackborough, recently wrote an article on how to properly speak to a 'disabled' person. She has kindly given me permission to quote what she wrote.

"I completely understand that it's difficult and daunting, especially if you haven't really interacted with disabled people before. It might be reassuring for you to know that even my closest family and friends occasionally have difficulty in understanding me. My speech tends to deteriorate further when I'm tired or stressed." – [Disability & Communication, Some Top Tips, article by Aideen Blackborough, Disability Trainer, Speaker and Author]

On a personal level, I can relate to this, when I'm tired or stressed, my own speech deteriorates to some degree, just like Aideen's speech, but that fact **does not** mean or give people the right to talk to me any differently. Sometimes, I struggle with my speech, depending on the situation. Personally, I'm better speaking to people physically on a one-to-one basis, rather than speaking to a crowd, or over a phone. Again though, this **does not** mean that I'm any less intelligent than the next person. The lines become blurred between struggle and unintelligence.

However I do get it. I suppose that it can be a daunting prospect to speak to a 'disabled' person, if somehow, you haven't had the opportunity to speak to a 'disabled' person before. The blurred lines become more blurred, when the actual choice of words come into question. Speaking 'to', and speaking 'with', a 'disabled' person does imply whether people respect a person with a disability or not, (in my own mind at least). Speaking 'to', for me, equals talking down to said person, (i.e. patronisation). Speaking 'with' a 'disabled' person, equals equality for me. You maybe thinking that I'm, in fact, overthinking, and/or overreacting a little too much, and yes, maybe to some degree I am, but what you must understand is that I've been the subject of

What is Ableism?

patronisation all my life, so I'm a little more hypersensitive than most people to terms and contexts of words, and if I am hypersensitive, it's only because of how society has influenced me. Don't get me wrong, I am not playing the blame game, or pointing the finger. I'm just saying what I personally experienced, believe, and how that experience and belief has shaped me as the person I am today.

Aideen's comment above, to me, does give a sense of understanding and forgiveness. Regardless of what you may think about my arguments in this book, and indeed my previous book, I am not totally oblivious to fear of the unknown and potentially offending. I just wish that there was more knowledge of the 'normality' of speaking with a 'disabled' person. It doesn't have to be this big thing. Speaking is a standard way to gain knowledge. Communication is the natural method of the human race to gain social skills. Without speech, humanity is lost. Just because of a small difference, why should that determine how people interact with each other? Why should that have any bearing or influence? It **shouldn't**.

Aideen's choice of word, 'interact', I must say, is a good term to use. The word alone just seems to lessen any potential fears a person may have. Interact doesn't necessarily mean speaking. Yes, it's true that this word could be considered counterintuitive, and maybe it is, but when it comes to society, you do have to tread carefully just in case you instigate something that you may not have intended to instigate. Unfortunately, you do have to walk on eggshells when it comes to society. One wrong move, (in this case, words), can do irreversible damage to how society perceives the world around them.

It is rather sad that Aideen Blackborough has actually had to write an article detailing the methods of speaking to a 'disabled' person, and I have gone back and forth in my mind on whether or not to actually include some of the points, but in the end, I have decided it necessary. It is sad to know that society has come to this, we are being taught on how to speak to another human being at the end of the day, but I do unfortunately get why it is necessary also.

What is Ableism?

Going back to the word 'normal', Aideen Blackborough has given a really good comment:

"...what is normal? Many people see me as "different" but that's ok. I'm proud to have CP and I wouldn't change it.... I consider that I live a normal life; I just have to deal with additional difficulties that most people don't. For example, taking my kids to school and there's a car blocking the pavement. I'm doing a normal, every day thing but I have to overcome difficulties that others don't even think about. Hope this makes sense?" – [Aideen Blackborough, Disability Trainer, Speaker and Author]

That word isn't very modern. 'Normal' shouldn't be a thing. It's just another way to label people. Like Aideen said, what is normal? The term is outdated and doesn't fit in with this 'modern society' we find ourselves, or claim to be apart of in my eyes, 'normal' is apart of the reason why segregation still happens. We are all 'normal', or we would be if society didn't make it hard to live a 'normal' life. To me, Aideen's comment **does** make so much sense. I get it. I've been where she has, sadly, as so many others who have a form of disability.

A recent TV advert of all things has given me a possible better understanding of the behaviours of society, by explaining the Seven Second Rule. Apparently, it only takes seven seconds to know if we love or hate something. The mind is a complex thing to understand and how anyone can make a judgement on something, (or in this case, someone) that fast, is truly beyond me. It just goes to show how humans are capable of great things, but just because we are capable, it doesn't mean that we actually use our capability for good. Yes, we are getting there, we're more accepting generally than we were in the past, and that's fantastic. We recognise the discrimination of how society was with racism, sexism, homophobia and other minorities and we are trying to put a stop to it. Nobody wants to be labelled with those terms that have been negatively ingrained in our minds for fear of being shunned, but nobody has a problem with being ableist. Even though people from my survey have said they know the terms 'ableism' and 'ableist', that maybe true in one sense, but I **really** don't know if people fully

What is Ableism?

understand the terms. I say this because people don't actually see it as an issue. People don't know that they are being ableist in most cases. 'Disabled' people are just seen as different and that's somehow acceptable? Media doesn't cover ableism in the same way as the other terms. We are just put into one category. Segregated from the rest of the world to be patronised, manipulated and judged without any proper rhyme or reason just because of our appearance.

Kerry Evans, the Disability Liaison Officer at Wrexham AFC, said she *"...hasn't experienced discrimination due to her disability, but unfortunately knows of others who have a disability that have been discriminated against." – [Paraphrase: Kerry Evans, Disability Liaison Officer at Wrexham AFC]*

However, others sadly have.

I recently put out a post on a social media page for 'disabled' people to participate in the second book, and I had some very lovely responses, saying that they'd love to be involved, of which of course, I really do appreciate their support. As stated, I purposely asked each and every single person who participated, how they would like to be identified in the book by name, or if they'd prefer to remain anonymous. The vast majority of participants gave me permission to quote their name and condition. I am stating exactly how every single person wanted to be identified. All quotes are the participants own.

On the subject of disability discrimination, one social media participant, Maddy C, who has long COVID and ME said:

"I, and any other wheelchair users, are being currently discriminated against by the charter train industry. These companies run private charters on the main line to various locations around the country. I used to love a trip to a city or a seaside. Unfortunately the law exempts them from providing accessible accommodation. I am currently fighting this. Every other provider of rail transport (preserved railways, narrow gauge railways etc.) has to provide access. This sector is in a loophole." – [Social media participant, Maddy C]

What is Ableism?

I will talk about transport accessibility for disability later in full detail, referring back to the above quote from Maddy C, but what I will say for now is that her quote is a perfect example of how society hasn't fully understood disability rights properly. It's not the job of 'disabled' people to fight for equality, equality should have always been apart of the mainstream society and this should never have to be a question. No company should ever have any right to have loopholes, especially when it comes to accessibility for 'disabled' people, especially when your company is providing a service to the public.

Speaking about the conditions that Maddy C has, you may think that long COVID isn't considered a disability, but in actuality, considering the long-term side effects, I believe that it could be identified as a form of disability.

"The most common symptoms of long COVID are extreme tiredness (fatigue), feeling short of breath, loss of smell and muscle aches." – [Symptoms of Long COVID - nhs.uk]

In context, the symptoms don't seem that bad, **but remember**, these are the most **common** symptoms. Meaning that there is a risk of further illness.

"Problems with your memory and concentration ("brain fog"), chest pain or tightness, difficulty sleeping (insomnia), heart palpitations, dizziness, pins and needles, joint pain, depression and anxiety, tinnitus, earaches, feeling sick, diarrhoea, stomach aches, loss of appetite, a high temperature, cough, headaches, sore throat, changes to sense of smell or taste, and/or rashes." – [Symptoms of Long COVID – nhs.uk]

Imagine having the latter symptoms constantly. Admittedly maybe not all at once, but for anyone to believe that long COVID isn't considered a disability, is ignorant. Long COVID **is** life changing, you only have to look at **any** of the above quotes from the *NHS* website, reread the quote from Maddy C, or even know someone yourself with the condition to come to that very obvious conclusion. It maybe relatively new to society to understand the impact of long COVID, but in my opinion, it doesn't get past the obvious fact that it **is** a disability.

What is Ableism?

Clair Girvan, a social worker and artist said:

"I have dyslexia, Autism, M.E, Likely POTS and found out yesterday I'm in early heart failure, I'm 42 and a social worker, no one understands the impact of my health issues as they are all 'hidden'..." – [Clair Girvan, disabled artist and social worker]

In many ways, hidden disabilities tend to create some level of controversy. People cannot 'see' a hidden disability, so it's extremely easy just to dismiss it outright or saying such incomprehensible things like *"You don't look disabled"*, as if it's a compliment! That is extremely offensive to both 'disabled' people who have a visible disability and also a hidden disability. Really it is like comparing, gender, race, sexual orientation, or sexuality. You just wouldn't do it today. Comparing disabilities is just another form of offending. This is what people don't understand, probably because disability discrimination has gone under the radar for so many years, most people are unaware of the harm they are causing. I say most, because unfortunately there still are those out there who deliberately discriminate against disability, (my past employment experience for one), but generally, the majority of people are genuinely unaware of the ableism that they project. I'd **really** love to think that if society was aware of the damage and harm they cause to those who have a disability, then they **would** stop once and for all. It's unfortunately a dream though of mine, sadly, I really **do not** think for one second that the society would change their attitude towards disability instantly. Realistically, it would take years to totally eradicate disability discrimination for good. Some people still have beliefs that are connected to race, sexual orientation, gender, etc., even in today's 'modern times', so I know that disability discrimination won't be wiped off the face of the Earth automatically. No, it takes time, campaigns, ambassadors, books etc., before any real sense of headway is made. It's a constant battle for equality, acceptance and justice. I think as long as we keep making noise to cancel out the negativity, disability will eventually have it's place at the equality table.

Referring back, it's absolutely astonishing how Kerry Evans actually hasn't experienced any form

What is Ableism?

of discrimination due to her disability, and yet, wonderful at the same time as it just goes to show that 'disabled' people can live as normal of a life as possible without the constant negativity. I do wonder why this is, because Kerry is 'disabled' but she hasn't always been in a wheelchair, she has Cerebral Palsy which progressed with a bleed age thirty which paralysed her right side. Whether because she wasn't always in a wheelchair, so people respect her more? That's what it comes down to, respect, and if you have a visible disability, or by rule, in a wheelchair, usually, that respect disappears. Not in Kerry Evans' case though, which is absolutely incredible, but why can't other wheelchair users and disabilities experience the same? You can't have one rule for one and one rule for the rest of the demographic. I must say that despite everything, Kerry Evans is such a positive and independent person and she *"hasn't let anything hold her back." – [Paraphrase: Kerry Evans, Disability Liaison Officer at Wrexham AFC]*

I would comment here about how 'inspirational' Kerry is, but inspiration has absolutely no bearing on trying to live a life.

I'm wondering if it's that attitude to life that make people treat you like an 'ordinary' person. Kerry herself drives a car, she has adaptations to her home which aids her independence.

In a way, she's experienced both an able-bodied life (with slight Cerebral Palsy,) and a life as a wheelchair user. This is what she told me. Even though Kerry has had a form of CP all of her life, thirty years of her life, she was mobile, (without a wheelchair). Maybe that's the difference? Maybe because she was mobile in the beginning, that has lead people to treat her 'normally' throughout her life up to this point? Kerry doesn't look as if she has any underlying issues, she just looks like a standard wheelchair user, (if there is such a thing), but she does have underlying issues, just like the majority of 'disabled' people in the entire world. People just see a wheelchair user and think "they can't walk". There is so much more to disability than thinking that someone just can't walk. There are hospital appointments, medication, pain, equipment, to name but a few things, and having to deal with constant discrimination, from the outside world, who knows absolutely nothing about the **person behind the disability**, on top of

What is Ableism?

everything else, is tiresome and just unacceptable. Yes, Kerry Evans hasn't experienced any form of discrimination in her life as I said, but others have, myself included. Kerry knows that too, as to reiterate her point, she knows of others who have experienced discrimination due to a disability. I like to believe that there are many others who have some form of disability and not have experienced discrimination, but I'd sadly just be kidding myself. Kerry Evans is the exception here, but society has to treat other 'disabled' people with the respect they wholeheartedly deserve, just like how Kerry Evans is treated, this needs to be extended across the board, all over the world.

When we met for the interview, Kerry herself, kept apologising, saying that she probably wasn't the best person to interview because she was so positive about her life. In a way, I found her just saying that, a bit heart-breaking if I'm completely honest. I wasn't disappointed with her answers, the opposite in fact. It broke my heart that by nature, disability always tends to have this negativity attached to it, like every single 'disabled' person must have negative experiences. Kerry's optimistic attitude is important and I told her that, because I want to show that despite having a disability of some form, that doesn't mean that you have to have a negative attitude to match. Kerry shows that despite her disability of *"...slight Cerebral Palsy..."*, *- [Paraphrase: Kerry Evans, Disability Liaison Officer at Wrexham AFC]*, she doesn't let anything *"...hold her back..."* , *- [Paraphrase: Kerry Evans, Disability Liaison Officer at Wrexham AFC]*. However, that isn't to say that the *Disability Liaison Officer at Wrexham AFC* hasn't experienced her fair share of a barrier in her life. Kerry's experienced *"barriers in her life in general society with venues such as hotels, (doors not being wide enough to access a disabled room). Venues would benefit from asking disabled people themselves how to design disabled facilities."* – *[Paraphrase: Kerry Evans, Disability Liaison Officer at Wrexham AFC]*.

I must say that I personally know what Kerry Evans is saying here, it would be more beneficial to **ask** a 'disabled' person to help design 'disabled' facilities. The way it is now, it **clearly isn't** working, and I'm thankfully, (or terrifyingly) not alone in this

What is Ableism?

thought. The amount of venues that I've personally encountered that have **claimed** to be 'disability friendly', just isn't. The struggles are real. You can't just install a grab rail in a bathroom or wet room of a 'disability friendly' room, in a hotel for example, but not have that room properly adapted to actually accommodate a 'disabled' person. If the room itself is inadequate in terms of space etc., that room **isn't** 'disability friendly'. It's nonsensical. There needs to be space to fit a wheelchair, hoist, carer or support worker, trusted family member or friend, as well as room to manoeuvre if required in any 'disabled friendly' facility. Anything less is just false advertising.

What good is it if somewhere is advertised as disability accessible, to only discover the complete disregard and disrespect of human rights? The amount of venues and public places, including places that offer 'disability friendly' holiday accommodation that fully aren't, is ridiculous. You may have hoists, ramps, widened doors etc. in these types of accommodation, which is great, but what they make up for in these adaptations, they severely lack in the bathroom of the accommodation. 'Disability friendly' accommodation should be accessible throughout. You just can't pick and choose what you adapt and what you don't. It's either all or nothing. What's the point of claiming to have 'disability friendly' accommodation if it isn't **fully** accessible? Really it's a form of trade description. The majority of bathrooms in these types of accommodation, are small. The layout is all wrong. A true 'disability friendly' bathroom should, and **must** have space. I remember going on holiday once in 'disabled friendly' accommodation, and the bathroom was very cramped. It was tiny, the shower was that small that I had to try and squeeze in it in a shower chair, but because the shower had a lip on it, it was extremely difficult to get the shower chair in the actual shower, and when I finally did, then trying to manoeuvre the shower chair to under the shower hose was just impossible. I felt literally crushed within that shower. The sink was just placed directly in front of the shower. It was ridiculous. It isn't just me, it's clear that others experience exactly the same, it's like nobody cares. As long as they don't have to deal with the lack of space, nothing else matters. Recently I

What is Ableism?

used a public 'disabled' facility of which I took a photograph to confirm my argument.

It's just completely heart-breaking how we as the human race, the most **intelligent** race, aren't as intelligent when it comes down to 'difficult' subjects. The topic of disability shouldn't be an inconvenience, somehow though, this is **exactly** how it feels if you are considered 'disabled'. The word alone just conjures up ideas of an almost 'weakness' or 'vulnerability'. We aren't 'vulnerable' or 'weak', or whatever you want to call it, we are human. We aren't going to break like a piece of delicate glassware if we try to do things. Having this Dickensian attitude only increases this ableist behaviour. You may think that you are being compassionate by helping, but there is a thing as 'too much help'. It's all about finding that fine line between letting 'disabled' people live as 'normal' of a life as humanly possible, and helping when **asked**. Doing absolutely everything for a 'disabled' person minimises any small chance of independence and freedom, to be apart of standard society, if capable. People need to start realising that 'disability' means 'differently abled', not an excuse to pass 'disabled' onto others to deal with. We aren't a pet. We deserve to be treated with respect and dignity. One of my social media participants, Brian Maddocks, came up with the perfect term:

"'Difability', not disability. It is only one letter change, but it changes everything." – [Brian Maddocks, social media participant]

Brian Maddocks' quote means that we need to defy the naysayers by showcasing our abilities. It would indeed be refreshing to have the chance to defy the term of disability and what it means to society, by showing what disability actually means to **us**. How are we **ever** going to achieve this simple request of independence, equality, opportunity and acceptance if we have absolutely everything done for us? That's no life, it's more like a prison sentence, but instead of actual prisoners, we are metaphorical prisoners trapped in a world where independence is constantly denied.

Whilst I was doing research, I was lucky enough to have a number of other high profile people who have been willing to contribute, from MPs to journalists who have written articles on disability. One of the participants who agreed to take part is

What is Ableism?

Dr. Sally Witcher, **"...a former CEO of Inclusion Scotland who has been 'disabled' since childhood..."** – [Scottish Herald]. She was kind enough to send me an article from a blog that she wrote about disability and has kindly given me permission to quote what she wrote:

"Down the centuries there have been many answers to the perennial question: "How do you solve a problem like 'disabled' people?". Some didn't mess about. The ancient Romans drowned children with impairments in the Tiber. The Nazis took a similarly uncompromising view of us, as 'useless eaters', unworthy of life. So they killed an estimated 240,000 of us, out of public view when the public protested. We've been segregated into hospitals and mad-houses, put into 'idiot-cages' in town centres, branded as evil, cursed, unnatural changelings. Conversely, others saw us as objects for charity, to be pitied and cared for. They even on occasion elevated disability to a holy state. We have found ourselves cast as heroic (yet still tragic) survivors; our purpose to entertain non-'disabled' people and make them feel good about themselves; eternally grateful

they're not us!" – *[Excerpt taken from the article: 'Accessible Britain? Careful what you wish for!'- By Dr. Sally Witcher, Bop Theatre Blog]*

I know that this quote may make people feel uncomfortable by it's content, but, to be honest these types of articles do exist, and I'm so pleased that they do, because it is showing that there is some hope for disability equality, by actually having articles which aren't afraid to say the truth. It's true that 'disabled' people often have to deal with this constant back and forth between pity and heroic, depending on what we are doing at that time, it is definitely quite jarring in a way to me that the back and forth behaviour from the past, has continued into today, without any improvement.

Going back to Dr. Sally Witcher's article, I personally feel that these articles are so few and far between. It would be better for articles such as Dr. Sally Witcher's to be highlighted more. These articles should be the first thing you see on the Internet if you're searching the term disability or any of it's related terms.

What is Ableism?

Yes, they may make you feel uncomfortable, but all of the important messages are when it comes to equality of any type, let alone disability equality. We are uncomfortable when people treat us as second class citizens, so I feel that society should have at least some of that uncomfortable feeling right back. Articles such as Dr. Sally Witcher's are designed to open up the conversation and move it forward. This is exactly what I meant when I said every single thing out there written on the subject of disability, that is easily accessible in the public domain, is designed to be used in a negative sense. It's just sensationalism, designed to harbour further segregation. With standard articles on disability, you just get the basic facts and figures, without any **real** information to start a proper conversation. With current articles on disability, you are just being fed the surface of the subject, there isn't any actual information that you can delve into and explore. It's just a generalised view, but if there was more exposure out there to articles that would highlight disability in a more positive way, but also be informative and interesting enough to grab the attention of people, then disability equality may stand a chance.

Some of the examples that Dr. Sally Witcher uses in the excerpt of the blog post are extreme in her comparisons, but it is true and it is about time something is said against this constant discrimination. People may think that either Dr. Sally Witcher, or even myself are just scare mongering, but we're actually not. I personally think that the world today has become timid. The thing is, to try and get a conversation going, sometimes controversy is the best way to move things forward. To hopefully make an impactful improvement towards subjects such as disabilities in this case. Steps desperately need to be taken to put an end to this constant battle for 'normality' and I personally think that Dr. Sally Witcher's article does just that. Sometimes we need to feel uncomfortable for an important topic to be highlighted. This is why I've decided to include the full paragraph of Dr. Sally Witcher's article, so that for anyone who reads this book, then they can make a judgement on themselves and their actions. I added an entire paragraph for it to make an impact on people.

What is Ableism?

Ableism comes in many forms, both subtly and blatantly, I've personally experienced both, most you may already be aware of if you have read my previous book, but so have many more in my position. It messes with your mental health if exposed to it often, but people don't realise the affect their attitude can have on 'disabled' people.

You may not think that asking someone who is 'disabled' what's wrong with them is wrong in itself, you may think that you are showing interest, but really, you are being offensive, you may think that you are being complimentary by saying to a 'disabled' person that they don't look 'disabled'. What's a 'disabled' person supposed to look like? The problem is that it's been ingrained in social culture that 'disabled' people are supposed to have our props, a wheelchair, is the most common, even the globally accepted disability logo has a person sitting in a wheelchair which isn't right in my opinion. There are many ways people can be 'disabled', and not all disabilities are visible. Also, a number of people can have the same disability but it can affect each person differently. Disability isn't one thing, it can be many things, so saying to someone that they don't look 'disabled', is just ignorant. Saying a 'disabled' person is inspirational is another form of ableism if we have a career for example. Why are we inspirational if we are doing what others do on a daily basis? The world needs to learn that it's not okay to single 'disabled' people out for what they may consider to be a landmark. Being 'disabled' isn't a life limiting thing, nor is it something to be commended. It's ableism that tries to make 'disabled' people limited. Before we get into the more positive aspect of this book, I want to share two instances of ableism that I've faced. One you may already know about but I'm going to delve deeper into the actual reality of the situation I found myself in, and another instance which I didn't cover the last time as I was still trying to process the experience. Both are considered to be a form of ableism.

You maybe aware of the first instance as I went into a bit of detail before, but I feel mentally stronger now to tell you exactly what happened. High school can be a difficult time for anyone, you have a certain pressure to look a certain way and be popular, I think I mentioned this before, but high school can be an eat or be eaten scenario for any child, but if you add disability into the mix, that pressure to 'fit in' can be a million times worse. To the outside world my high school liked to have a positive reputation, equality for all was the main selling point. Mum and dad fell into this trap as the school presented itself very equality driven, in reality though, it was segregation that was the main focus. I have heard that the school in question is better now with a lot more focus on inclusion, but nobody should ever be proud to say that something is better now if it should have always been and more importantly, advertised itself as being something greater than it actually was in the past. The key thing I experienced during this time was the level of segregation. 'Disabled' pupils were treated the same way as each other, there wasn't any room for individuality, independence or potential. We were never allowed to go outside with the other able-bodied pupils at break times or lunchtimes, no, we were forced to stay in one room until the school bell rang for lessons. To make it worse, every single lunchtime or break time we had to be 'babysat' by a support worker. They would take it in turns, they had a rota of who was 'looking after us' that day. It was demeaning. You had the 'disabled' pupils and the able-bodied pupils, it was like '*West Side Story*' but more intense. I know that sounds dramatic, but it's the truth, it was a 'us vs. them' scenario. What made it worse was the fact that because the people who were supposed to be in charge were treating the 'disabled' pupils differently than the able-bodied pupils, I believe that the able-bodied pupils took note of this and decided to treat us differently too. Children, especially the age of high school, are very suggestible and when they see something that is treated as 'normal' by segregating the 'disabled' by the exact people who are there to guide and educate, of course it's going to have an effect on their perceptions. It's inevitable. We were all thrown together in one group, people have said to me that the way we were treated was only my experience. I'm sorry, but no, other 'disabled' people my age who went to the same high school as me undoubtedly experienced the same as me. It affects you, I know it did me. Any confidence I had before high school was quickly and cruelly snatched away in the last three years of me being there. Before then, it was great, in my first two

What is Ableism?

years of high school, 'disabled' pupils were given a choice about where they would like to spend break times and lunchtimes, either in the room, or outside with the other able-bodied pupils. There was very little, if any, segregation happening in those first two years. We were allowed to mix with others if we wanted to, we weren't bound by any disability label, it was fantastic! What changed? The SENCO. The first SENCO thrived on making 'disabled' pupils feel happy and equal. As soon as the first SENCO retired, that's when everything started falling apart in my opinion. Any freedom we had was quickly replaced by isolation and separation. I've said this before, but a SENCO is basically someone who is in charge of making 'disabled' pupils feel equal by meeting the needs of every single child individually. Once my third year rolled around, the atmosphere definitely became more hostile towards the 'disabled' pupils.

The relationship between the new SENCO and the support workers seemed a bit too friendly, as if it wasn't treated as a job. I just got the sense that the SENCO treated the staff unbelievably close, far closer than a person in their position should have. It's absolutely fine to develop friendships but I felt like the level of friendliness was inappropriate for a job like that, and ultimately affected the standards of care towards the 'disabled' pupils. It's no secret anymore that during my GCSE's, myself and my family had an uphill battle with the replacement SENCO just so I could be provided with what I was entitled to. Their behaviour during this time, if they had won the battle, would've negatively affected my future if it wasn't for mum and having the inside knowledge from my sister-in-law, Ceri, who is an English teacher herself. I personally think that too much focus was put on disability as a whole with the replacement SENCO, that ability and potential became lost or obsolete. I definitely noticed a change in approach comparing my second year of high school to my third. Whether the school in question would like to admit it or not, their attitude and actions during this time with 'disabled' pupils was unapologetically ableist. Segregation, patronisation, ignorance and even bullying to a degree all played a part in making everything seem impossible for the 'disabled' pupils.

What is Ableism?

"Bullying is often aimed at certain groups, for example because of their race, religion, gender or sexual orientation." – [House of Commons Library (Bullying In UK Schools)]

Yes, this is a small part of bullying, but disability **should** and **definitely needs** to be added to this section of the *House of Commons Library*. Disability discrimination shouldn't have to go unpunished. By not stating disability in the bullying in UK schools, I feel that it gives permission for disability discrimination to carry on. *'Out of sight, out of mind.'*

"The Conservative Party in its 2019 Manifesto committed to "help teachers tackle bullying, including homophobic bullying'" – [House of Commons Library (Bullying In UK Schools)]

I need to ask, where were the *Conservative Party's* promise to also tackle disability bullying in schools? Maybe they did, however, I really do believe that it should have been stated in their two-thousand and nineteen Manifesto, and not just highlight homophobic bullying. Of course that is extremely important these days, all forms of bullying behaviour is, but I truly feel that disability doesn't have the same level of exposure as other topics. This is **exactly why** disability equality is moving further and further into extinction. People often seem to leave out disability in general terms. This **isn't** fair, not in the slightest.

"Children with disabilities are up to three times more likely to be bullied and up six times more likely to experience violence than their peers, according to research." – [Irish Times]

These statistics are absolutely horrifying. The statement is from the *Irish Times* admittedly and from twenty-twenty-one, but even though it's a newspaper article from Ireland, and from two years ago (at the time of writing this), it really just confirms to me that disability discrimination sadly still exists in schools no matter the location, and this is a massive issue. Something definitely and desperately needs to change. From my research so far, to me, it seems that disability bullying and discrimination in schools is still as concerning as it was when I attended my high school.

The high school thrived on appearances to the outside world, that it was this wondrous place with equal opportunities for all, whereas, in reality, it

What is Ableism?

was filled with unjust treatment of pupils who where considered 'different'. Teachers of the school were amazing I must say, I had two teachers in particular who encouraged me to be the best person I could by saying that I should think about a career in ICT and I have a good imagination for storytelling. It wasn't the teachers I had a problem with, it was the people who were ultimately there to provide us with the tools we needed to succeed and make sure we were safe and happy.

I think that power is a dangerous thing, and I think that the new replacement SENCO abused the power they thought they had. The moment they arrived, the equality atmosphere definitely disappeared and I unfortunately never saw it return in those last three years. The 'ableist' attitudes **definitely** became more apparent in those final three years. I personally felt attacked, like I was being punished just for having a disability. I felt that there wasn't any chance for 'disabled' pupils to feel as part of the mainstream school life. The ethical issues that this denial creates are huge. I studied ethics in university as a part of my course and I can tell you now, knowing what I know, the experience in the latter years of high school were unethical to say the least, and that's being kind.

Ethics definition:- "Moral principles that govern a person's behaviour or the conducting of an activity." – [OED]

Basically ethics in layman's terms are standards that we all live by, some have high standards where people treat others equally with respect and equal opportunities, and there are low standards, where people basically don't care for others at all.

I don't think looking back now, that the SENCO had any proper experience for the job, or any morals or integrity for that matter. I think that they just thought that it was just a job and that was it. There wasn't any heart in it, I personally felt as if the 'disabled' pupils were left to fend for themselves in this new, scary environment which the disability team had unapologetically created. I felt like an outcast in those final three years. I felt like we were bait, ready for our prey to eat us alive. It was terrifying. I used to blame the able-bodied pupils for making me feel 'inadequate'

What is Ableism?

and 'different', but now I have absolutely no doubt in my mind that it was the disability team that helped to create this division between the able-bodied pupils and the 'disabled' pupils. We were looked upon as monsters, but vulnerable people too, people that nobody would want to be seen with, let alone bother with. We were 'labelled'. I feel that the way the disability team treated us at the time had a major affect on how the able-bodied pupils saw us. That is ableism right there. The school can try and deny it but I know first hand what I saw and experienced.

To say that the school is better equality wise now is a bit difficult for me to be okay with. I'm ecstatic to learn that the school has improved with the treatment of disability, but I wholeheartedly stick to my thoughts that it should have always been at a high standard disability wise in the first place. It wasn't a time where disability was considered a 'vulnerability'. It's the twenty-first century, disability should have always been a part of the mainstream. Somehow though, I think that the school in question mustn't of had the message between two thousand and six to two thousand and nine like the rest of society. It had every opportunity to pave the way to promote disability and diversity as a great thing, but it ultimately lost that opportunity to change perceptions. The *Disability Discrimination Act of 2010* came in a year after I left high school. It's a shame that it didn't exist before two thousand and ten, otherwise I feel that the high school would have violated the Act on numerous occasions.

To have someone say to me that it was only my experience in high school is ignorant. Unless people meant that it was just my experience as I was part of the 'disabled' group, but again, that attitude is both ignorant and discriminatory in itself. Society doesn't understand the level of effort it takes for a 'disabled' person, like myself, to get themselves up in the morning for another day of segregation, discrimination and judgemental ignorance that somehow we just have to accept and take on the chin, not only in education, but in everyday life as well. You think when I was in high school, the daily abuse just happened to me? I wish it did. I'm not trying to be nasty here when I say this, I'm just being honest, the amount of discrimination that I witnessed in high school towards other, less academic

What is Ableism?

'disabled' pupils was frequent, and some of the bullying behaviour came directly from support workers, with them talking about 'disabled' pupils behind their back, (myself included). Nothing was ever done to sort it out may I add? To me, the whole school was just a large playground for staff and pupils to target the ones who were considered 'vulnerable' and 'easy targets', which were unfortunately the 'disabled' pupils. I overheard able-bodied pupils say some really nasty things about some 'disabled' pupils also, there was absolutely no rest-bite or escape. I know that you get bullying in schools, but the content I heard was inexcusable to say the least, some of which was directed at me. I'm not going to divulge the bullying directed towards the other 'disabled' pupils, as I don't think it's my place, that isn't my story to tell, but I'm also not going to divulge the bullying directed towards myself either for three reasons, one, I've grown, both mentally and emotionally since then, two, I've made my peace with it, and three, I now feel and understand that it wasn't really the able-bodied pupils fault, they just jumped on the bandwagon. I have told mum about everything that went on, so at least I'm not bottling that negative experience up anymore. My conscious is now clear in this regard. What I will say is that everything that I experienced in those final three years, was just the tip of the iceberg to the despicable behaviour that was constantly going on under the radar. I truly believe that these attitudes and actions enhanced when there was a management change in the disability team of that school. I know for a fact that if the first SENCO was still working in my last three years of high school, then my experience and other's experience would've been a more positive one. The timing of it all was too convenient for my liking. It wasn't 'perfect' when I first started the high school, nowhere ever is in today's society, but it was far better than what it became.

It's the lack of understanding that is missing and it's sad to think that people still have the same beliefs as the past, where attitudes towards other things have changed. I can't work out how most things nowadays, like racism and sexism for example are frowned upon, but ableism still exists? It's so unbelievably unfair.

What is Ableism?

I'm not sure why people think it's okay to treat 'disabled' people so disrespectfully, I'll admit that most people today are unaware of their attitudes and actions towards the 'disabled', but there are those who know that they're being disrespectful. There's a bigger issue if you are 'disabled' and you are suffering from your mental health at the same time. Some people think that they can take advantage and treat you horribly because you **appear** at your most 'vulnerable'. I've come across this numerous times, most I've told you about before, but there was one instance I left out as I was still trying to process the experience. I'll tell you what happened now. I'm now ready.

During the first lockdown, I was feeling the loneliness and depression as everyone was, I just didn't see the point of getting out of bed, I mean, you couldn't do anything if you did get up, you were stuck in the house. I understood the complexity of the COVID-19 situation and understood the seriousness of it, but just being in your home everyday with nothing to do, of course that's going to play negatively on anyone's mind. When the first lockdown was ending and the rules were relaxing a bit, mum suggested to me that I should apply for a part-time job in a company, just something to tide me over until my proper workplace was back up and running.

I emailed the company and asked if there was any chance of part-time employment. Now, bear in mind I have said before that I don't really like using the phone, as I get tongue tied and my heart starts racing. When you write a CV, you must include your contact details, including your phone number, I explained this in the email I sent that I couldn't use a phone due to a combination of my CP and anxiety. I had a reply the next day, just basically saying that they aren't looking for anyone currently but they'd bear me in mind for the future. I was disappointed but understood. I just accepted that the company wasn't interested and tried to move on.

I was in my bedroom one day when the phone rang and mum picked it up, I heard a lot of commotion so I went to see why. As soon as I went downstairs, mum said to the person on the phone that I was in the room and said that they could speak to me. Apparently mum said she panicked when she saw me and didn't know what

What is Ableism?

she was doing at the time, but so did I. I had a major panic attack and refused to speak to the person on the other end of the phone. I'm fine going on the phone if I know beforehand and can get prepared for it. I'm terrible when it's just sprung on me that I need to use the phone there and then. It sounds ridiculous, but that's me and I don't really care what others think. I just can't use the phone. Mum eventually explained that it was the owner of the company and they wanted to speak to me. I was annoyed because I explained on the email I initially wrote to apply that I could do anything but use a phone and I explained why. So they should have took that information on board and respected me. I'm just going to say that ignoring the reasonable requests of 'disabled' people, is a form of ableism because it just shows a complete disregard of 'disabled' people along with obvious disrespect.

As my mental health was at rock-bottom at that point in my life with everything I dealt with beforehand, I had a full-blown panic attack and just couldn't take the phone from Mum to speak to the owner. Needless to say that the owner wasn't impressed but Mum asked if we could go to meet them face to face one day the next week. The owner half heartedly agreed to the meeting. Now I completely understand that my attitude wasn't the best, but you have to try and understand that I felt so alone mentally during this time in my life that I just couldn't function properly. I hated the entire world and at that point, I couldn't see past the fact that the owner called me on the phone, when I specifically said that I could do anything they needed me to do, but answer the phone. I made a point to emphasise it. I made it clear and even explained why. I felt disrespected.

The day came when I thought that I was going for an interview, I got ready, both physically and mentally, I basically psyched myself up for what potentially lay ahead. Mum came with me, for moral support really above anything else, she was telling me about the easiest route to the company when we were on the way there, as I was going to be making my way there in my powered wheelchair, for independence more than anything. I was working out the safest route for me to drive.

What is Ableism?

As soon as we got there, something didn't seem right. We went in, there was a receptionist on the desk who never said a word, strangely. They were just doing busy work it seemed to me, to avoid having to speak to us. Then two employees came out from the back of the company, and because we were invisible to the receptionist, we asked the employees where the owner was as I had an interview with them regarding a chance of part-time work. The employees both went to the office to get the owner, which literally took fifteen minutes. In that time, mum and myself were waiting in front of the reception desk, the receptionist still doing busy work and not interacting with either of us. The atmosphere in there was strange. I felt like I was in the way and wasn't welcome. After fifteen minutes of waiting, another employee came from the office, but they seemed a bit frustrated by mum and myself being there. They literally bounded up to us and asked what we wanted. My anxiety at this point was understandably through the roof, so mum explained and the employee immediately said that the owner wasn't there. We were confused to say the least. The employee then went on to describe my potential role in the company, including making and receiving **phone calls**, and that I would be only covering the days that employee was off for the day, (so basically as and when.) Their attitude came across as a mix of aggressive, defensive and passive all at the same time. I didn't want to work in a place like that. I explained about my anxiety with phone calls, but they basically implied that it was the job, and I had to deal with the phone if I wanted the job. We asked where the owner was and they said that the owner was in Chester and didn't know when they were going to be back. It was ridiculous, considering we arranged the interview for that particular day. It was demeaning. I felt like a child in trouble at school. I had enough at this point and asked mum if we could leave. When we were leaving, the employee who was disrespectful somehow had a personality transplant it seemed as they said that it was "nice" to meet us. That was laughable to me.

We left the place and I was in complete disbelief, how can any company today, be so ignorant? This is unfortunately the world we live in though, a

What is Ableism?

world where disability discrimination goes under the radar.

Mum felt responsible for it all, she kept apologising for making me do that, which made me more angry with the company as they made mum feel guilty for trying to help me. It wasn't mum's fault, and I told her that, the fault was solely to be blamed on the company and the company alone. Mum wasn't to know what was going to happen. It's just the world we live in, the people who consider themselves important and look down on those who they consider are beneath them on a hierarchy standpoint, ultimately takes advantage of that pretend power and tries to control those who they consider less fortunate than themselves. I don't think I have to say that this is a form of ableism. Ignoring the reasonable requests, being talked down to, being ignored, made to feel insignificant, all of these things I felt in that one instance. It's not a surprise to say that again my mental health deteriorated significantly because of this, and it was at rock bottom anyway due to the pandemic. It was just so disrespectful the way I was treated, as if I was a nuisance. I know that I should have spoken with the owner of the company on the phone that day, but my anxiety was through the roof and I just couldn't. I had a panic attack. I don't really think that the owner actually read my initial email I sent. If they did then they would've read as to why I felt uncomfortable using a phone, and that I preferred email communication. I will admit, my first job in a local visually impaired charity, after I finished university, involved me making and receiving phone calls, which I absolutely hated, but with it being my first job after university, I didn't want to 'rock the boat' as it were. It was absolute hell, if I'm brutally honest. I always had to pluck up the courage every time I had to make a phone call or receive one. I'd have a massive drink of water beforehand to try and stop my mouth from drying up. It was an ordeal, something of which I have absolutely no intention of reliving. I think that is one of the reasons why I left that particular job, I just couldn't handle being forced to do something that I'm not comfortable with. I didn't want to go through that again. I couldn't go through that again.

According to the *House of Commons Library*:

What is Ableism?

"The EA 2010 prohibits disability discrimination in various areas of life, including services, employment, education and the disposal and management of premises." – [House of Commons Library (Disability Discrimination)]

If disability discrimination **is** illegal, then **why** does it happen? I personally experienced this, as you now know (or knew previously), in at least **two** sectors where it is prohibited, namely education and employment. Maybe the education system can justify this simply because of the fact that the *Disability Discrimination Act* was first established in two thousand and ten. (I left school in two thousand and nine), it's unfortunate and unfair but that is just how everything seems to go. What I cannot understand is why employers still feel that they can discriminate against disability so blatantly? It just doesn't make **any** sense. Are employers aware that discrimination against disability is illegal, or just don't they care? I would like to believe the former in an ideal world, but knowing what I know and unfortunately experienced, in reality, I unfortunately do think it's more likely to be the latter. I'm not just saying that for effect, I honestly, hand on heart, really believe that employers don't care.

I remember when I was fired from my first proper graphic design job, because the manager was basically apparently very uncomfortable with me working there because of my disability, which is absolutely ridiculous. I'm not going to go into that experience again (what actually happened,) as I already have in 'CP Isn't Me', but when I was eventually, (and unfairly may I add,) fired from said job, I initially looked everywhere for any unfair dismissal due to disability discrimination. Low and behold, shockingly (maybe not if you look at it from a different angle) when I eventually found the information, long story short, because I was initially hired on a voluntary basis, I had no case to bring forward, nothing at all. Essentially, I just had to accept it. In no way though is it acceptable. In my opinion, there is absolutely no difference between a paid job and a voluntary job, absolutely everyone should have the same rights law wise when it comes to disability discrimination. What message does it send to employers? That it's okay to discriminate against disability, as long as they are working on a

What is Ableism?

voluntary basis, you have absolutely no obligation to make and treat a 'disabled' person with respect and dignity? I'm sorry, but that attitude is Dickensian. We **desperately** need to look into this unrealistic view of volunteering if you have a disability. It **definitely** needs to be re-evaluated. The way it is now, is just unethical, immoral and ignorant. It should not matter if a 'disabled' person **chooses** to volunteer at a place of work, it's **that person's choice** at the end of the day. Sometimes it isn't even a choice. Sometimes, 'disabled' people need to weigh up the pros and cons of having paid employment, as it may affect their benefits. Now, you maybe thinking to yourself, *"Why in the world would a 'disabled' person need to think about benefits if they are offered paid employment?"* A valid question admittedly, but disability is far more complicated than you might imagine, (on a practical level anyway.)

I, myself, personally volunteer at the motorsport company I work for, (would I like to be offered income? – Yes, of course I would, as I can only imagine anyone else would in the same position. It's only natural.) Is voluntary employment ideal?

No, it **definitely** isn't to an employee ('disabled' or otherwise). Volunteering always seems to benefit the employer, as they are getting the work, but not paying for it. Demographics, such as disability, have drawn the short straw really if they opt for voluntary work. You may argue that demographics, such as disability should be happy to be getting out there, doing something practical to help, and meet people, of course that certainly is one aspect of volunteering, but in another way, volunteering if you are considered 'disabled' is just another way to label. It really does feel like disability is being targeted and penalised. In an ideal world, absolutely none of this would ever be an issue, there wouldn't be any rules on employment for 'disabled' people, everyone would have equal rights and opportunities as everyone else, without the constant negativity hanging over us. Why shouldn't disability be treated exactly the same as the able-bodied demographic? It shouldn't make any difference how you identify, everyone should be treated exactly the same in regards to opportunities (if able and willing), and respect. A 'disabled' person's benefits should never be allowed to come into question. I think that the word 'benefits' extends that disability label, that so many people like me are trying to eradicate. It almost certainly seems to help spread the message that disability is not something that is 'normal'. In social understanding, benefits always equal weakness or vulnerability. So much so, that some people in society see claiming benefits as a solution to unemployment. It's the 'easy way out'.

'Disabled' people have 'benefits' really, to make the day to day cost of living with a disability a bit easier to manage, **not** because we are incapable. It costs so much being 'disabled', most of those benefits ultimately are spent on items and services that help to manage or cope with either a disability, impairment of some kind, or a long-term health condition. These costs are called *Disability Related Expenditure (DRE)*. – *[**Majority of Information Gathered on Subject of Disability Benefits taken from Real.org.uk]***

I personally think that society generally, wrongly assumes that disability is just a easier alternative to living. Yes, some 'disabled' people cannot work, (I'm not delusional,) but so many others **are**

able to work. Trying to differentiate this seems to be the difficult thing for people to understand, (employers, especially). It's time now to revaluate this assumption on my own personal opinion and start to champion disability for what it actually is, and most importantly of all, what it actually means.

In a way, I hate the terms 'disabled' and 'disability' for what they can do to a person's sense of worth and their mental health. It's only what society has been taught to believe. Disability is just a term, we shouldn't have to be labelled as such, yes the term is ultimately used for identification, but the majority of 'disabled' people choose **not** to be identified as that term, because then, once you are, that's it, there's absolutely no going back once that branding has taken place. Once 'disabled', always 'disabled' in society's eyes anyway.

Disability is just one small part of a person, not the whole package. The whole world is so blind-sighted by the false narrative of disability, that it's no wonder why ableism, and indeed disablism, exists. The thing is, the information written out there is just for a small minority of 'disabled'

What is Ableism?

people, but it's written in such a way that makes you believe that all disabilities are the same. That's so **not** the case.

Everyone is different able-bodied or not, but we all do the same thing, yes, some of us live in a different way to others, but that's great. Ultimately, it does just come down to personality. If we can just let a person's personality shine through just for a moment, I know that people wouldn't have a problem with disability or any other barrier that makes a person feel uncomfortable. It's the discrimination that takes priority above anything else and it shouldn't. Absolutely **nothing**, disability wise, or even other demographics should ever make a person feel uncomfortable. If we all looked and acted exactly the same as everyone else, that would be boring. I for one am not prepared to live boring and I assume that you wouldn't want that either?

"In order to be irreplaceable, one must always be different." – [Coco Chanel]

Our differences make us who we are. Our likes and dislikes, our mannerisms, what we love, what we hate, who we love, who we hate, our sense of humour, our style, everything that make us who we are, makes us unique. Just because some may look or act differently to another, doesn't give anyone the right to judge, patronise or discriminate.

We are going to take a deeper look now into disability discrimination, the different examples of disability discrimination, where it's most prominent and what can be done to try and stomp disability discrimination out for good. I've already touched on some areas, including discrimination in education and employment, but I want to research further into these areas now as I feel that is the next step.

Chapter 3

Disability Discrimination in Culture

"In complete darkness, we are all the same, it is only our knowledge and wisdom that separates us, don't let your eyes deceive you." – ['Interlude, Livin'... In Complete Darkness', 'Rhythm Nation 1814', Janet Jackson]

We've talked about 'ableism', so now we must talk about the main thing that causes 'ableism'. Discrimination. It's a horrible word, but it's now time to look at the root cause of why 'ableism' exists in the first place.

"I am fortunate enough to have been the Member of the Senedd for Wrexham since 2007 and in that time, it is clear from my casework and regular correspondence with constituents that, sadly, disabled people regularly face additional difficulties. Whether that's physical and the literal obstacles in houses, buildings and our towns and communities, or it could be the hurdles and

blockages created by organisations or people's attitudes." – [Lesley Griffiths, Member of the Senedd for Wrexham]

There are different types of discrimination, but most of these thankfully are now being recognised and rectified for the most part. Of course, you still have instances of discrimination, but people now are aware and the majority tries to adjust their ways and mind-sets into this fairly new way of thinking. Disability however, seems to have missed this adjustment in attitudes, through no fault of it's own by the way. I really don't think disability discrimination is well known, I like to think that is the case anyway, but you never know today.

For this chapter, I'm actually going to lean a bit more into Government findings into discrimination and see if there is any realisation that strategies need to be improved. This will be very interesting, if I do say so myself.

First though, to understand why disability is misunderstood today, we must look at the past to see how people's negative attitude towards the subject contributed to modern society's viewpoint. There is always a cause to any action.

Discrimination in Culture

Attitudes Towards Disability in the Past

Unsurprisingly, disability was never treated equally in the past. As far back as the medieval period, it's safe to say the disability wasn't treated respectfully at all. The level of inhumane treatment was relentless and unbelievable to put it mildly. There wasn't any respite to the horrific behaviour.

Collective Treatment of Disability

Disability was disrespected during the early days. There was no proper information out there about the different types of disability, or disability in general. As a direct result of this lack of understanding, society mistreated disability, either by being 'curious' or terrified of it. Derogatory names would be given to 'disabled' people and some would even be 'warned-out' of town in New England in America.

Shockingly, the term 'billies in bowls' would unfortunately be a common expression to describe someone who *"moved themselves around by sitting in a small wooden bowl and propelling themselves with two small wooden blocks." – [HistoricEngland.org]*. Of course there were other derogatory names and terms for different forms of disability, some are too offensive to mention, but of course you had the unpleasant terms, 'idiots', 'imbeciles' and 'lunatics'. These terms are horrific in themselves, I refuse to add some of the others. The terms I've mentioned are tame in comparison, believe me. Compared to society in the nineteenth and twentieth centuries, where everything ran on appearance, wealth and the class system, disability would unfortunately be seen as an extraordinary thing. If you weren't deemed 'normal enough' to 'fit-in' with the social hierarchy, just because you may have had a disability of some form, to differentiate between, what would be considered to be 'normal' society, and disability, these derogatory names would help to separate the two, placing a metaphorical barrier.

The nineteenth century saw the majority of this inhumane treatment.

"...Negative attitudes towards people with learning disabilities existed around the world. At one time in the USA, people were only allowed to get married if they had a certificate

to say they were normal and well. It was also common practice in some countries such as Sweden to stop people with learning disabilities having children by sterilising them. This is still sometimes carried out today, for example in Australia." – [The Langdon Down Museum]

I cannot personally believe the level of inhumane treatment. Not to allow people to get married just because they may have a learning disability of some form, unless they had a certificate to confirm that they were well enough? It's inconceivable, but this was unfortunately the reality of disability during this time period. I would say that at least nothing like this happens today, but I personally never realised that forms of this abhorrent behaviour still happens today in Australia. Sterilising people with learning disabilities? This is something that you would imagine belongs in the past. How anyone this day and age can so blatantly do this to another **human being**, is terrifying. If you didn't understand why I felt the need to write my books, then this is definitely a good indication. We say that we're more understanding, more knowledgeable, more modern today, but how can we be if mistreatment still happens? I really cannot understand the reason why people sterilise others with learning disabilities. The only 'logical' theory (and I will say logical in quotations as really, mistreatment of disability in any way isn't logical), but the only 'logical' theory I can think of is maybe, Australia somehow thinks that if they sterilise people with learning disabilities, then there won't be a chance of more people who have learning disabilities being born? Of course if this is the case, there's no actual problem in having a learning disability at all. People who have learning disabilities can live a full life today. I really can't understand why sterilising people with learning disabilities is a thing still in Australia.

For context, I decided to research this sterilisation procedure in Australia just to see if I have understood the above quote correctly, to see if there's any truth to the claim, as even though I know that disability discrimination still unfortunately exists, it does seem a little farfetched to me. It seems extreme.

"It is common in the legal commentary to refer to child sterilisation as if it is a gender neutral issue, but the overwhelming majority of sterilisations and certainly all the cases heard by relevant Australian courts and tribunals, involve female children with intellectual disabilities. There is social problem at the centre of the debate about sterilisation. Sterilisation is a procedure that is notorious for having been performed on young women with disabilities for various purposes ranging from eugenics through menstrual management and personal care, to the prevention of pregnancy, including pregnancy as a result of sexual abuse." – ['The Sterilisation of Girls and Young Women in Australia', Australian Human Rights Commission]

I can understand sterilising for actual health reasons, the type of health reasons which can be dangerous and even fatal, if not undertaken, however sterilising people with learning disabilities has absolutely no justifiable reason as to why it happens, other than believing nonsensical ideas of stopping hypothetical pregnancies without consent, where the potential infant could be born with a learning disability of some form. Forcing anyone to do something against their will is inhumane and a criminal offence in the UK, and by rights, I would imagine other countries too. Obviously if unconsented sterilising is a thing in Australia today, then it isn't a criminal offence, and if it is, then Australian Government definitely needs to rectify this ASAP. I'm not saying to ban sterilisation altogether, as it does help to rectify actual health issues that may cause actual harm down the line if nothing is done. What I am saying is to criminalise unconsented sterilisation which includes sterilising people with learning disabilities against their will. It's inhumane and goes against all that we, as a 'modern' human race likes to celebrate.

Disability may have been seen as 'unique', a 'curiosity', and/or a 'hideous thing' back in the nineteenth and twentieth centuries, but the true hideous thing was in fact social attitudes towards the subject. It's really unbelievable how people were so focused on shutting the topic down by finding horrific methods to either hide disability away, or indeed, use disability for their own personal gains.

Discrimination in Culture

Asylums/Institutions

The most common practice to 'deal with 'disabled' people' from the eighteen hundreds to nineteen-fifty was sending them to live in asylums or institutions. From my research, a lot about the asylums/institutions were surprisingly positive, stating that 'disabled' people who were committed, basically, had their own little community. There were workshops where the people could learn different skills.

Typical asylum/institution housing 'disabled' people with learning difficulties in the 19th-20th century

"Craft workshops were managed by local artisans. As well as this, patients' boots and clothing and staff uniforms were made on site in tailoring workshops. There were also bookbinding, carpentry and mat making activities. As many as 150 women were worked in the laundry. We also know that patients kept canaries as pets, and cats roamed the estate hunting vermin." –

['Daily Life in the Asylum, A bustling, isolated community', HistoricEngland.org.uk]

Workshops? Shops? Activities? Even being able to keep canaries as pets? This sounds like an idyllic retreat, not a place of isolation.

Apparently, the 'disabled' people who were housed in   Buckinghamshire County Asylum near Aylesbury, and Middlesex Asylum in Hanwell, had the opportunity to also grow their own food, to generate an income of some form. Historic and monumental events were celebrated in these asylums/institutions, including Royal coronations

etc., there were regular dances, also having resident chaplains were a regular feature of the asylums/institutions, which were specifically designed to make 'disabled' people feel more freedom and gain more social skills ironically. I know for a fact that Denbigh Asylum in particular did exactly these things, in order to make the surroundings feel more 'normal', sounds idyllic right? It couldn't be. Not to put too fine of a point on it, but these

Denbigh Asylum
Denbighshire, North Wales
United Kingdom

123

people were still trapped against their will in these places, forced to form a small community to make everything seem a little less depressing. To live a life of pretence. Scratch the surface though, and I can guarantee you that this 'idyllic lifestyle' the owners and staff members created, was just a rouse, something of which could be deceptive to the untrained eye. It really didn't matter how much it was dressed up, the cold reality of it was 'disabled' people were still segregated from the rest of society. No level of artificial freedom was going to change that. There were still strict schedules that had to be followed, everything was micromanaged.

"These "insane asylums" subsequently turned into prisons where society's "undesirable citizens" — the "incurables," criminals, and those with disabilities — were put together as a way to isolate them from the public." - ['Nine Of History's Most Infamous Mental Asylums And The True Stories Behind Them', Natasha Ishak, All That's Interesting]

This is the truth of it all. Just because you may create a world with everything a human being needs to live, really you are taking away the whole point of life by deciding to isolate people for no apparent reason whatsoever, other than they have something that you may not understand. Yes, it was the eighteen hundreds and disability was seen as an 'unusual' thing, but even back then, deciding to isolate people just because they may have a disability is disgraceful. Creating a world for disability is just that, a creation, a fake existence. It isn't worth it. Hiding things that you don't understand ultimately just adds to the problem of disability discrimination. I do personally think because of this attitude in the Victorian era, disability today isn't as 'normalised' as it could be. It's a shame. A great potential was missed in my own personal opinion. If 'disabled' people had the same level of opportunities as everyone else in society in the Victorian era, equality may have been a thing today. Who knows?

People with mental health issues and learning disabilities were treated significantly worse in these asylums/institutions.

Discrimination in Culture

"The Mental Deficiency Act of 1913 meant that people with learning disabilities could be forced to live in asylums, many never returning to their families..." – [The Langdon Down Museum]

Having no say in your life, forced to be isolated from your family and the community in general is absolutely upsetting. Being denied to be apart of your family just because you may have a learning disability of some form? It's barbaric. Nobody would dream of treating another human being this way. In my personal opinion though, it has gone too far the other way. There's no happy medium. The word 'compromise' doesn't exist in the world of disability. People are too caring towards any 'disabled' person, so much so, that it's suffocating in a way. Disabilities are seen and treated as 'fragile', to the point where we are treated as children. We're wrapped up in cotton wool, overseen by a society who have no idea of **us**. Do you know how that feels? To be constantly treated as a victim? Your **every move** analysed? Your freedom, your independence just taken away? You have no input in your life. You always have to be seen and treated as a 'disabled' person. People have to constantly be with you in case "something happens". You're looked upon both sympathetically and empathetically. To you, empathy may not seem to be a bad thing, but look at it from a 'disabled' person's perspective. You go through your daily routine, a routine that can vary from day to day, both socially and personally. People's reactions to you change constantly. Staring, patronising behaviour, judgemental behaviour, assumptions that aren't based on true reality, sympathising, not to mention the personal side, the constant pain, the equipment, the constant battles that we have to face day in, day out, just to get what we're entitled to. The mental health side of it all. and you want to throw empathy into that mix? Unless you have lived it, you can't empathise with it. It's actually offensive to empathise with something that you have no proper idea about. We don't deserve to be empathised on top of everything else. We deserve respect and action. None of these traits society thrusts upon us is going to change anything, dedicated action is. The sooner society realises this as **fact**, the better.

Discrimination in Culture

"At first, institutions aimed to teach skills to people with learning disabilities so they could be discharged back into their own communities. But over time they became places of containment. Fears about the health of the general population were sparked by the eugenics movement in the early twentieth century. People with learning disabilities came to be seen as a threat to a 'healthy' society." – [Royal College of Nursing]

People with learning disabilities being seen as 'a threat' to society? Sometimes I do despair at the level of inhumane treatment of disability, even in the early years when disability was still somewhat of a 'new concept' so to speak. Being locked away just from basically what was a rumour **does not** justify the ridiculous response. It seems to me that disability was treated like a scapegoat. If there was an issue (often health related), 'disabled' people were automatically blamed without question. They were society's excuse for all the negativity. It's so funny to me how quickly attitudes changed. I believe that society had so many issues quickly developing, panic set in, and disability became the new 'punching bag' of sorts. Disability was seen as a 'vulnerability' in the nineteenth century, (even more so to a degree than today in many ways). It still is today like I say, but at least there is some awareness of disability, regardless of how limited that awareness is, understanding desperately needs to be improved and more action definitely needs to be undertaken today, if we are actually ever going to achieve full disability equality, but awareness is much better today compared to the nineteenth century, but then again, that definitely isn't saying much.

"There was a new class of medical professional, the 'alienist' (later known as a 'psychiatrist'). At first, alienists believed asylums were peaceful places where patients could be restored by 'moral treatment'. But by the end of the century, they had lost their 'therapeutic optimism' and believed that most patients were 'incurable'. The asylums contained 'chronic' and dangerous cases, and most of the inmates never left." – ['Disability in the 19th century', HistoricEngland.org.uk]

It's quite telling how people in the nineteenth century mistreated disability even in the beginning when the initial intentions were pure, made in good faith. Maybe foreshadowing for what was to come? Referring to psychiatrists as 'alienists', gives me a good argument for this theory, the word 'alienist' to me just proves that disability was an alien concept in the past. Maybe intensions **honestly** did come from a good place in the beginning, but psychologically, maybe those honest intentions were intentional in themselves, to mask the true thoughts and feelings? It does make a lot of sense to me.

'Freak Shows'

The fifteen hundreds unbelievably saw the beginnings of what was horrifyingly referred to and advertised as 'Freak Shows' in England, but didn't reach the pinnacle of popularity until the mid eighteen hundreds in both the UK and America.

"Hundreds of performers, from conjoined twins Daisy and Violet Hilton to the extremely small-statured General Tom Thumb to William Henry Johnson, a Black microcephalic man also known as Zip the Pinhead, made their living on the sideshow circuit. It became a viable and

hypervisible career path for disabled people at a time when we were thought of as pathetic or revolting creatures that needed to be kept hidden out of sight."

['Before The ADA, There Was The Freak Show', Kim Kelly, Author, 'FIGHT LIKE HELL: The Untold History of American Labor']

TOP: CONJOINED TWINS, DAISY AND VIOLET HILTON
BOTTOM: WILLIAM HENRY JOHNSON, 'ZIP THE PINHEAD'

This is just disgusting to read.

"Early freak shows occupied a very general category that could refer to nontheatrical exhibits such as fetuses in jars or exotic or deformed animals as well as exhibitions of humans. In this context, the term freak was considered a pejorative way of referring to humans, in performance or not, and was rarely used by professional performers or promoters."
– ['Freak Show', article by author Michael M. Chemers, Extracted from Britannica]

These shows were basically used to showcase people with a wide range of disabilities, but also as a way to deceive society. For the public to 'marvel' at the 'uniqueness' and the 'disgusting creatures', all for a profit. It's interesting to note that 'professional' performers and promoters never actually used that particular term. This just screams to me desperation. Desperation of needing customers that badly that the promoters of these shows were actually ready and willing to dehumanise and degrade the 'performers'. There isn't any actual doubt in my mind that the 'performers' reluctantly agreed to advertising these shows as 'Freak Shows' because simply, 'disabled' people didn't really have any choice or say in the matter, which is utterly heart-breaking. After all, what other option did they have? Workhouses? Asylums? These people were treated like toys, simple as that.

The term, 'Freak Show' is arguably widely recognised in general society, even today. We may not know why fully they were referred to as 'Freak Shows', or what the actually were in the first place, but it goes without saying that these 'Freak Shows' were obviously well established and renowned for us, as society today, to even have heard of them in some capacity.

A lot of 'disabled' people during this time period were forced to 'perform' in these abhorrent shows.

"It became a viable and hypervisible career path for disabled people at a time when we were thought of as pathetic or revolting creatures that needed to be kept hidden out of sight." – ['Before The ADA, There Was The Freak Show', Kim Kelly, Author, "FIGHT LIKE HELL: The Untold History of American Labor"]

I think it's safe to say that humanity, or even logic for that matter, didn't come into question. 'Disabled' people were 'hired' to 'perform' in 'Freak Shows' as a means of providing a platform for the 'people' who offered this type of 'entertainment' to the general public. It was a case of wanting fame, and the more 'strange' the 'performer', the more likely the 'Freak Show' in question would gain popularity. These 'people', wanted to be known as the best in the business, so the more 'peculiar' the disability, the more likely 'disabled' people would be forced into a life of turmoil, as word would've spread and 'people' such as PT Barnum would find fame and respect for having the best show.

"Up until the 1940s and especially during its Victorian heyday, the sideshow—or "freak show"—was one of the only sources of gainful employment available to people like me..." – ['Before The ADA, There Was The Freak Show', Kim Kelly, Author, 'FIGHT LIKE HELL: The Untold History of American Labor']

There isn't much more that I can add to the above comment from Kim Kelly. It speaks for itself, and speaks volumes.

Abhorrent 'Acts'

Not to single out any of the 'disabled' people who were an 'attraction' at these shows, as every person condemned to this disrespectful life mattered, but a few people have stayed in my mind since researching, and I will name a few of these people who unfortunately went through this horrific treatment, as an example of how these shows deceived the public, but also mistreated 'disabled' people. These people mentioned though are more than likely only a small percentage of the amount who actually 'performed' in these shows.

Joice Heth

Advertisement for Joice Heth

Her name was Joice Heth, and she was **purchased** by PT Barnum in order to 'perform' at his 'Freak Show'.

"Barnum launched his career in the mid -1830s with his exhibition of Joice Heth, an elderly enslaved African-American woman. Heth had been exhibited by others with little success, but Barnum brought her to New York, advertised her age as 161, and claimed that she had been nursemaid to the young George Washington." – ['The Joice Heth Exhibit', The Lost Museum]

To reiterate, and for it to sink in, Joice Heth was an enslaved African-American woman, who was also blind, may I add? Joice was **purchased** by PT Barnum after **little success** at other shows, and was given the ridiculous title of *'George Washington's 161-year-old nurse'*, (as seen left),

Discrimination in Culture

which of course wasn't true. There wasn't any evidence for this of course, but these shows never ran on facts or evidence, they ran on lies and hearsay. The title was designed to create more appeal to PT Barnum's distasteful 'attraction'. The public had no choice than to believe such nonsense.

Her task was basically to recount tales to a captivated audience about her time as 'George Washington's Nurse'. Being as infamous as he was, I think PT Barnum saw an opportunity to use George Washington's popularity and (for want of a better word) fame for his own personal gains. To capitalise on a well-known public figure by adding false information to his life. George Washington passed away in seventeen ninety-seven, and I heavily doubt that the family couldn't object to this blatant lie, as laws weren't made to protect any person's likeness or usage of name, until nineteen eighty-eight when the *Berne Convention Implementation Act*, and similarly in nineteen seventy-eight, when the *Copyright Act* came into practice.

Joice sadly passed away at the age of eighty in eighteen-thirty-six, of exhaustion from the gruelling schedule of constantly being on display, and made to 'perform'. You may think that eighty isn't a bad age to pass away, but you must remember the life she led up to that point. She was enslaved, more than likely tortured, then purchased like an object, and condemned to a life of 'performance' and deceit. Yes, again the old argument of, it was a 'different time', but everyday must have been traumatic, not only for Joice, but others too. I can imagine sadly for Joice the prospect of death didn't seem so bad in comparison. As if this mistreatment wasn't disgusting enough, after her death, PT Barnum then ordered a public autopsy to determine her true age. Was there no end to his abhorrent actions? Dignity and respect wasn't given to Joice Heth even after death. PT Barnum had the audacity to cash in on one of his 'curiosities' after the woman took her last breath. 'The Greatest Showman' PT Barnum, he was not, in my own personal opinion. He was just a despicable excuse for a human being, with absolutely no integrity whatsoever. Even after his 'displays' had passed away, he still wouldn't let the **people** rest. It seems to me that if the opportunity to make money presented itself, there was no hesitation in exploiting the dead. The 'Show Must Go On' mantra springs to mind. It's absolutely shocking and disgraceful.

No Shame To Exploit

These 'people', responsible for the absolutely disgraceful treatment of the 'disabled' people, had no problem at all in showcasing disabilities as 'extraordinary'. Even advertising 'disabled' people doing 'ordinary' things **despite** their disabilities. It's unfathomable.

"It was a brutal time to be different, and faced with the known horror of imprisonment or the uncertainties of the stage, some people decided to take what seemed like the best option available: joining the freak show." – [Kim Kelly, Author, 'FIGHT LIKE HELL: The Untold Story of American Labor']

Some 'disabled' people did have a choice between being apart of a 'Freak Show', being committed into an asylum, or being forced to work in a workhouse however, but a lot didn't have that luxury of choice. Their fate was decided for them. When you actually think about it though, those choices wouldn't be considered a 'luxury' in today's day and age, but back in the time period I'm talking about when disability discrimination ran rampant, having the choice between an asylum, 'Freak Show', or workhouse, I'm guessing, **would** be an exciting prospect or the best option sadly.

You may have noticed that I referred to the owners of these 'Freak Shows' as quote, unquote 'people', as I personally believe that the owners couldn't be real human beings. Real human beings have compassion and integrity, which these owners obviously never had, if they were comfortable enough to exploit 'disabled' people as they did, (living **or** dead) without any guilt or remorse for their actions. Profit should never be an excuse to act immorally. A 'different time' it may have been, but there still should have been a limit, at least a personal limit, if not a societal limit. These 'people' didn't have a conscious in my own personal opinion. People had intelligence even in the fifteen hundreds onwards, mistreatment of

Discrimination in Culture

'disabled' people in this time period, should have been noticed by the public, the actual brutality of the situation. It would've been common sense to see someone who was being mistreated. It's just cowardice, plain and simple. It's a form of bullying.

Admittedly, the popularity of these shows grew in the eighteen hundreds, despite them being established much earlier. You may ask why? Why did it take so long for these types of shows to gain momentum, and why did these shows gain momentum in the first place? Historian and *Labour* Councillor, Dr. John Woolf, startlingly has the answer:

"On 23 March 1844, a six-year-old dwarf marched into Buckingham Palace. His name was Charles Stratton, AKA General Tom Thumb, and he was 25in tall. He was dressed in a court suit, and a cocked hat framed his blond hair and rosy cheeks. Towering above him, at 6ft 2in, was the 'greatest showman', PT Barnum.... The pair had an audience with Queen Victoria and her retinue of royal guests who were spellbound as Tom performed skits, tricks and impersonations

for more than an hour. Victoria was in hysterics when Tom withdrew a small ceremonial sword and started battling with her spaniel. Later that day, the Queen wrote in her diary that Tom was "the greatest curiosity, I, or indeed anybody ever saw". Without realising it, Victoria had given the

Charles Stratton
AKA General Tom Thumb

freak show her royal seal of approval. An entertainment revolution was about to occur." – ['The greatest show on earth? The myths of the Victorian freak show', article by Dr. John Woolf, extracted from History Extra]

Having the Head of State at the time, indirectly promoting this extremely bizarre level of discrimination, that society then revelled in, says a lot about this time period. The Queen gave a 'green light' of sorts to society to then go and exploit disability without any moral compass, or anyone to tell society otherwise. In my mind at least, Queen Victoria had blood on her hands by indirectly promoting such shows. The popularity of

Discrimination in Culture

these shows grew after the sad passing of Joice Heth, her treatment (or lack of) was absolutely despicable, if the treatment of Joice is anything to go by before Charles Stratton had an audience with Queen Victoria, you can probably imagine how worse the mistreatment had gotten since the approval from the Queen at the time. I personally doubt this, but any small shred of blocking any mistreatment after Queen Victoria met with Charles Stratton and PT Barnum went straight out of the window. Also, for PT Barnum to then go on and try to exploit another person with Charles Stratton, to Queen Victoria of all people, just goes to show the level of his ruthlessness, his disregard of human life, and his barbaric character.

You maybe asking yourself, why would society base their thoughts on Queen Victoria's beliefs? This would be a valid point, but you must remember that under Queen Victoria's rule, Britain had a successful time period with the expansion of industry, economic growth and the growth of empire. So of course with this positive track record of helping to revolutionise Britain, Queen Victoria had a lot of influence on society. People looked up to Queen Victoria to make the correct decisions. It was that trust that then gave Queen Victoria a platform. The power. The upper hand. The privilege to have society trust her judgement without question. If the Queen expressed joy over something, people would inevitably listen and follow suit. It maybe inconceivable, even laughable today, basing your judgement on Royal opinions, but it's not much different from basing our opinions on media today. We pride ourselves on our independent thought (which really isn't true. Today, royalty is just replaced with media's influence). We rely on media today to shape our beliefs, thoughts and opinions, which is dangerous. Back then though, royalty had the most influence. Royalty was today's media.

"With great power, comes great responsibility."
– [Former UK Prime Minister, Winston Churchill]

Former *Prime Minister*, Winston Churchill may have become *Prime Minister*, years later, after the death of Queen Victoria, but Winston Churchill's quote is appropriate as it perfectly describes people of influence.

Being in power, you must be aware of the level of influence you have. If you are in this position, you constantly have to be mindful of your actions. This is more suited to media today admittedly. The saddest thing is a 'Freak Show' and most modern media outlets in the present aren't that different from each other. They are both money driven for the most part and will happily deceive individuals for profit. Not all media outlets are money driven of course, there are those who base their information on truth rather than sensationalism to gain interest and therefore a profit, but taking into consideration the world's reliance on media to retain information, there undoubtedly are those who do unfortunately take advantage of their platforms and just publish unreliable content just for greed. Although not directly linked, 'Freak Shows' did work and operate under the same mantra as the unreliable media of today.

I do wonder if Queen Victoria never had this type of 'entertainment', if in fact 'Freak Shows' would be as popular, if the Queen at the time, never 'endorsed' that cruel form of discrimination so openly, without worry? Yes, it may have been a 'different time', and disability was seen as an extraordinary thing, but it was still inhumane, especially if you know how some 'disabled' people were forced into performing in these infamous shows.

"Some of the performers had been kidnapped and were forced to go onstage against their will. Others were mistreated by abusive staff members or by people in the audience, who did not see the performers as real people." – ['Inside The Tragic Stories Of 9 'Freak Show' Performers', by Erin Kelly, extracted from All That's Interesting]

This is absolutely disgraceful. Nobody with morals would ever dream of forcing anyone to do something without consent today. (It's against the law in many respects, depending on the situation someone may be being forced to do something against their will). This was the reality of disability in this time period, there was no law to state otherwise. There was absolutely no consideration for the person. Having a disassociation with disabilities never helped to rectify this mind set. Disability was seen as a pretence strangely, as an illusion. Maybe that's why people didn't really see any issues with the mistreatment? Maybe it was easier to disassociate rather than confront? Or

Discrimination in Culture

1800's 'Freak Show' Poster of an Amputeed Woman

more likely, maybe it was because people didn't really understand disability? I mean this could be the case, as people automatically put 'disabled' people into institutions etc. Disability was seen nothing more than a 'curiosity', if Queen Victoria's diary entry is anything to go by?

I'm guessing that 'Freak Shows' were seen as sadly the best option to a 'disabled' person (for those who were given a choice), at the time, as I can imagine the 'people' running these abhorrent 'shows' tried to entice 'disabled' people with the promise of fame and a life of ease, compared to the alternatives. Why else would 'people' feel the need to use disability? Money drove everything, and still does in many ways. There's an argument that the incentive of money is much worse today, but you cannot take away from the absolute disgusting treatment 'disabled' people faced during this time period, appearing in these shows.

"...The most popular attractions were oddities with extraordinary talents, who could do supposedly normal things despite their disabilities. A famous example of this type of act and sort were Siamese twins, so called because of Chang and Eng, the original twins were born in Siam in 1811 and brought to America in 1829. Midgets were frequently advertised as being much older than they actually were. Hirsute or bearded attractions would range from Jo Jo the Dog Faced Boy, and the famous fake show, Hairy Mary from Borneo, which was in reality a monkey." – *['National Fairground and Circus Archive', The University of Sheffield]*

Deception was the main feature at these types of shows. As long as it brought in a profit, integrity was left at the door, so to speak. You can actually apply the term 'con artists' to these 'people'. They had absolutely no issue with creating a false narrative. As long as the 'story' was good, and it made money, by alluring the public, who cared?

Discrimination in Culture

These people with disabilities were disrespectfully treated, and for what? Entertainment? It is absolutely shocking, disgusting and unfathomable how individuals with a disability was so blatantly put on display to 'perform', be gawked at, ridiculed, objectified, basically made to feel like an outcast by society. Cruel names were attached to these **people** to make them seem more interesting. Normality didn't sell, peculiarities sold. These names would demean, belittle and lower self-esteem and confidence to those who were shamelessly exploited. The saddest thing about all of it was the acceptance of these 'disabled' people. What was the alternative? An asylum or workhouse? The lesser of evils it may have been, but at the end of the day, it was still evil, no matter which way you look at it. These were human beings, with thoughts and feelings. What I can't wrap my head around is where were the families of these 'disabled' people? Being the time period it was, I can sadly hazard a guess.

I'm only surmising here, but given the fact that disability was treated as a 'peculiar thing' during the medieval period onwards, I would think that having a 'disabled' child would in fact be shameful, as parents and families of said 'disabled' children may have actually been shunned by society, labelling the family, (which would be ironic in itself, having no problem in labelling the 'disabled' family member, if it meant the shame would be removed from the parents or family). So maybe parents and families of 'disabled' children opted to remove said child in order to keep up appearances? Knowing now what I know about the fifteen hundreds onwards, it isn't farfetched in my mind to suggest this as a possible reason for parents and families not stepping in to save their children from such disgusting and disgraceful treatment.

Chang and Eng Bunker

A little backstory on conjoined twins, Chang and Eng Bunker:

"Chang and Eng, joined at the waist by a tubular band of tissue about 3.25 inches (8 cm) long and about 1.5 inches (3.8 cm) in diameter, were born of a half-Chinese mother and a Chinese father. Their anatomical peculiarity caused them to be sought after as children, and they even had an audience with the king of

Discrimination in Culture

**Chang and Eng Bunker
The first known Siamese twins**

Siam. In 1829 Chang and Eng in the "hire" of a British merchant left Siam, and throughout the following decade they travelled around the eastern United States and in Canada, Cuba, and Europe." – [Encyclopedia Britanica]

Travelling the world, having people want to meet you can be an exciting prospect when you're young. Getting the attention over something you can't control, (especially in the eighteen hundreds) and all you have to do is keep 'performing'? The appeal of it would sound idyllic on the surface. I'm guessing that this was the approach to getting Chang and Eng Bunker involved in this horrific lifestyle? These 'people' strike me as the type who would make their 'attractions' believe that their life was wonderful, keeping up the pretence, scratch a little deeper though, and it is obvious that it was all just a front. These 'people' were like vultures waiting for prey, and when they had their prey, there were only three things on their minds, exploitation, money and power. They could sugar-coat it or deny it all they wanted, but this was the harsh reality. People often try to entice others by offering something that would be hard to say no to, only for their selfish end goal of doing it for their own benefit.

"Things started to change in the early 1800s. In 1829, 18-year-old conjoined twins Chang and Eng held one of the first freak shows in Britain: they were exhibited in a commercial, permanent venue; they had a manager who introduced the act; there were visual and textual accounts of the show; and there was a performance. The Siamese Twins, as they were known, performed acrobatics and somersaults to an audience who paid half a crown for the pleasure. They could ask questions, touch the connecting ligament and purchase an exhibition pamphlet which told the twins' fabulous story. The show was endorsed by members of the Royal College of Surgeons who were given a private performance and were drawn to the mysteries of the twins' physiology, while the

average punter was enticed by the exotic spectacle. In seven months, 100,000 people came to see The Siamese Twins in London." - ['The greatest show on earth? The myths of the Victorian freak show', article by Dr. John Woolf, extracted from History Extra]

Chang and Eng were really another two people of which society could stare at in 'wonderment'. The brothers were again put on display for all the world to see. Admittedly, I couldn't find any information on whether the conjoined twins actually enjoyed it all or not

Maybe in hindsight, these 'Freak Shows' offered an alternative life, much more appealing in theory to a 'disabled' person? Better than being caged and chained to walls in asylums? At least they would have an opportunity to be apart and contribute in some way to society. If I lived in this period, and was lucky enough to be given the choice, I sadly know I'd opt for these shows. An opportunity to travel, see new things, experience life, receive attention, rather than be hidden away in asylums or workhouses, being tortured for no apparent reason whatsoever. Theory can seem better than reality, especially during this time period.

Thankfully the appeal of the 'Freak Show' ended in the nineteen-forties in America, when attention began to shift. Coincidentally, this was the exact time when *"several federal laws made discrimination against people with physical disabilities illegal, and the exhibition of "extraordinary bodies" was outlawed in some states." – ['Sideshows', Lynchburg Museum]* Unbelievably however, it took about thirty years for the UK to catch up.

I personally cannot understand this. Why did it take so long for the medical profession to reconsider disabilities? I did think at first, maybe it was the fact that the *NHS* wasn't founded then, but I realised that the *NHS* was founded just after World War II.

"The creation of the NHS in 1948 was the product of years of hard work and a motivation from various figures who felt the current healthcare system was insufficient and needed to be revolutionised." – ['The Birth of the NHS', article by Jessica Brain, Historic UK]

Discrimination in Culture

I'm guessing that the struggles after the war to make ends meet was another incentive for the creation of the *NHS*. For context, the *NHS* was founded on the fifth of July nineteen forty-eight. This baffles me if I'm honest. This just goes to prove that disability has always been an afterthought in society, even to the so called 'medical professionals'.

1932's Banned Film, *'Freaks'*

Directed by Tod Browning, *'Freaks'* was a banned nineteen thirty-two film which really just exploited disabilities. The promotional poster alone is enough to understand why the film was banned in the UK and USA. It is still technically illegal to show this film publicly in parts of the USA.

"A circus trapeze artist, Cleopatra, takes an interest in Hans, a midget who works in the circus sideshow. Her interest, however, is in the money Hans will be inheriting and she is actually carrying on an affair with another circus performer, Hercules. Hans'

1932's Banned Film 'Freaks'
Promotional Poster

fiancée does her best to convince him that he is being used but to no avail. At their wedding party, a drunken Cleopatra tells the sideshow freaks just what she thinks of them. Together, the freaks decide to make her one of their own." – [Synopsis of 1932's banned film, 'Freaks', IMDB.com]

From the get go, you can probably see the controversy of said film? It is said that Tod Browning wanted to pay tribute to the people with disabilities who were working in what was horrifyingly referred to and advertised as 'Freak Shows'. It's also claimed that he also wanted to pay tribute to his own life as a child, being a part of the travelling circus himself. I would imagine that Tod Browning innocently titled the film as '*Freaks*', probably in a way to attempt to pay homage to those who 'performed' at a 'Freak Show'. I can imagine that Tom frequently came into contact with the shows from time to time growing up, and saw no issue with creating a film which was based around the subject. Disability was seen as this unusual concept back in the past, even in the early thirties when disability was starting to be properly recognised. It's with films like this, the disability equals fear angle, that did absolutely nothing to help minimise the false perceptions, films like this only helped to accelerate this ridiculous belief that disability was something to fear, no matter how much evidence you had to say otherwise. I mean the genre of the film is classed as horror.

"Inspired by Tod Robbin's short story Spurs and his own experience of growing up as part of a travelling circus, Browning wanted to pay tribute to the people with disabilities working in what was then called 'freak shows' in an attempt to destigmatize them. Badly mistreated and disregarded by society, the so-called 'freaks' adopted a code of ethics that stated 'the hurt of one is the hurt of all and the joy of one is the joy of all'. Browning wanted to celebrate this solidarity and highlight, to audiences in 1932, that they are people too." – ['One of Us: What Freaks Tells Us About Evolving Attitudes Towards Disability on Screen', Tanya Charteris-Black, Independent Cinema Office, (ICO)]

The mantra of the 'Freak Show' performers, never translated to the screen. This was obvious when the film:

"...was refused a certificate in the UK on the grounds that it "exploited for commercial reasons the deformed people that it claimed to dignify". The film was labelled as 'grotesque', 'abhorrent' and 'loathsome', some of the able-bodied actors were blacklisted and many of the actors with disabilities returned to work in circuses or went on to feature in films that presented them as 'monsters'." – ['Certification and Censorship', 'One of Us: What Freaks Tells Us About Evolving Attitudes Towards Disability on Screen', Tanya Charteris-Black, Independent Cinema Office, (ICO)]

If you are trying to destigmatise disability by creating a film, obviously, the term 'freaks' doesn't convey disability in the best light. It was nineteen thirty-two granted, and I understand Tod's reasoning behind him naming the film *'Freaks'* to a degree, but still, there **should** have been some foresight that a film such as *'Freaks'* would end up being controversial and even banned? Granted, maybe there was some element of 'shock' aimed towards disability itself, maybe that was one of the reasons why it was controversial and eventually banned? I can't honestly believe that it was banned solely for the mistreatment and exploitation of disability. Society today still struggles in a lot of areas when it comes to disability equality, so I highly doubt that people in the nineteen-thirties were outraged by the exploitation of disability. Don't get me wrong, there may have been a few outraged by the exploitation, but for it to be banned on exploitation alone? I'm having trouble believing this unfortunately.

Even the promotional poster continues with this level of discriminative language by asking the horrendous question, *"Can a full grown woman truly love a midget?"* This is wrong on so many levels. The poster alone suggests that it would be extremely unusual to fall in love with a 'disabled' person. Referring to the trapeze artist as 'beautiful', whilst using derogatory terms for the side-show performers of the film, would subconsciously encourage society to wrongly believe that 'disabled' people aren't as attractive as able-bodied people. Only marrying the leader of side-show performers for their inheritance, again subconsciously this is a dangerous thing to advertise. Also, by having the inheritance as the main plot point of the film and the worry of the 'beautiful trapeze artist' only marrying the leader of the side-show performers for that reason alone, subconsciously encourages the idea of 'disabled' people are vulnerable and can be easily manipulated for another person's gains, and no able-bodied person would ever fall in love with a 'disabled' person. This is a barbaric message to send out.

I personally haven't watched the film, I however did watch a clip of said film, both for context and to see if my analysis of the synopsis and promotional poster was actually misinterpreted somehow. The clip I watched was the 'One of Us' scene. Basically, it was horrifying just by the ableism on display. I sat with my mouth literally open when watching the scene. It was designed to create a sense of horror. The side-show performers chant 'one of us' whilst a challis is passed around for each side-show performer to drink from. The challis eventually gets passed to the trapeze artist, all the while the side-show performers are chanting *'one of us'* on a constant loop, becoming more menacing as the challis is passed to the artist. The whole scene is passed off as a terrifying scenario.

"Browning, who once travelled with a circus, cast real carnival performers—including people of short stature, conjoined twins, bearded ladies, microcephalus, and limbless sideshow performers. He contrasted their honesty and integrity with the degeneracy displayed by the true monsters in the film, the so-called "normal" people. Called "ghastly" and "repellent" by critics, Freaks was banned in several places—including in the United Kingdom for some 30 years. Though it later attained cult status, the controversial film effectively ended Browning's directorial career." – ['Freaks', Britannica]

The aftermath of the film was horrendous in itself. It's really sad to see that the able-bodied actors who appeared in the film, were automatically blacklisted from appearing in other films after. For the 'disabled' actors to be reintroduced into

'Freak Shows' to 'perform' after the film wrapped just really is telling just how society received the film. I must say that I'm extremely pleased to learn that the negative reviews actually contributed to the complete ban on the film. Granted, it could have been an ableist attitude as to why the film was banned, but to be completely honest, I do believe that society began to recognise disability discrimination to a degree. Whatever the reason, I'm just pleased to learn that proper action was taken. A lot of awful things happened to the people involved in the film after it was over. I would like to now say that we're getting there, and we are up to a point, but again, so much more can, **and needs** to be done to improve disability relations with society.

Let's be like the people of nineteen thirty-two, and do our bit to stomp out disability discrimination for good. Everyone can do something to end disability discrimination indefinitely in time. People just need the **right** information to be able to weaponise.

Discrimination in Culture

Misconceptions

There are many things which people still don't realise. For example, take wheelchair users, people often only see what is in front of them, a person in a wheelchair. Nobody actually realises the other things involved with being in a wheelchair. Of course everyone is different and it **is** dependent on the individual's condition, but more often than not, wheelchair users often have underlying issues that they have to deal with. Disabilities in general tend to have underlying issues which the public are unaware of if you have a mild form of a disability. Of course it is more noticeable with severely 'disabled' people, but with mild forms, it can be a totally different scenario. I'm not saying that to confirm vulnerabilities. 'Disabled' people can do, and achieve great things, if only we have the opportunity. I'm just saying that disability is far more than just sitting in a wheelchair, if you are indeed a wheelchair user with a mild disability. Physiotherapy sessions, pain management, spasms, medication, operations are just some of the things a 'disabled' person has to deal with. It isn't a picnic, not by a long shot, but we can manage it in our own separate ways. What will make it easier is if society cut us some slack and actually allow us to be involved in everyday 'normal' life without any questions.

Main Character Syndrome

Managing Director of *1st Enable Ltd.*, Jeff Dawson said basically, (and I will paraphrase here, as I was lucky enough to have a meeting to discuss ideas for this book), that **"we all could be considered to have a disability if we really think about it, both physically and hidden. Things like glasses being a physical indicator of a possible disability."** – **[Paraphrase: Jeff Dawson, Managing Director of 1st Enable Ltd.]**

Yes, you did read that right, glasses could be considered a disability. Something that most of the world has worn at least once at some point in our lives. A universal common denominator that everyone can relate to. Jeff did make me think a bit about this. He said basically, in order to teach about disability effectively, basically you need to find something that most can relate to and take notice of. There lies the potential for true change. It's all well and good just describing a disability that has no bearing on another. Yes, your speech maybe intriguing, informative and inspiring, but like Jeff explained, *"once the speech ends, that audience returns to their own heads, their minds, their worries etc."* – *[Paraphrase: Jeff Dawson, Managing Director of 1st Enable Ltd.]*

It is true, individuals often only see themselves as the 'main character' in their own personal lives. It can be considered a narcissistic trait, but unfortunately, because of the world we live in today which is extremely fast-paced, and reliant on social media.

"Main character syndrome is when somebody presents, or imagines, themselves as the lead in a sort of fictional version of their life." – *[Psychology Today]*

You basically need to have a topic that will capture the attention of everyone, preferably, something that everyone can relate to in order to get the desired effect. It sounds (again) so superficial, but this is unfortunately the world we live in, especially with today's technology and complete lack of privacy with a social media obsession. By having a topic which is relatable, it is more likely to have the desired impact of it staying with them, according to Jeff. Also though, it is extremely important to talk about other disabilities too. Only then, can we truly try and make other disabilities heard. Maybe having a fifty-fifty approach could be the way to go? Starting by talking about something that everyone can relate to, to grab attention, and then change the topic slightly to the intended subject. By doing this, there is a possibility that people will be more interested in the actual topic. Also, by explaining about something relatable first, you maybe subconsciously explaining how 'normal' you are to society, (for want of a better word).

Being Born With A Disability VS. Developing A Disability: Public Opinion

Recently, I asked a question on social media:

QUESTION

"Is there any difference between being born a disabled person and developing a disability during life? What are your views? Be truthful."

This is a **very** good question to get to the heart of social views on disability. To delve a bit more into the psychological aspect, as a 'disabled' person myself, I thought that it would be a good area to cover, to see how people's attitudes differ between being born with a disability, and developing a disability.

"I think people who are born with a disability are used to being the way they are, because they don't know any different. I think developing a disability later in life would be a lot harder to deal with maybe?" – *[Natalie Copnall-Aspin, social media participant]*

"Yes I think if your born with a disability, you learn to use things and approach things differently. If a person/persons get this in later life, they have to adapt and if your elderly it can be very different situation... not only the person has to adapt, but also the person looking after them/care as in my case, me..." [Shirley Cummings, carer and social media participant]

"For me, it was easier to grow up with my disability. I've never known anything else. I really feel for the people that lose their functions later in life. Their mental health

suffers way more than mine does." – [Bridget Dandaraw-Serrit, social media participant]

This is true. I do believe not knowing the difference in a way, is easier to adapt to a 'disabled' life, (speaking from experience). Whereas, if you develop a disability of some form for whatever reason during your life, it maybe a little harder, both physically **and** mentally to adjust to your new way of life. For me, I've never known what it's like to be able-bodied, so for me, there isn't a comparison, because I have nothing to compare my life to if this makes sense?

Going back to Kerry Evans, the DLO of Wrexham AFC, she, on the other hand has experienced, (as she's said) both a life as an able-bodied person and a 'disabled' person, yet her outlook on life is extremely positive. This attitude is a wonderful thing to have witnessed for myself. Kerry, (as mentioned), has had a number of different disabilities since she developed her disability, but obviously, she hasn't let that define her. She hasn't let that one **small** part of her, take over. It could have been so easy for Kerry Evans to develop mental health issues because of what she went

Discrimination in Culture

through (and continues to go through), but Kerry **refuses** to her disability identity her, become her. She's respected. So why can't other 'disabled' people have that **exact same** level of respect? There is abs no difference at all between Kerry Evans and other people with disabilities. **Nothing at all**. I do wholeheartedly believe that it's basically down to the fact that Kerry was able-bodied during the first part of her life, somehow, Kerry has managed to steer herself away from the negative experiences of life, and instead replaced it with a positive outlook on life. It's fabulous to see, and to see first-hand.

Examples such as this does give me hope.

There is actually a page on the *Government UK* website dedicated to teach the public the proper terms to use for disability. *Gov.UK* says:

"The word 'disabled' is a description not a group of people." –[Gov.UK]

The website goes onto say:

"Avoid medical labels. They say little about people as individuals and tend to reinforce

stereotypes of disabled people as 'patients' or unwell." – [Gov.UK]

This is exactly what I like to see. A little bit of backup. I'm pleased to see that Government is trying to stop disability discrimination by adding it to their website , but there has to be more that could be done. Although a starting point, one page on disability discrimination just isn't enough to change perceptions. It's just putting a sticking plaster over a wound. A wound that is growing day by day.

Disability Discrimination In Society

Just adding something, such as disability discrimination to a Web page, and thinking that it will make a difference, is just a lazy way to say that you acknowledge the situation, (especially if you are in a position of power like Parliament is.) Some text on a Web page isn't enough, and it is frightening to think that the Government may believe that it is enough. Unfortunately, unless something is put into the public domain today, (especially in media,) then I really don't think or see any actual possible change. Society is so engrossed and obsessed with media today, that it would be better for this type of information to be put on television adverts and social media platforms, in order for it to make a greater impact and impression. I can see why Government added disability discrimination to their website, and again, I am grateful that they did, especially with them dedicating a whole Web page to the subject of disability discrimination. However, this will not do anything to improve relations between disability and able-bodied people unfortunately. Realistically, nobody is going to search for this type of subject unless it is put in front of people. Nobody would see the need, unless researching for a project etc. I know that sounds harsh, but unfortunately it's true, people aren't going to look for disability discrimination, simply because the subject doesn't affect them. Government would have a better chance of changing perceptions of disability if they actually thought about new ways of bringing this subject to the masses.

I'm now going to speak about the difficulties I've faced, and likely so many others have faced who are in my position.

- **Public Transportation**

Buses

As I've already said, public transport is a God-given right to **everyone**. Nobody should ever feel excluded from general society just because they maybe differently abled.

Transportation has always been a point of contention for me personally, take your standard bus for example, yes their is room for wheelchairs, there's a sign in the spaces that say those spaces are reserved for disabled people. What I can't understand is, why there is only **one space per bus**? In my mind, there should be one **either side** of a standard bus. What if two wheelchair users want to go out for the day and they need a bus to take them from point A to point B? They wouldn't be able to, as there is only **one space reserved for wheelchair users**? Or, like in my own personal case, I wasn't able to board a bus, simply because there was another wheelchair user in the one disabled space provided. I had to wait **three** times a particular day, just to board a bus to get home. (Just a side note:-because of the bus I was forced to board had a different route, I had to change buses a further **twice**, just so I had the guarantee that I was going to get home that night.) All for the sake of an extra disabled space on a public bus? You wouldn't see able-bodied people having to struggle in the same way. Why is disability an afterthought?

A particular bus company was very forthcoming in their advertising campaign of their new buses that were kitted out with the latest tech. Society somehow has this fear of technology one day taking over, but they aren't as afraid if it means having charging ports and *WIFI* on public transport? In my opinion, this bus company should have always thought about the people first, gimmicks, second, because that's all it was at the end of the day, a gimmick, a ploy to rival competitors. No thought was given to potential passengers when coming up and instigating this poor excuse to boost numbers using their bus service, let alone any thought for wheelchair users and 'disabled' people alike. All that they cared about was the business. That, in my eyes was, (and still is,) the main focus. That is a truly sad conclusion to all of this, but unfortunately, also a very real and apt one, something

that all businesses, given the chance would potentially opt for as a cheaper alternative to spending money and including **everyone**.

On a recent day out, I was actually legitimately amazed to see that there is an actual bus company, *'Llew Jones'*, with specific 'disabled' access vehicles. (Above)

"We also have a range of Wheelchair accessible vehicles in our Executive and

Standard Class fleet. Whatever your requirements, our family run team of professional and experienced staff are dedicated to ensuring we meet our client's needs. – [LlewJones.com]

Transportation of any kind should have disability at the heart of their companies. It's not fair that 'disabled' people always has to compromise where the rest of society can go about their daily business with very little issue. It isn't the fault of 'disabled' people that we in fact have a disability. It's an utterly ridiculous logic. It does obviously feel like disability is being punished for existing. Government should by rights really look into this transport issue for 'disabled' people, and come up with a realistic and strategic plan to introduce more accessible features onto their transport vehicles. One bus company isn't enough. *Llew Jones* isn't really pioneering this, they are just creating a transportation system that should have already existed years ago. It's so obvious what needs to be done, however, because we now seem to live in a self-obsessed society where we are very much antisocial in a physical sense, which of course is ironic as we love to socialise virtually for the most part. I do wonder if *Llew Jones* would ever consider to work with UK Government to improve transportation for disability? It would be the ideal scenario.

Trains

I was recently sent an article about how train transportation has improved greatly for 'disabled' passengers, and I am truly thankful to the journalist of the article in question for granting me permission to use it and quote what was written.

"Travelling by train can be a daunting prospect for someone with a disability. But with the help of those with first-hand experience of the challenges, Northern is steaming ahead with changes to make its services more accessible."
– ['Rail passengers hail 'life-changing' new

Discrimination in Culture

It's true, travelling if you have some form of a disability can be daunting, you have to be mindful of so many things, including but not limited to, having enough space to fit a wheelchair, or, if you are anxious or have a disability such as autism, finding out how long **exactly** your journey is going to last, things which able-bodied people often take for granted. I do think that is partly why society doesn't see disability as 'normal', but rather 'abnormal', because society itself never really appreciates the things someone who is considered to be 'disabled' has to constantly think about, and always has to be aware of. Society thinks of disability as 'abnormal' because they instigate the 'abnormalities'. I think if the whole planet had a disability of some kind, then there is no question in my mind that accessibility would be the main focus of society, because everyone would be the same, then adaptations all over the world would have to be made to help people live as 'normal' of a life as possible. Society is selfish in this regard in my own opinion, if it doesn't affect them, then they don't care if anyone else has a difficulty. As long as they are managing in life, then that is all that matters.

However, I am very pleased to learn from Helen Carroll's article of the much needed improvements that have now been implemented by this particular rail service, granted, a little too late in my own personal opinion, but better late than never.

Actually asking people who know **first-hand** about what is needed to include disability, is **a major** turning point in the progression for change. I'm glad to read from Helen Carroll's article that the rail service in question, actually took the time to ask those who have a disability the improvements that needed to be made and implemented. If only other services and public facilities had the same mind-set. It's common sense really, if you are doing something that potentially helps another person, especially if it is something potentially to improve their lives, then of course, asking that person how to design that thing, is something that is **always** going to be beneficial.

Nobody can ever second guess things as important as inclusion and equality. There does need to be some input from the demographic you are designing for. Maybe again, people are frightened to ask for fear of offending, but it's going to be more offensive to a person if their needs aren't met properly. I think it's a very British thing to be honest, the 'stiff upper lip' mantra of the UK has somewhat become the most integral part of the country. We are scared to do things, ask questions, ask for help etc. because of this mantra that ultimately makes absolutely no sense in today's world. How can we change perceptions if we are scared to ask the fundamentals of humanity? It is ironic how we claim to be more 'open-minded and accepting', when we are terrified to ask a 'disabled' person for help in designing something that could potentially benefit them. How does that work or make any sense? It doesn't.

"As the largest train operator in the north of England, Northern recognised that more needed to be done to help make UK train travel less inaccessible for the nearly 15 million disabled people across the country. After the company sought advice from Stephen Brookes – former rail sector champion and now rail policy adviser for Disability Rights UK – NAUG was set up." - ['Rail passengers hail 'life-changing' new initiatives for all disabilities' (Article by Helen Carroll for the Liverpool Echo)]

Northern is setting the example that other companies need to now follow. They have actually sat down and realised that more needed to be done to include everyone. It is true, doing anything if you have a disability of some kind is quite the experience, and for the most part, not in the good sense of the word. So seeing a company take initiatives to change their service to include disability is a fantastic thing to finally see.

"The organisation has been instrumental in the following: making Northern's services

accessible for mobility scooter users; the design of a new type of accessible toilet "pod", the first example of which has been installed at Guide Bridge station (with plans for another 82 on the network), and dementia-friendly signage at Buxton station." -   ['Rail passengers hail 'life-changing' new initiatives for all disabilities' (Article by Helen Carroll for the Liverpool Echo)]

This is absolutely game changing in my own opinion, even though accessibility should have always been a fundamental right to everyone in society by now, to see some actual thought go into the push for equality is monumental. People are now actually sitting up and realising the mistakes of the past, **and what makes the biggest difference is just the involvement of asking those in the know**. Actually investing in the people the accessibility on these trains are designed for is so obvious, yet ingenious. This is what I personally meant by progression. It's such a small difference to ask 'disabled' people their opinions on what should change to include disability, but in the end it will help to make a big impact on the perceptions of society, as we won't be seen as 'disabled' as much because we have the facilities that **we** helped to design and get installed.

I'm not going to go into much more detail here about the positive impact that this train company will ultimately have as I need to discuss further the other points in this chapter, but what I will do is add one more quote from the article of the other ways that disability is being included into the everyday train journey on this one rail service.

"Northern has won two national customer service awards for its app, Accessible Travel Simulation, designed for travellers who are anxious – including those with autism. It enables them to "virtually" experience a journey from the comfort of their own home, including interactions with staff, and is being used widely as part of Northern's Try the Train scheme." - ['Rail passengers hail 'life-changing' new initiatives for all disabilities' (Article by Helen Carroll for the Liverpool Echo)]

Discrimination in Culture

There are so many other examples of how this rail service is helping disability by incorporating things such as a virtual train journey on *Northern's* new app, to help to calm passengers who are anxious or who have autism, which is just amazing that a train company actually, again, took the time to design an app that helps in such a way. I applaud them for their efforts. It's the little things, the small details which I personally appreciate. 'Disabled' passengers can also ask for assistance online before they travel if required, especially wheelchair users, like myself, who require a ramp to board a train. Like I say, simple adjustments, but it will make a big impact in the accessibility argument. There is much more to this article that I can't write about here regrettably, as I need to move on to other subjects in this book, but the article needs to be shared to be known of how much of a positive impact *Northern* is making. I would urge anyone and everyone, 'disabled' or otherwise, to take some time and read Helen Carroll's full article, as it is not only monumental for the equality of 'disabled' people, but you really get an insight into what a 'disabled' person deals with on a daily basis.

I can't help but wonder if whether other transport services followed the same example as the railway service in Liverpool, maybe disability discrimination would lessen? I do wholeheartedly believe that people judge disability simply because there is no basic easy accessibility to the fundamentals of society, which undoubtedly **will, and ultimately does** make a person with some form of disability **look** 'vulnerable' to an able-bodied person. If **all** companies, **especially** everyday fundamental companies such as transport services made it easier for a 'disabled' person to access a service without difficulty, then I believe that people's perceptions would be altered for the better. It's the obstacles that society creates which ultimately impact on a disability, **not the disability** itself.

Public Facilities

"Facilities being offered must provide equal access to toilets for disabled customers / visitors and employees, to the same

standard as non-disabled people. This means meeting their Equality Act 2010 obligations." – [Accessible-Toilets.co.uk]

Facilities for 'disabled' people are compulsory. Everyone should have access to restrooms etc. regardless of ability. It's just common sense and a part of our human rights. Nobody should **ever** feel excluded or uncomfortable. Everyone deserves to be treated as everyone else.

Apparently, a **standard 'disabled' toilet** should have dimensions of **at least *"2200mm deep x 1500 wide." – [LAN Services Ltd.]* A 'disabled' toilet realistically needs to have enough space to fit a wheelchair, hoist, 'disabled' person and their support worker(s) if needed, and enough space to accommodate **everything and everyone** who uses a 'disabled' facility. Nothing should ever be an obstruction. I'll be honest, I really don't think companies who have the contracts to build these types of facilities, actually are aware that there needs to be space with absolutely no obstructions whatsoever. The amount of facilities I've used when out in public with very little space to fit myself, my wheelchair and my mum is ridiculous. Usually, it's either a sink or a hand-dryer in the way of the toilet, which I always have to try and manoeuvre around awkwardly. Thankfully, my disability is mild, so nine times out of ten, I can manage (with difficulty – difficulty that shouldn't ever be an issue), but because I'm slight in build (thanks to my CP), I can just about squeeze myself in-between any obstruction. Think though about other 'disabled' people, I'm lucky in a sense that I can just about manage to use a 'disabled' facility, but what about others with a disability? People who aren't as able as myself, how are those people supposed to manage obstacles?

The people responsible for building these facilities aren't 'disabled' themselves. This is the problem. They are companies hired, therefore they're there just to do a job. They must have to build from a premade plan, as literally almost every single 'disabled' facility is built exactly the same way. I really think that the companies who build these facilities miss a trick. Just by asking a 'disabled' person how to design a 'disabled' facility, would be a clever way of getting to know about different disabilities, what's needed, what's going to work and what isn't, (in accessibility terms), and just generally make disability appear more 'normal' than ever before to society, as of course, it should be. Working with 'disabled' people on 'disabled' facilities makes so much sense and would both be beneficial and have incredible potential for both understanding and 'normalising' disability to a twenty-first century society. If other companies followed the same example as the railway service in Liverpool, then maybe disability would have a fighting chance of being recognised as 'normal'

On a recent day out, I had to use a 'disabled' facility. As you can see, (I hope that the photograph justifies the issue), the sink is directly in front of the toilet. This is just one of many typical issues a 'disabled' person faces daily. For more severely 'disabled' people, it's virtually impossible to use, a public 'disabled' facility, there are exceptions of course, but those exceptions are so few and far between. I recently took a trip to Cardiff Millennium Centre, whilst I was in the city to promote *'CP Isn't* Me', and I used the 'disabled' facilities there. I must say that I was pleasantly surprised how spacious the facilities were, with different types of equipment to cater to numerous different disabilities. I shouldn't have to say that I was pleasantly surprised, as space and equipment should just be a given in a 'disabled' facility, but sadly like I've said, unfortunately, this isn't the case. The majority

of public 'disabled' facilities are designed like the image shown, c r a m p e d   a n d unequipped, which defeats the whole purpose of a 'disabled' facility.

I've spoken before about my own personal experience with the 'disabled' facilities whilst I was in university. How ridiculously small they were in comparison to other 'disabled' facilities that I used previously. Basically, those facilities in university were standard able-bodied facilities with just a 'disabled' logo sticker stuck randomly on the facility door. (Of course, the 'disabled' facilities – or lack of – weren't the only issues that any 'disabled' student/visitor faced whilst in this particular university. If I struggled, then of course others also obviously struggled). I'm not going to write about all of the missing aspects here, as I have done so before in *'CP Isn't Me'*, I'm only discussing the ridiculous excuse of facilities in this section to make a point.

When I flagged up the issue with the facilities to the university, (the disability team to be precise), I just felt that I was being humoured, there wasn't really any actual intention to rectify this, (or any other) issue for that matter, that I brought to the attention of the university. I've said this before, but only **one** 'disabled' facility was 'adapted' when I attended university, (and I do use the term 'adapted' loosely), as only **half the wall** was extended, when I, (with my mum **and a social worker**) clearly asked for the entire wall to be extended so that I could access the facility easily with my powered wheelchair, two support workers, a hoist and room to manoeuvre. It wasn't too much to ask, just for my dignity and my rights as a **human being** to be met.

"If someone doesn't cooperate with their duty to make adjustments, the Equality Act says it's unlawful discrimination." – [Accessible-Toilets.co.uk]

Although I've personally experienced difficulties with public 'disabled' facilities in the past, they weren't as bad as the experience in university.

Companies who build these facilities **should and need** to comply with the *Disability Discrimination Act of 2010*. Saying that though, it works **both ways**, the people who are responsible for the Act should, and desperately **needs** to look into 'disabled' facilities. I do wholeheartedly believe that if they did, then the facilities would undoubtedly be improved. As it stands now, it doesn't seem like any review or follow-up is being implemented. That is a shame if true. It's no good just putting things into law just because it may 'sound good' to the public, without any real proper monitoring of an Act. That is immoral.

"If I have to feel thankful about an accessible bathroom, when am I ever gonna be equal in the community?" – [Judith Huemann]

Dropped Kerbs

"A dropped kerb is a section of pavement that's lowered to make it easier for people with disabilities to get from the pavement to the road or for vehicles to drive across." – [TotallyDriving.com]

Dropped kerbs in a public place are **essential** to promote disability independence. It is this level of 'normality' that every single 'disabled' person should be entitled to. It's just basic human rights at the end of the day, but kerbs don't tend to work in favour of disability somehow. Either there are no dropped kerbs, there is **one** dropped kerb on one side of a road but none on the other, which is obviously highly dangerous, as a 'disabled' person cannot access the pathway on the other side of the road. The amount of times I've personally come across these issues is absolutely ridiculous and unacceptable. (Side note, dropped kerbs are often on a slant, which makes it difficult for wheelchairs to pass them easily.

Wheelchair users often have to fight the laws of gravity just to not suddenly drive into the

road into oncoming traffic. It's terrifying, believe me. I dealt with this in the past and how I wasn't killed in the process, I don't know?)

Whoever put these in place, should have asked wheelchair users beforehand on how dropped kerbs and the design of dropped kerbs should be implemented.

I recently took a photo of a 'disabled' parking bay, (right), in a public place where there was only one dropped kerb for about **three** 'disabled' parking bays. The dropped kerb was

Discrimination in Culture

a bit further down to where dad originally parked the car. There were cars already in the other 'disabled' parking bays when we pulled up. I was in my powered wheelchair (which isn't the smallest of chairs), and I had to try and squeeze myself in-between the car and the small gap to the dropped kerb. Yes, I could have gone the other way (the other side of the car), but I ran the risk of driving into oncoming traffic, and I obviously wasn't going to attempt that.

This isn't a 'one-off'. There are numerous dropped kerbs that have **exactly the same** issues. Dropped kerbs are supposed to be there for both safety reasons and independence. The amount of drivers who I've personally seen parking **by a dropped kerb** is just awful. It doesn't show any respect or equality for disability whatsoever. According to *TotallyDriving.com*, it's also against the law to park on a dropped kerb. There are so many issues with dropped kerbs that are just being allowed without question. The law desperately needs to reinforce the laws on dropped kerbs.

The law otherwise is just failing disability and therefore encouraging disability discrimination.

Whoever designs these dropped kerbs and think that it's acceptable to have a dropped kerb on one side of the street and none the other, is just ridiculous. It's just laziness in my own personal opinion. The way the dropped kerbs are slanted is just too much. I get that the kerbs need to be designed to make it easier for a wheelchair user to use on a **slight** slant, but not to the extent where it seems to impact on safety. The designers definitely need to go back to the drawing board and redesign these dropped kerbs, and to reiterate, by asking a 'disabled' person their thoughts on the redesigns. Yes, it's a radical idea, but it just might work.

Aideen Blackborough has actually raised this issue of pavement parking, which obstructs accessibility to 'disabled' people by campaigning.

"I first initiated the campaign following an incident in October 2022. Whilst carrying my youngest child, I was almost tipped out of

my wheelchair due to dangerous pavement parking. Despite alerting the council and my children's school, nothing has improved. In spite of the Headteacher's pleas, parents continue to park on pavements around the school, often forcing me into dangerous situations. Last week, two similar incidents occurred." – [*'Pavement Parking Campaign Update', Aideen Blackborough, Disability Trainer, Speaker and Author*]

If you aren't 'disabled', it won't affect your daily routine if you come across obstructions, it maybe an annoyance, but you can just walk around the obstruction (usually a vehicle parked on a pathway), without too many difficulties. A 'disabled' person who comes face to face with an obstruction doesn't have that 'luxury' of choice. I say 'luxury' in quotations as accessibility shouldn't ever be a 'luxury', accessibility is **necessary**. This however, doesn't just affect disability, people with prams and buggies experience exactly the same issue.

Obstructions to 'disabled' people are dangerous. Obstructions are a safety issue. Wheelchairs, especially powered wheelchairs aren't designed to squeeze past an obstacle, depending on the person, a wheelchair has to accommodate that person's weight, so many wheelchairs are bulky. Yes, some powered wheelchairs are allowed to use the road instead of a pathway, but this can be a major safety issue, and a compromise that we shouldn't have to make. This option isn't a solution.

I personally had this same issue on numerous occasions during my lifetime, mainly as a child, where a car was parked on a pathway, so mum and dad have had to find a dropped kerb (which are few and far between), and take me onto the road directly onto oncoming traffic, just because of somebody's incompetence.

There's another area of improvement with dropped kerbs, they are too sloped. If a 'disabled' person is using a pathway and wants to carry on that pathway, we almost always have to be mindful of dropped kerbs as they can create major safety issues themselves. I personally have spun into the road into oncoming traffic when trying to use a pathway, especially as a child, which has a dropped kerb. A lot are too sloped, and therefore gravity comes into force. If something is too sloped, and you are trying to use a pathway in a wheelchair, there is a real danger of the chair succumbing to gravity and the chair being forced into the road. I personally am now wary of passing a dropped kerb in my powered wheelchair, for fear of potentially being forced into the road. I use my manual wheelchair because of this fear, as much as I can, eliminating my independence. UK Government desperately needs to rectify this. If a fatality is caused due to either pavement parking or sloped dropped kerbs, then they may take action. This attitude isn't good enough, disability is really an afterthought. I'm personally am extremely happy that Aideen Blackborough is fronting this much needed campaign, which I fully support, but again this shouldn't be left up to 'disabled' people to highlight the obvious issues, there should already be awareness and plans to rectify issues which cause a danger to disability. You can show your support for Aideen's campaign by contacting her directly on her website, aideenblackborough.com or by using the hashtag #QuestionMarkWhereYouPark on *X* (formally *Twitter*).

Disability Discrimination In Education

Bullying is sadly nothing new in places of education, according to a research paper on the subject of bullying from the *Department of Education*, it is noted that bullying behaviour was first recorded **" ...in the 19th century, although the term bullying was not mentioned, the pattern of it has been described as interpersonal violence in everyday life." – [A Time Line of the Evolution of School Bullying in Differing Social Contexts, a research paper by Hyojin Koo for the Department of Education]** and it is something that I personally lived through as you may well know, and I can imagine so have many others in my position, so I know all too well about this. Schools are supposed to be a place of safety, to teach children about the world, and in

Discrimination in Culture

my eyes, that also means teaching children about different demographics, including disabilities. Even though Kerry Evans said she hasn't felt discriminated against, she *"...was bullied in school." – [Kerry Evans Disability Liaison Officer at Wrexham AFC]*

Bullying

Being bullied in school is so despicable anyway, but to be bullied over something you can't control, like a disability of some form, somehow makes it a thousand times worse in my eyes. I'm not trivialising bullying behaviour or favouring which is worse in terms of the intended recipient by any means, bullying in any context is absolutely awful, and just shows how insecure others are in society. All I'm trying to say is that if you are able-bodied, then there is a slight chance that the bullying behaviour may die down overtime, as an able-bodied recipient of this bullying behaviour may change their appearance to try and 'fit in'. You may think it's a superficial way to look at it, but in all honesty, the whole world today is superficial, and I personally feel that the world today has gotten worse overtime with this learned superficial attitude. If you're 'disabled' and bullied, unfortunately there isn't much that you can do to change perceptions, especially in education, trust me, I've tried. 'Disabled' people don't have that luxury. We can't decide and say one day, "*I don't feel like having my disability today.*" This isn't an option. It doesn't help having that label hang over you, that's the barrier that makes it difficult to 'fit in'. That, coupled with a person's physical appearance if a person has a physical disability, we stand no chance. We are automatically categorised as 'different'. There is absolutely no logical reason for this. I think it maybe a coping mechanism for able-bodied children to bully the ones who may look a little different from everyone else. Stress of exams, homework, peer pressure, disruptive home life, can all play a part on a child's mental wellbeing, and so children may turn to bullying behaviour as an outlet, a form of therapy almost. They maybe trying to pass the pain, the pressure, the stress, being attention starved, whatever a child maybe feeling, and passing those feelings onto a 'weaker' child, to make themselves feel better, (for a while at least). Managing whatever struggles they were feeling before bullying. I'm **definitely not** condoning bullying of any form, I'm just trying to work out myself why some children feel the need to bully, whereas other children don't. I'm not a psychologist, so I really cannot answer it, it's just my own personal theory.

A study by the *Centre For Longitudinal Studies* found that *"Forty per cent of children...reported that they were bullied by other children 'some of the time' and a further 9 per cent said they were bullied 'all of the time.'"* – *['Are disabled children and young people at higher risk of being bullied?' - A Study By The Centre For Longitudinal Studies]*

This definitely needs to be looked into. The study states it was conducted in two-thousand and seventeen, (which isn't too long ago if you think about it). The same study goes onto say, *"Our research demonstrates that there is an association between disability with bullying in both early childhood and adolescence, even after other factors that affect the risk of being bullied have been taken into account."* – *['Are disabled children and young people at higher risk of being bullied?' - A Study By The Centre For Longitudinal Studies]*

Disability inclusion and equality is apparently improving in schools today (namely high schools) from an anonymous source, but has it **really**? I know that the study is from six years ago as of writing this book, but has the education system really had enough time to right their wrongs? Six years may seem a long time on the surface, but for what I personally experienced, it would definitely take longer to make sure every single issue with disability in education is fully rectified. By some miracle it is, the education system itself needs to review **why** they allowed the discrimination of disability to happen at all. Like I've said, inclusion should have always been apart of the standard education experience, not just because the *Disability Discrimination Act of 2010* was introduced and made law. However, the quote from the *Irish Times* admittedly has me questioning the reliability of my source. I do wonder if that is why the education system is apparently more welcoming of disability today, just to make it look like they are more ethical in their approach to comply to an ever accepting

Discrimination in Culture

world? I say 'accepting' loosely as nobody can really ever trust that society creates this 'accepting attitude' towards a number of different topics themselves, it's more likely that some people say they believe in something, just to **appear** more modern to match with this ever changing modern culture, that we have somehow found ourselves. Who **really** believes in what they present to the public? To be clear, I'm **definitely not** saying that every single person in the world has the exact same belief system. There are those who see no difference between able-bodied people and 'disabled' people, however I do think that there needs to be an uprising in those who believe in equality in every context.

Places of education never want to be seen as anything less than welcoming, especially today. The amount of backlash it could cause a place of education would be immense. The uproar and scandal of being labelled as 'ableist' is a greater concern to the education system than it is making sure proper access and inclusion is implemented. Like I've said before, image is everything, (especially in high school,) yes, the battle for popularity is something usually pupils and students battle for, but it can also work on another level. Schools today have to be seen to be compliant with the law, to set an example to the pupils and students, but to also appeal to the public. Yes, this version of 'image' is on a grander scale, but the argument is a valid one in my own opinion.

I'm also wondering though, by extension, whether the education system itself felt it necessary to change their attitude towards disability, or whether in fact, they were pushed into it because of the law? Unless we look into this in more detail, then we are ultimately going to be left with more questions than answers, and that is something that I personally am **not** prepared to let happen. I believe that is why disability discrimination has gone under the radar for so long, because people are afraid to ask the more pressing questions for fear of being offensive. 'Disabled' people aren't really going to call out any research, if it is done to ultimately try and change perceptions. After all, that's what we want. As long as the research is conducted respectfully to the subject matter, then it's a great tool for change. Nobody should ever be afraid to ask questions about anything, let

Discrimination in Culture

alone, discrimination. It is a bit counterintuitive how society is seen as more 'politically correct' (or 'PC') in recent years with topics such as religion, race, sexism, sexual orientation, gender equality etc., but people still it seems hasn't had the memo to include disability in this new 'PC' world. Why is this?

Saying that, I've just recently learnt that the *Disability Discrimination Act of 2010* **wasn't the only disability act**, there was another act nine years **before** in **two-thousand and one**.

"Special Educational Needs and Disability Act (SENDA) 2001 – extended disability discrimination legislation to schools, colleges and universities and gave disabled children many more rights in mainstream education". – [The Alliance For Inclusive Education]

How can this be? The level of discrimination against my disability when I   attended high school, and probably others in the same position as me felt during the early two-thousands was unapologetically immense and cruel.

From what I personally experienced, (again, especially in my high school), I can honestly tell you now that disability rights were never included in mainstream education back in the early two-thousands, (mainly high schools). I'm not speaking for other schools, colleges or universities during this specific time as I don't know, I hope disability rights in mainstream education were included, but you never know, all I can go by is my own personal experience of **my** high school, and having a disability in the early two-thousands. My high school must've missed the Act in question from two-thousand and one. In no way would a school allow such disrespect for 'disabled' pupils by choice and rest easy. Morals and ethics never allow decency to slip. That's what I like to believe anyway, yes, I maybe naive, but sometimes you **have** to be a bit naive to save your own sanity, not denial, never denial. Saying that though, you never want to show your naivety to the world as people often think that you are just a pushover if you announce your naivety to the world.

I'm saying I'm naive to my past high school experiences, not saying that I'm lying, being economical with the truth or seeing everything with rose-tinted glasses, you couldn't to be fair during the period when I attended high school especially. I **know** that disability inclusion was non-existent in my high school during the early two-thousands, I'm **choosing** to ignore, not forget the experiences, nobody can ever forget a time in their lives when they were made to feel insignificant about themselves. It will stay with me for the rest of my life probably. To be honest, for all of the difficulties that high school gave me (disability wise), I'm glad I stuck it out, I'm glad that I finished the high school, because without those experiences, I don't think I'd be where I am today. Yes, I have mental health issues partly as a result, but since writing, I've recognised a resilience, a strength inside me that I personally am proud of. I absolutely hated my five years in high school, don't get me wrong, I was alone, depressed, isolated every single day for five years, but I'm proud that I stuck it out, finished with six GCSE's (in the end, after all the ordeal with a separate invigilator), went onto college, met some great people, finished with two diplomas from said college in computing, and went onto university and finished with a Honours degree in graphic design. Finally managing to get a graphic design job in the motorsport industry. I'm a great believer in everything happens for a reason. Without those experiences in high school, I really don't think I would have had the determination to succeed in life. Those experiences helped me to be defiant later in life, of course I suffered mentally for a while, but I've recently recognised the strength within myself. Without the experiences I had in high school, I probably wouldn't even be writing as I wouldn't have anything to actually write about.

I just want to take a moment now to speak to the high school directly.

You probably will never read this, but I just want to say thank you. Thank you for the discrimination, thank you for the bullying, thank you for latching onto one part of me and running with it for five years continuously. You see, without those negative comments, actions etc. I probably wouldn't see my strength, granted, later in life, but that doesn't matter one little bit. I'm strong now. I'm not the shy and quiet girl I once was. Without you, and the negative experiences, I

Discrimination in Culture

wouldn't be where I am today. It's that defiance. I'm a qualified graphic designer, and now an author, I own my own small part-time business. You have made my life what it is. I **choose** to ignore what happened in the past, never forget. I can't forget. I know that it happened, I will never recreate history, if it happened, it happened, you can't deny that. You cannot change the past, but you can move on and prove to everyone who doubts you, wrong. I don't dwell now, I progress. That is what my personality is now. I was a smiley, happy girl when I first started at your high school, with confidence and self-worth. During those five years, you knocked me down to a shell of my former self. It took me **a long** time, but I'm more confident and determined than ever before. You cannot take that away from me.

From what I hear from anonymous sources, you have improved your attitudes towards disability. If that is true, all I ask is that you keep improving by learning from your mistakes in the past, and **be** a more inclusive school. It's just not good enough to claim that your school is the best and equality driven, if in reality, it isn't. Saying those things just to reel people into believing that you are a great school with values, morals, ethics and equality for all, when it is anything but, is immoral. Actions speak louder than words.

"Students with reported disabilities are more likely to drop out from higher education and less likely to achieve a first or upper second-class degree. Those who reported a mental health disability have the highest drop-out rates." – [House of Commons Library]

If this statement was written in the early two-thousands, then I'd be more inclined to believe that this is the case, but this statement was written on the twenty-second of February twenty, twenty-one, only **two years ago**, (at the time of writing this book.) How can this **still** be true? If disability in education has improved so much since those inconceivable years of disability discrimination in education? Either, the *House of Commons Library* are out of touch with the improvements in education, or in fact, no improvement has been made at all. Either way, this **definitely** needs to be looked into. Whichever way you look at it, it definitely isn't a good or positive representation of disability. Whatever the reason is for the statement, I really do believe that the *House of Commons Library* is just focusing on one element when they made that claim. Disability, not the **person**. This in itself is just perpetuating the idea that disability, and even mental health issues, limits the capability of a person who has either, some form of a disability, or mental health issue. No wonder disability and mental health always get a bad wrap in society, with such a negative outlook. The research needs to be reviewed and brought up to date if in fact, disability equality has become a reality in education. There isn't any difference between able-bodied people and 'disabled' people. I'm personally proof of that. This statement by the *House of Commons Library* doesn't encourage people to think differently about disability. Quite the opposite. There are different severities of different disabilities, yes, the more severely disabled the person, the less likely higher education is expected, **but not all** disabilities are the same. This is what I meant by people categorising disability as just one thing. If a 'disabled' person has the capability and determination to enter into higher education, why should that be denied? It doesn't make **any** logical sense. It's just not a fair conclusion to make. Also, incorporating mental health into this unjustified comment, is unbelievably unfair. By denying people who just happens to have some form of a mental health issue, makes that person feel more unwanted and worthless. It's the job, **and the responsibility** of Government to make **every single person in society** feel equal. Not to take away a possible dream in just one paragraph. It's as if Government is trying to pass the blame onto the people who have a disability or any mental health issue for the total disregard of disability, and mental health equality. Basically what Government is saying is that *"Higher education is only suitable for the able-bodied as they are more likely to get a job at the end of the course. It would be a complete waste of time and taxpayer's money to put a 'disabled' person or a person who has a mental health issue through higher education, because at the end of the day, these people will only drop out due to higher education being so difficult for a 'disabled' person, or person with a mental health issue to cope with. It's much more beneficial to put time* *and effort into able-bodied people, as they will keep the economy going."* You can try to correct me all that you want, but this is what I personally get out from the statement. Nobody can deny it, it's there in black and white. Favouring able-bodied people over 'disabled' people and people with a mental health issue is just disgusting. Let me tell you, putting all of your time and energy into the able-bodied and relying on them to keep the economy going is foolish. The economy is worse today (as of writing this) in twenty, twenty-three than it's ever been, (especially after the pandemic). Absolutely everybody, able-bodied or otherwise, are struggling to get a job. What I'm trying to say is that by denying a person's right to education, you are basically denying that person's right to life, and for what? The **possibility** of an able-bodied person getting a job? I wouldn't pin my hopes on that. Whether they realise it or not, employers need educated people more than ever who have qualifications. Disability or mental health issue? It doesn't matter in the slightest. It doesn't make **any** difference whatsoever. We cannot keep having our lives decided for us, it's immoral and unethical to make the suggestion, or imply that people with a disability or a mental health issue shouldn't have the same opportunities as everyone else. It is **definitely not** something that can just be accepted. This is part of the reason why disability and mental health are always looked upon as being 'abnormal'.

There were so many issues with accessibility in my university, far too many to mention honestly. Yes, I should have spoken up about the total disregard of disabled students. I get that, and I did consider the idea of becoming somewhat of an advocate and ambassador for disability rights in the university, but realistically, I just couldn't. Basically, I personally felt like the whole thing would be a waste of time, as I tried to improve the university before by asking to adapt one 'disabled' facility to no avail. I also had to take into consideration my workload, the essays, the lectures, the presentations and the most time consuming thing, the dissertation. I had to weigh up what was more important at that time, so, I learnt to just live with the issues as best as I could. It wasn't ideal for studying, but I personally felt as if I didn't have any choice. The university (disability team) ultimately made me feel like this. There was always excuse after excuse as to why accessibility couldn't be apart of the university, (mainly, usually due to budget), so I basically just gave up and accepted it. I was powerless before, but I'm not now.

I did try to highlight issues with accessibility really, and disability in general in my own way during my final year at university, as I made my dissertation about the topic of Ehealth (Electronic Health), but I spoke about whether Ehealth was basically helping or hindering to a 'disabled' person, both on a physical and a mental level. Whether it was worth all of the upheaval to get technology that is designed to make a 'disabled' person independent, ultimately backfires as certain types of technology only confirms a false narrative of disability equals help. We all need help at some point in our lives, nobody bats an eye when an able-bodied person asks for help (depending on the individual asking of course), a person with a disability has next to no chance of ever being seen as 'normal' as our 'props' are constantly seen. It is ironic how something that is designed to help disability, can ultimately do the opposite. I guess the dissertation was a reflection if the rejection I thought I overcame during high school.

Yes, the education system apparently is more accepting and accommodating towards disability today, but if this is true, the education system must have known of the improvements that needed to be made beforehand, it had to have been recognised years previous for changes to be made today. I'm only going by the source I have who initially told me about the improvements made today. Also, I'm a bit doubtful that the education system itself knew what needed to be improved unaided to ensure disability equality fully. Unless they employed a 'disabled' person within Government to specifically provide information about how to improve disability inclusion in education, I really cannot imagine that disability equality has really been realised to it's full potential. How can it be? It goes back to the old adage of unless you are considered 'disabled' yourself, you really cannot understand what needs to be done to improve equality. You may **think** that you do, but do you really? Yes, you may have all of the necessary qualifications that say that you have knowledge of how to improve disability

Discrimination in Culture

equality, but qualifications don't mean one little thing, compared to lived experience. Has the education system as a whole for example, actually sat down and asked 'disabled' pupils and students **themselves** their thoughts on what could be done to improve disability equality? Or, (more likely – from personal experience), have they just made 'improvements' (what they consider themselves to be improvements) without any proper research?

Yes, from the outside world looking in, it probably looks better, but do 'disabled' pupils and students actually feel free and equal in schools, colleges and universities? Or is it just a case of having to go along with what has been put in place to make the education system keep up appearances, and look good whilst doing it?

In an ideal world, bullying wouldn't exist, but it does unfortunately. Children can be cruel. Nobody can actually stop bullying behaviour from happening, no matter how many improvements you **think** you have made. Nobody can police everything, no matter how well you think attitudes have changed in the education system towards disability. Children often see a difference and latch onto it. Yes, maybe it's a case of not knowing the situation, but it is abhorrent. No matter how many improvements the education system makes to now try and improve disability equality and inclusion, children unfortunately will always find a loophole. What about after school, or online? Maybe able-bodied pupils and students 'behave' in schools, colleges and universities where their bullying behaviour can be monitored and called out, but what about the times when they are unsupervised? What happens then? Now, I'm not saying that **every** child in the entire universe acts like this, no, the majority of pupils, (especially in primary schools) are just inquisitive and more often than not, see absolutely no difference between themselves and a 'disabled' pupil, because guess what? There **isn't any difference at all**.

Again, I do think that the toxicity of society today, have given children (especially high school ages) a complexity about image. Everything is run on image today as I've said, if you don't look a certain way, then you are automatically tossed to the bottom of the pile, no questions asked. However, I really do believe wholeheartedly that

Discrimination in Culture

young people today (especially high school age) have so much pressure placed upon them that they may need a way to release that pressure, and so bullying is a direct result of that pressure. By nature, 'disabled' people are, or do look a little different from the rest of society admittedly. Even if a 'disabled' pupil has a hidden disability, if able-bodied pupils find out, then it is literally World War Three. Disability is the biggest barrier a person can endeavour, especially if you are in high school. It's that labelling that ultimately barricades you into this unjustified 'disability box'.

People often talk about physical barriers when it comes to disability, but in a way, it's the invisible and emotional barriers that ultimately creates somewhat of a distance. Reactions are often the most common barrier a 'disabled' person can face.

Chapter 4
The 'Disabled' Apartheid

"Returning hate for hate multiplies hate, adding deeper darkness to a night already devoid of stars. Darkness cannot drive out darkness; only light can do that. Hate cannot drive out hate; only love can do that." – [Dr. Martin Luther King Jr.]

It's true, even though Dr. Martin Luther King Jr. Was speaking about race relations with that quote, it works on so many levels today. If we aren't prepared to have the discussions we so desperately need ,(in this case, with disability), how are we ever going to progress as a society? This closed attitude will continue to build and build until one day, it'll be too late.

It sounds extreme, but people in South Africa from nineteen forty-eight to nineteen ninety-four regrettably went through Apartheid, where people were segregated just for their skin colour. Thankfully that ridiculous segregation ended years

The 'Disabled' Apartheid

ago for race, but it seems that 'disabled' people are still going through their own version of Apartheid today. Again, I do truly think it comes down to a basic lack of education.

I'm not trying to make light of what people had to go through years ago, through no fault of their own. No, I would never do that. The treatment of race relations was despicable and disgusting years ago, and should never have happened in the first place, regardless of whether 'it was a different time' or not, discrimination of any kind should never have a place in society.

Whether we realise it or not, there is still a social division happening, but we have replaced one demographic for another. We've replaced race for disability.

This is just my own personal opinion and I feel it's a valid one, however uncomfortable it may seem. Segregation and judgement. This is the reality. It still goes on. You may not realise it because it isn't constantly talked about today for disability, not like how it was for race. Years ago there was an obvious problem which needed addressing and thankfully it finally was addressed for race. The whole world doesn't seem to be satisfied unless it has something (or someone) to judge. When Apartheid ended for race, I feel personally that people had to look for another thing to segregate, but this time people would have to pass judgement secretly to save from being called out for the newly established backwards thinking, and so I feel that was when ableism was unfortunately born.

Ableism, in my eyes anyway, seems to have taken over in a big way, and it segregated people, much like Apartheid did years before. I'm not trying to offend, I'm trying to make my point by taking something that most people are aware of and eventually realise was wrong and just replacing race for disability.

As the well-known saying goes, 'two wrongs don't make a right.'

It's true, people can't just replace one demographic for another and expect there to be no repercussions. If people believe this, then there is a definite problem we all face as a collective.

The 'Disabled' Apartheid

I genuinely came up with the 'disabled' Apartheid analogy myself, but I was curious if there were any articles that could backup my analogy, as I was aware that it could cause backlash if I couldn't find evidence that could confirm it. There was something that I found and it comes from an article by Stephen Naysmith in the Scottish newspaper, 'The Herald':

"Disabled people face a catalogue of unfairness, as damaging and discriminatory as that experienced by black people in apartheid-era South Africa, a leading human rights expert is set to warn." – [Excerpt taken from an article by Stephen Naysmith for 'The Herald' newspaper in Scotland]

Comparing ableism to Apartheid may sound shocking when you first hear it, but really there isn't any difference between how race was treated back in the day to how disability is treated today. Once you get over the initial shock of it, there really is a strong case for it. After my research I came to this realisation myself about the 'disabled' Apartheid, I decided to search the terms disability and Apartheid, not thinking that anything would come of it, I just thought that this was my own personal view and there wouldn't be anything that could backup my analogy. However, I was surprised to see the amount of articles backing up my claim and quite shocking, most from South Africa. Clearly, there are still problems with Apartheid in South Africa, but directed towards disability. I genuinely think that if it is still happening in South Africa, then there is no reason to say that the disability Apartheid has spread out across the world. It may not be as well-known as the race Apartheid was, but it is a thing, and the frightening thing is, we may not be aware that we are contributing to this version of Apartheid. Ultimately, it comes down to the treatment of disability, (an obvious reason), but because people seem to segregate disability and put it into it's own group, into the 'disabled' umbrella', this version of Apartheid will continue to grow.

Stereotyping, stigmatisation, patronisation, ignorance, intolerance etc. Can all be a part of the argument that there is some sense of this discrimination happening, but just swapping one demographic for another. There is an unspoken separation, but just because it's unspoken, doesn't mean it's not happening. At every turn disability seems to bear the brunt of the ridicule which is cruel and quite frankly, wrong. I don't know why, maybe people fear disability because it's not as openly discussed as other subjects today, maybe because it isn't a shared experience, or it could be a little bit of both. Who knows why actually people treat others differently, but I personally have a good idea of how this stigmatisation happened.

Intolerance of disability has been taught. It has mainly been taught by the media, when I say intolerance, I mean the learnt behaviour of intolerance. People are constantly told that the 'disabled' cannot do things the same way as everyone else, that the 'disabled' are different, that the 'disabled' are vulnerable and need protection. I have a great example to backup my claim, which I will make further down this chapter.

In my own opinion though, it's the terms 'disabled''' and 'disability' that automatically puts us into that world, that cage, that prison, which disallows us to be involved in everyday 'normal' things. Our lives are dictated for us and we have no say about how we want to live. Our independence is ripped away from us, and all because of two words. If we let those two words overpower us, we will just crumble as a society. People need to be taught the difference between all disabilities and severities. I accept that not every 'disabled' person can do the same thing as everyone else, I appreciate that. It would be patronising and ignorant in itself to believe such a thing. I've said this before but nobody is bionic, however much we like to think we are. Everyone is different and unique. We all have different skills, strengths and weaknesses that set us apart from the next person. However, society still has an obligation to learn not to tar everyone with the same brush, and learning the difference between all disabilities. Not just passing the buck by saying that people can learn about disability in care work. You may learn the job, but you may not understand the full package. The person. Unless people learn earlier in places of education about disability, then any attempt to learn later down the line, will ultimately be a lost cause, it'll be too late, as media and other propaganda would have brainwashed people into thinking that disability is

The 'Disabled' Apartheid

just one thing, and should be treated as one thing. This is why I feel passionate about mandatory disability education at an early age, and it's not just me saying it, the large majority of all participants surveyed ('disabled', able-bodied and carers) said the same. The support is definitely there, we just need to see support and implementation of this much needed want.

At the same time, until society, as a whole start to realise this need, then it's only right that the 'disabled' are taught about how to handle the segregation they will undoubtedly face in life. It's only fair.

The subjects discussed in those PSE lessons when I attended high school mainly catered for able-bodied pupils. Where was the focus on disability? Yes, there were crucial lessons for getting a job and running a household, income and expenditure, all of the basics a 'normal' person needs to learn in life, but nothing was aimed at the 'disabled' pupils, for example, how hard it is to try and get a job if you're 'disabled', 'disabled' rights, the responsibility of society to make a 'disabled' person feel included in life and not just out of pity, managing your own money if you have to pay for your household expenses plus any care you may need. Possible discrimination, etc. The basics for 'disabled' people to learn, to prepare us for what actually lies ahead after you leave the education system. Ceri said that the PSE lessons are fortnightly and still an hour out of normal teaching time. The whole school takes part so no lessons are missed anyway, exactly how it worked when I had PSE lessons. It would be so easy and beneficial in the long run to dedicate one of those PSE lessons to disability, the positive impact that would create by just having an honest discussion about disability in those lessons that are designed to teach children about life, would do the world of goof for everyone involved, (including the adults).

The thing is, education can't just stop there, judging by my own survey research, a lot of people still need to be educated on the fundamentals of disability. To the question of whether disability would help or hinder society's current views, one participant of the able-bodied survey answered:

The 'Disabled' Apartheid

"Definitely a help, do you think it might be a little uneasy for a 'disabled' child in a classroom though whilst the discussion is going on?" – [One Participant's answer to Able-bodied Survey]

This is a valid point to be made, it could prove uneasy for a 'disabled' pupil or person whilst the discussion was taking place, but I personally think that it's all about how the education system chooses to handle it. Maybe having 'disabled' guest speakers invited into the discussion so it's not just a one-sided approach of able-bodied trying to teach other able-bodied about disability, or having some sort of day where everyone had to 'live' (for want of a better term) like a 'disabled' person for a week, (staff members included) for everyone to try and see what we have to deal with, or maybe even more of a project where able-bodied have to team up with 'disabled' for a week, and by doing so, learn about the person behind the disability label, then do a presentation with the 'disabled' person on what they discovered, and in turn the 'disabled' person can discuss what they discovered about the able-bodied person? I don't know, I'm just brainstorming, but what I will say is that educating disability maybe an uneasy thought to begin with for everyone involved, but the constant labelling and ableism is far worse in my opinion. It's all about the execution of educating disability, if it's done in a sensitive way for that initial uneasy feeling to pass, then I truly believe that it would be beneficial. After all, disability is just the same as every other thing being taught in places of education, and it should be recognised as another factor of life.

"...Most able bodied people I have asked about it are more socially embarrassed to ask or talk to anyone who has any disability. However the people or carers with disabilities are willing and happy to talk. It's always per circumstance but the attitude (to me) seems to be ignore vs help or talk to anyone with a disability." [One Participant's answer to Able-bodied Survey]

If able-bodied people are "embarrassed", as this one participant put it, to even talk to a 'disabled' person, then education I feel would potentially remove any 'embarrassment' felt by either party, and I can say wholeheartedly that it's not just my opinion anymore, others like me feel the same

The 'Disabled' Apartheid

way about disability education with the majority of the 'disabled' participants in favour.

It could be considered selfish on my part I suppose, forcing the idea of disability education onto society, but all I'm trying to say is to think about it, and try to see the potential within the idea of equality for all. There is a call for more education about the subject, the results from my own survey research alone proves this with a majority of the 'disabled' people surveyed agreeing that education on this subject needs to be taught, and again there seems to be an overall majority vote in favour of education from both able-bodied people and carers.

I can't speak for every school at this time as I don't know, I can only go off by what I personally experienced, but if those PSE lessons in other high schools were anything like mine in my high school, then there's absolutely no question that the school board should've looked into incorporating disability into those lessons. After all, those lessons were all about learning about life, the do's and the don'ts, learning how to be accepting of others, and yourself, essentially how to manage your life. It's just common sense that disability should've and could've been a part of the lessons. Disability is a very important part of life, after all, there's approximately '14.6 million people' – [House of Commons Library] who are currently living in the UK alone with some form of disability (as of January 2023), maybe even more once this book is published and in circulation. Why is there that many people who have a disability in the UK and still attitudes towards 'disabled' people are still from prehistoric times? I just find it baffling. Disability desperately needs and deserves to be apart of the curriculum if we continue to divide. I'm not sure what it is, I don't know whether people think that disability is a contagious disease, or that people may offend others with disabilities if they do decide to start a much needed conversation. It's more offensive to treat 'disabled' people as second class citizens than to embarrass not only us, but yourself by always treating us like babies. That's the reality, people treat 'disabled' people like little babies, because you may think that we can't understand you or hold a conversation. That's what I meant by referring to the Seven Second Rule, people take

The 'Disabled' Apartheid

one look at you, and within seven seconds, someone instantly makes a judgement, which is usually only based on appearance alone. Appearance can only tell us so much, but it's that complete disregard for personality which lands society in hot water. When you're young and happen to have a disability, you don't mind so much being wrapped up in cotton wool, it's nice, you feel loved and cared for, ill be honest, you feel like you don't have to learn how to do something properly as everything is done for you. As you get older though, you start to acknowledge the lack of independence that the whole world seems to put on you. It's that lack of independence that ultimately stops any possible chance of normality. That's why people see 'disabled' people as 'vulnerable', you're not allowed to have your own mind and be independent. I believe it's that lack of independence from an early age that greatly impacts negatively on any possible chance of future independence. It's just a never-ending cycle. The more someone does for a 'disabled' person as a child, the more a person will automatically do for a 'disabled' person when they're older. There's another disadvantage to this constant lack of independence too. People can do too much for a 'disabled' person that they can sometimes get reliant on people to do basic tasks. Able-bodied children are taught to do things so that when they're older, they are able to function as a part of society, no questions asked. 'disabled' children though, they don't have the chance to learn basic life lessons as they are deemed 'incapable' and 'vulnerable'.

As I've said, I know that some 'disabled' people can't help themselves and that is fine, I'm not talking about the seriously 'disabled'. I'm talking about people such as myself. They see a difference and instantly they are there to 'help', which is great, but in the right context. Disability is different. There are many different forms of disability, some more severe than others. This is what people just can't understand. Everyone is unique, we don't all look identical, it's called genes. Everyone has different genes from each other, but nobody bats an eye when a person sees someone with a different hair colour than themselves. How is disability any different? It's the same thing, but because you aren't around

The 'Disabled' Apartheid

disability twenty-four seven, you immediately become more aware of disability when it's in front of you.

I think it doesn't help when 'disabled' people are put with a support worker who only patronises a 'disabled' person by being constantly molly coddled in front of society. I'm lucky now to finally have Judi as my support worker, I've said this before but Judi treats me like a normal human being. It's a refreshing change as there have been support workers in the past who would just baby me, not letting me live my life. It didn't matter if I had a degree, I just felt embarrassed and ashamed about myself strangely for letting support workers patronise me. Vulnerability is just thrust upon the 'disabled' and we're just expected to accept our fate. For me, it was that intense level of 'support' that just made me feel suffocated. I felt as if I couldn't do or say anything because I was constantly being judged by what I said and did. This is an amalgamation of a number of different support workers I had to deal with throughout several periods in my life before Judi. There were a few support workers during college and university however that treated me as a normal person which I loved. However support workers such as Judi and the ones from college and university are a dime a dozen unfortunately. This is why I'm lucky enough to have Judi, I don't take her for granted now I have experienced the problem with support.

When Ceri asked me to review a book for her class, I remember writing:

"...my own disability became the elephant in the room in high school, like I felt underappreciated for who I actually was at the time. I felt, (as Harriet herself felt,) the support workers made everything worse as they were there to just do their job and that was it. No friendship developed in high school with any support worker I had, nor any peer. I felt like there was a stigma to who I was at the time." [Excerpt taken from Samantha Maxwell's review of the book 'Speechless' by Kate Derbyshire.]

Harriet was the main character in the book I reviewed, but even though she was just a character, I saw parallels between her and myself. There's almost an invisible barrier that blocks 'disabled' people from the rest of the world. The

The 'Disabled' Apartheid

book focused on the character of a high school pupil with Cerebral Palsy and the obstacles she had to face daily just to try to feel accepted. I focused on my experience in high school and used that to compare the experiences I've had in high school. Unfortunately though I've come to realise that those obstacles are not just confined to high school if you're 'disabled', they expand into everyday life too. I just want to say right now that treating disability as an issue or disadvantage does absolutely nothing to help disability. You should be building us up, not tearing us down by insensitive and hurtful comments you think are acceptable. People cause the barriers, not disability. Being 'disabled' is just one part of a person, it's a minor difference, but people blow it out of proportion and make it the one main trait. The be all and end all. Seven seconds isn't enough time to really appreciate a person for who they are, I don't care if it's scientific evidence, people who have a heart and a brain will see that it takes far longer to get to know a person than just seven seconds. You cannot make a judgement based on first appearances. I think society is so wrapped up in itself these days that we tend to forget that it's about building relationships with each other. The whole world seems to have been sped up, everything seems to be rushed. Technology doesn't help, instead of talking face to face, we've replaced it with social media and screens, everything is virtual. Yes the world should make strides in technological advancements, but at what cost? By gaining technology, we've lost ourselves. You maybe thinking that I'm going on a tangent about something completely unrelated. This is a book about highlighting ableism and trying to stop it by positive responses, which of course it is, but if this book is about the uncomfortable incredible of ableism, we cannot ignore the elephant in the room. I think technology is a wonderful thing, but it can also cause so much damage to society, disability included.

Social media platforms mainly are used to talk to friends or family, share pictures and just feel like one big community. However, there is a very toxic side to social media too which can play a major part in enabling ableism and ableist attitudes, more often than not, without people realising they are a part of the problem.

The 'Disabled' Apartheid

Take social media platforms, they can be a cruel place, they harbour the most offensive views on any topic possible, and what is most frightening, the people who share negative views and behaviours do so because there is an antimony to it all. People can create a profile different from who they are, this gives some sort of undeserved 'power' to a minority of people who believe that they can say what they want, to who they want because they are 'protected' by a screen. In reality most people are scared of the consequences of expressing negative opinions and behaviour, in public, it's just you against everyone else. Online, because people have the illusion of their comments only being visible to just them as more often than not these people who post negativity and hatred are on their own in a room, they believe that they are safe because only they can see it, or maybe they just crave this need to belittle others to make themselves feel better, but they are not brave enough to say it in public. A screen gives a person anonymity to say or do whatever they want.

Some 'disabled' people use social media platforms as a way to communicate and socialise with the outside world. According to a UK Government document I found online though while doing research says:

"The internet and social media can be a powerful tool for 'disabled' people to use to make their voices heard and engage with services. However, 'disabled' people are subjected to a high-level of abusive behaviour online and offline. This is under-reported and under-prosecuted." – [House of Commons Petitions Committee, Online abuse and the experience of 'disabled' people, First Report of Session 2017–19]

It's a shocking read to say the least. It's very interesting but very hard hitting when you actually read through it. To have the level of abuse constantly thrown at you because you're 'disabled' is horrific to say the least. How the owners allow such abuse to take place is beyond me. To me, social media platforms can be like a virtual playground with children who are just so nasty to one another, but in a virtual space instead of a physical space. That's what I personally compare it to anyway. People who have mobility issues will

The 'Disabled' Apartheid

use social media platforms as a means to speak to friends or family, it's a bit of escapism. A few hours away from the constant reminders of what being 'disabled' truly means. To have someone or a group of people say something negative about a person especially if they are 'disabled' just isn't right. For many 'disabled' people, those few hours on social media platforms is sometimes the only bit of pleasure to look forward to, to feel normal with others without the constant reminders of appointments and other things, and to have someone else feel the need to abuse in those few hours behind a screen, is immoral, cowardly and, quite frankly, pathetic.

Nobody should ever be made to feel insignificant to another, we all bleed, we all breathe, and yet, we struggle to find a way to live as one society, and for what? Labels that are outdated? It would be funny if it wasn't so hurtful. Ableism goes under the radar because it's just viewed as an acceptable way to behave, disability is something that has poisoned the minds of society into thinking that it is something to be sympathetic to. I remember once I was at a party and this one person said to me "It's a shame isn't it?" to which I replied, "What is?" not knowing what the reply was going to be, "That you're in a wheelchair." I was understandably taken aback, but I was quick to reply to the insensitive comment "Well, not really, I've done quite well, all things considered, I've got a graphic design degree and work in a motorsport company now designing for the different levels of motorsport, my disability is just something I have, and I manage." In other words I was really saying that I'm not just defined by my disability, I can, and do have other traits, so unless you can be bothered to treat me as an equal, then just leave me alone. It's that stereotypical attitude that drives me so mad. Needless to say that person who said such a ridiculous statement was shocked and didn't know what to say. Ceri was with me when it happened and later she applauded me for telling that person the truth about myself and subsequently, disability. I am in a wheelchair, but that isn't it, people think that 'disabled' people are just bound by their own disabilities and nothing more, that we cannot do anything for ourselves or lead a 'normal' life. The stigma of disability will always be apart of life unless we actually start to sit up and take notice of

The 'Disabled' Apartheid

our actions and more importantly, hold our hands up, and take full accountability and learn how to change our attitudes towards disability as we have with other subjects that have unfortunately plagued society in the past. Society must take note that there is a problem with how they treat 'disabled' people. In the review I wrote for 'Speechless':

"Personally, since high school, I didn't want the label of disability as in many regards, just the word alone has negative connotations. Don't get me wrong, I'm happy and accepted who I am and proud to be who I am. All I'm saying is that I don't like the negative connotations that word can conjure in the mind of society in general." – [Excerpt taken from Samantha Maxwell's review of the book 'Speechless' by Kate Derbyshire.]

That is still true today. As much as I have become comfortable with my disability and am proud of it, I still have an issue with the label of 'disability'. The word is negative, it conjures up negative behaviours towards the 'disabled', it's seen as something that is life limiting. Disability is treated as this one thing, this one classification that people like to use against you. You can't do this, or try that just because you just happen to be 'disabled', people treat you like a baby if you're 'disabled', it doesn't matter what you have done in your life that's considered 'normal', if you have your trademarks, such as a wheelchair, walking stick, walking frame, cane, or anything else that can identify you as having a disability, then you're automatically different from everyone else in society, and ultimately punished for that by being categorised unfairly. Your abilities don't count for anything because of the 'DIS' always overshadowing the 'ABILITY' part. When I asked the question in my survey to whether the terms 'disabled''' and 'disability' automatically puts a negative attitude towards a person in the minds of society, in a way I was glad to have received this response. I actually felt relieved to know that it wasn't me just imagining it. The fact that this response came from the able-bodied survey too, is a bonus as it just goes to show that some able-bodied people share my theory as to why disability is treated so poorly.

The 'Disabled' Apartheid

"Unfortunately it often does. I suppose because it has the prefix 'dis' it focuses on what isn't rather than what is. It's easy to focus on what a person will need than what they might contribute." – [One Participant's answer to Able-bodied Survey]

People can be shallow when it comes to disability and the fact that they are unable to understand how their comments and treatment affects the overall outcome of disability as a whole will always be apart of the issue. It's always focused on the negative, what we can't do and how we can't manage. There is a stigmatisation there. I think that because this false narrative has been a part of mainstream culture for so long, it's become a major part of how society negatively interacts with 'disabled' people in general, whether they realise it or not, everyone does it in some way. I can come to that conclusion myself, just by looking at the answers from my surveys.

A lot of the participants who took part, basically said that they would offer help to a 'disabled' person if they saw that they needed help. On the surface, this is great, it's basic humanity, and it's perfectly acceptable to offer help if a 'disabled' person is nonverbal, but it can be a little degrading and come off as patronising if people offer help without a 'disabled' person asking in the first place. I wonder if people would be willing to help other able-bodied people in the same way if nobody asked? A lot of able-bodied participants had said that they feel sorry for a 'disabled' person. This baffles me to be honest, because others have said that they would interact with a 'disabled' person the same way as they would an able-bodied person. I guess it just comes down to how an individual perceives a 'disabled' person, again, going back to the Seven Second Rule.

I'm now going to list the different examples of ableist attitudes that people often say to 'disabled' people for you to try to get a better understanding of it and to let it sink in.

- Asking someone what is "wrong" with them

- Saying, "You do not look 'disabled'," as though this is a compliment – it's not

The 'Disabled' Apartheid

- Viewing a person with a disability as inspirational for doing typical things, such as having a job

- Assuming a physical disability is a due to laziness or lack of exercise

- Using public facilities that are for people with disabilities, such as parking spaces and/or toilets

- Asking if a person's disability is real

You may think that I'm only "saying these things" to cause a deliberate uneasiness. I'm not. This is the reality of what 'disabled' people face on a daily basis, whether you like it or not, it's the truth. Forget the 'facts' about disabilities that you may find in books or online. It's time to face up to the real fact that people often say or do uncomfortable things in life. We like to uphold this image of a 'perfect world', but this world is just filled with fakery with very little substance or accountability.

"One of the most cowardly things ordinary people do is shut their eyes to facts." – [Lewis Carroll]

It's true, I really do think because of the fast paced, cancel culture we have somehow become over the years, our ability to properly fact check has been hit hard. Real facts don't get the attention, but other 'facts' do?

I recently, (as of writing this) attended a concert to see The Jacksons, (my first in four years, as of writing this.) There was a platform for 'disabled' people to use, of which I was on, alongside a few others. We were all having a great time when some people standing in the crowd turned around, saw everyone on the platform enjoying themselves and said, (and I quote):

"Oh look! Even disabled people are enjoying the show!"

Excuse me? Why is this unusual? Why do we always have to be grouped together and pitied?

Understanding Ableist Language

Unfortunately, there are many examples of ableism in everyday language. Terms such as 'dumb' and 'lame' were originally used to describe disabilities, many years ago, but today, people use them as synonyms for 'stupid' or 'bad'. People

The 'Disabled' Apartheid

also misuse words in a way that trivializes conditions. For example, a person may say, "I am so OCD." This type of language is unacceptable and immoral. Why would people ever feel the need to say these things to a 'disabled' person? What on Earth possesses people to think that it's an acceptable way to behave? You may not think that comments like this happen or actually think that there's a problem with these comments. All of these statements are the exact equivalent to racism, sexism and homophobia. There's another branch of ableism that I would also like to make you aware of, something of which I originally put at the start of this book, but I want to say why these terms are offensive and considered ableist.

Inaccessible Design

Designing buildings, public spaces, products, and technology that only caters to able-bodied people is an example of ableism. This includes, having low tables in cafés and restaurants, educational environments where basic 'disabled' access is non-existent, websites that have no text enlargement feature, or any other accessible features, and sidewalks with obstacles that make walking and driving a power chair/manually pushing/propelling more difficult.

Education Discrimination

Schools refusing to make disability adaptations, such as low tables, inaccessible toilet facilities and just basic equipment a pupil or student may need to learn, failing to understand a disability, or trying to 'teach' a pupil or a student not to have their disability, for example, a teacher may decide to punish a pupil or student for having a disability such as dyslexia, rather than adapt how they teach.

Employment Discrimination

Employers may be biased against those who have a disability, as they may believe 'disabled' people are less productive employees compared to able-bodied employees. They may also refuse disability accommodations to existing employees or allow workplace bullying to go unpunished, or in my case, just fire a 'disabled' person for no particular reason whatsoever just because their disability makes the employer feel uncomfortable.

The 'Disabled' Apartheid

All of these things are considered to be a form of ableism. There's no way to get around that. You may think that it's political correctness gone mad, but it truly isn't. It's hurtful, derogatory and discriminative and should be stopped now. I've unfortunately experienced the majority of these things at some point in my life, and I fear that others in my position may have too. Ableism has gone on for far to long, and I for one am totally sick of it. It's exhausting to constantly put up a fight just so that you can have some sort of 'normality' without the funny looks or comments. Don't we deserve a break from the constant negativity? It seems that it doesn't matter how much you try to distance yourself away from the labelling, as long as you have something to identify you as 'disabled', the world does nothing to encourage your dreams. When you're 'disabled', you sometimes feel like an animal in a cage at the zoo, just there to provide people with some sort of entertainment and wonderment. It is utterly crazy that people behave so terribly. Disability is an alien concept to society. People don't seem to know how to interact with people who have a disability, they just seem to revert to the same old way of treating us a vulnerable.

I want you to imagine how you would feel if you were constantly being patronised and discriminated against through absolutely no fault of your own, when all you want is to be treated as an equal member of society? Would you be angry with people for not giving you a chance to explore your potential? Everything is focused on 'no' when you're 'disabled'. We can't do this or that, it grates at you after a while. People just can't seem to connect the fact of disability and normality strangely enough. It's difficult for anyone to get a job today for example, but if you are looking for work and have a disability, then you can just forget about it. Your chances are minimal at best. Nobody is willing to hire people with disabilities, from my experience. It makes me angry with the school system that they give 'disabled' children false hope by letting them go to PSE lessons as everyone else, which of course is great, and they should be, but if the reality is that disability has no place in the real world, why allow 'disabled' children to believe they have a chance when so clearly in 'modern society' we don't? Obviously

251

The 'Disabled' Apartheid

this desperately needs to change as the education system is just setting 'disabled' people up for a fall.

It doesn't matter to an employer that you may meet the requirements for a job with numerous qualifications and knowledge, if you have anything to imply you are 'disabled', the amount of qualifications you have doesn't matter. People are superficial. They only see one thing – disability.

If the education system can teach the differences between all disabilities, but also make a point to say that we are normal and should be treated the same way as everyone else, then the world would be a more progressive place. As it stands now, society is basically kidding themselves, to truly be modern, we should and must accept disability as another factor of life. It's not just about teaching children however, although it's a start, disability education should be compulsory for all businesses, councils and other authorities that make up society. It cannot carry on the way it currently is, people must learn to incorporate all diversities, not just pick and choose what will ultimately work best for them in the long run.

The 'Disabled' Apartheid

People must learn to accommodate disability wherever they are situated.

If places accommodated more for disability, then I feel we wouldn't look so 'alien' to society. I've been in cafés where all they have are low tables, it may look stylish, but it isn't practical. It's style over substance. I've been known to sit by a low table in a café or coffee shop as all of the normal tables were full and come home in complete agony as my back was forced to sit in an uncomfortable position. Restaurants have more or less the same approach, but with tables which have bars along them that when pushed by these tables make them too low and I've hurt my knees, coming away with bruises, trying to squeeze in. There's a blatant issue with this lack of access. We look more 'disabled' sometimes because society thrusts it upon us. You may think why don't I just ask someone to move so that I could have a better seat? I do most of the time, and to be fair, nine times out of ten people are kind enough to move for me, but you must understand that it makes me even more uncomfortable as then people are more aware that I need a higher table because of my disability and they are more sympathetic as a result. It's not sympathy I want, it's action. We're only treated differently because society is influencing us to be.

It even can be a challenge outdoors in a park or at the seaside for example trying to eat, the wooden tables you often see dotted around are not disability friendly at all, you have two planks of wood as seats either side to accommodate able-bodied people, but nothing to make disability feel welcome. No space for a wheelchair user. The 'disabled' just have to try and manage on the end of the table where there's often a piece of wood obstructing access to a wheelchair so the 'disabled' are left to try and cope eating from quite a fair distance, and in doing so, putting strain on themselves which isn't good for posture or dignity to be completely honest. Outdoor wooden tables that accommodate disability do exist, my parents and I have seen them and used them, so they do exist , but we've only seen them in three areas, Anglesey, Tenby and Oswestry. They look like ordinary wooden picnic tables, but the difference is that they have a space cut out of the benches for wheelchair users. How? A piece of the wooden seat, designed for able-bodied people has been removed to accommodate wheelchair users. It's so ingenious yet so simple, and I don't know why these are not distributed across the UK and beyond, because honestly they are amazing. I know it sounds ridiculous to say, but to go for so long having to cope with the constant pain and uncomfortable feeling you have to endure when trying to eat by an ordinary wooden table when things like this are already invented it's honestly a miracle. I'm not saying that for effect either. You honestly feel a part of mainstream society sitting by a 'disabled' friendly wooden table, and I believe that if they were distributed more, than it would make the economy thrive too as more people who are 'disabled' would feel like a part of mainstream society in pubs and restaurants for example, especially in the Summer months, when it's too hot to be inside. Bringing more money in which in turn would help the economy grow a bit more. Everyone helping everyone. We need more inclusion. By having more of these style of disability friendly tables outside, I feel that everyone would benefit. It would be a small change, but a massive step in the right direction

The 'Disabled' Apartheid

to make all people feel wanted and would benefit society in the long-term too. I do have a tray which clips onto my wheelchair for when we're outdoors eating and there's no table of any kind, but I'm sure you can appreciate that I don't care too much for the tray as it makes me look more 'disabled' than what I am to the general public. I want to be clear, I'm not ashamed of my disability to reiterate, nor do I ever have a problem with more severely 'disabled' people. Of course I don't. I do have a problem with labels that stop people seeing the real person in the wheelchair. I feel like my tray signifies and shouts 'DISABILITY' and when you've had to deal with discrimination throughout your life because of your disability, it's that unfair label that I try to avoid having thrust upon me daily. I do have to use a tray sometimes when there's no other choice, but I prefer not to, because of those negative connotations that disability can conjure up in people's minds. It's shocking that I try to hide my disability as much as possible, I mean don't get me wrong, it's obvious I'm 'disabled', I'm constantly in a wheelchair, but I personally feel that what I lack mobility wise, I have to make up for intellectually to try and prove to people I'm not an 'average' 'disabled' person (whatever that is.) I tend to push myself too much in the knowledge department as I feel that if I don't constantly show my intellectual side, my disability will take over and become the driving force. The one personality trait. I don't want that anymore. It's sad, but society has made me feel that I constantly have to prove myself to others for a chance of being accepted for my personality and not just my physical appearance. I suspect that so many others like me may feel the same way as I do in this regard. Personally, having something as simple as a tray, designed to make life easier, ultimately makes everything worse as the possible label and barrier is cemented in people's minds.

When I was in university, I wrote my dissertation on Ehealth, (Electronic Health), and whether it actually helps or hinders a 'disabled' person to live as 'normal' of a life as they can. I guess, it's always been a part of the problem for me personally, not so much the equipment side of it, but the acceptance side of disability. I believe my dissertation was the starting point of me actually being proactive to highlight the issues that

The 'Disabled' Apartheid

disability ultimately comes with. I mean, I have been gifted a wider platform now thankfully to fully express my concerns, but my dissertation was the beginning of something I didn't really think bothered me until I started writing about it. Saying that, the equipment side does seem to play a role of the discrimination and labelling behaviour 'disabled' people face. It's an excuse to be ableist in my opinion. Equipment maybe needed to help people live a (what can be considered) 'normal' life, but equipment such as wheelchairs, hoists, walking sticks, walking frames, splints etc. should never be the focus. That equipment is only there to provide 'disabled' people help if and when needed. It's not an excuse for anyone to use against a disability. It's there to give assistance, not create obstacles or barriers. Yes, I'll admit that sometimes, the equipment given and adaptations that are made for 'disabled' people to feel independent and more like apart of society isn't always the best, case in point the total disregard of 'disabled' access in my university, but 'disabled' people should never be penalised for their means of living.

The 'Disabled' Apartheid

It was different when I was a child, the whole world seemed less cruel towards disability, or so it seemed to me. Everyone seemed much more accepting of disability. Able-bodied children loved me as they thought I was 'cool', both in school and outside of school, which I loved because I was popular. I had tons of friends in infant school and primary school, including Rebecca and Stacey (twins), Shannon, Lucy, Jasmine and Emily. This friendship group meant the whole world to me, admittedly. I loved school at this point, mainly because of my friends. I was never made to feel any different, I was always included in everything. I somewhat took it for granted at the time if I'm completely honest. If I'd had known what laid ahead, believe me, I wouldn't have taken anything for granted. These group of school friends treated me as one of them. My wheelchair was just an extension of me to them I feel, but the chair wasn't me to them. My friends saw me first. I remember on school trips, I used my manual wheelchair for ease of access, and my friends used to argue over who was going to push me! I had to make up schedules to say who was going to push me and when, so that everyone could have a

The 'Disabled' Apartheid

chance! It's funny to me now, going from having a lot of friends in infant school and primary school, arguing on school trips who was going to push me round, to absolutely nobody bothering with me in high school because I was in a wheelchair, it is a bit difficult to understand really, but again, I guess the reason for this is simply the image aspect of high school, compared to infant school and primary school.

I also had a lot of friends back home who would call for me after school, or on the weekends to go and play outside with them. There was one friend in particular, Elika, who always stuck by me, admittedly I wasn't fully aware of how unique that relationship was, because I was so young, I couldn't grasp the actual real friendship we had as children. Nobody does when they're in the moment. Looking back now, knowing what I know, I'm just so grateful to Elika, Rebecca, Stacey, Lucy, Shannon, Emily and Jasmine for always seeing past my disability, and just wanting me for me, and that is something that I will always cherish.

Elika (outside of infant school and primary school), was that one friend that would always be there for me no matter what, every chance we had, we would be together, Elika would come on days out with myself and my family or come over for tea. She just helped to establish that 'normality'. Again, I never felt different whilst Elika was around, she made sure of that. Again, she made sure that I was included in everything with our larger group of friends. She was amazing in her approach to me, there was never any negative behaviour with Elika, or with any of my school friends when any of them interacted with me. It's known that children can be cruel with each other, but none of my friends growing up was ever like that, nor did they feel sorry for me. My disability is visible, and some children can get obsessed with this one feature and make it the one personality trait of a 'disabled' child. Able-bodied children unfortunately bully others who are seen as different from another, but I honestly cannot remember any animosity from either Elika, Rebecca, Stacey, Lucy, Shannon, Jasmine or Emily during this time, and that counts for something, especially today when society runs on negativity. So I just want to take this opportunity to say thank you so much to each of my amazing friends back

The 'Disabled' Apartheid

then. You all made me feel normal. I truly appreciate your kindness and really ignoring my Cerebral Palsy, because by simply ignoring the disability, you all saw me. That means the absolute world to me. I know that we don't really see each other anymore, (if at all), but honestly, you're all amazing, I truly mean that. I will always love each and every single one of you for seeing me, and not my disability. I will never forget your kindness.

People have said some cruel things to me and about me since, that when I look back at those times, I smile. Nobody ever showed any discrimination towards me or my disability that I remember, up until two thousand and four, the year I started high school. As soon as I started high school, that feeling of 'normality' changed forever. I sometimes miss the years pre two thousand and four, where I didn't feel like I had to fight to be seen and treated as 'normal'. I would say that the friendships I made when I was young, undoubtedly helped me feel that sense of 'normalcy'. Creating a place where I could see myself as 'normal', giving me a clear example of what it means to be 'normal'. It's true that I really don't like to be classed as 'disabled', not because

The 'Disabled' Apartheid

I'm ashamed of myself or the actual term. I'm ashamed of how society has developed into this backwards thinking mess and think it's absolutely fine to bunch disability into one thing, when it's definitely not one thing, disability is many things, and two people who have the same disability may not always present the same way.

It definitely needs to be realised that disability comes in many forms and by grouping disability together, you are just perpetuating the narrative. There are many different forms of disability in the world, Downs Syndrome, Cerebral Palsy, Bells Palsy, Spina Bifida, Asperger's, and ADHD, are just a handful of examples of different forms of disability, there are, of course, many more, but I cannot list them all here, but all disabilities have different levels of severity. Some are more complex than others. People need to know the difference and learn to adapt their ways of thinking.

I long for those days of happiness shown through the level of humanity I was constantly shown from my family and friends when I was a young child. It gave me greater knowledge of how different

The 'Disabled' Apartheid

society is today, compared to how it was when I was young. It gave me a reason to fight for equality. Without that constant in my life, I don't think I'd be able to fight as I would think that is just how disability is treated. I again just would like to thank my family and friends of that time especially Elika for always seeing me, not my disability.

As time passed, I became much more aware of this Apartheid state of mind against disability. It became clearer as I got older. I used to put the patronisation down to the fact that I was a child, but when you get to the preteen stage of your life, and there are still obvious issues with how segregated and patronised you are from the rest of the world, there's definitely something wrong. Again, you may think that I was naive, but for the longest time during my preteen stage, I always wondered why adults spoke to other able-bodied children my age at the time with such respect? Whereas, I was just getting the segregation, discrimination and patronisation on a daily basis with society. Of course, unlike the Apartheid of yesteryear, it wasn't ever flaunted, but you'd get the patronising, sympathetic look from people or even be spoken down to. An unspoken separation. However, just because it's unspoken, doesn't mean that it's invisible.

I believe that it's because modern culture is so obsessed with media. We seem to live by it. It's the be all and end all. Media does nothing to remedy any preconceived ideas about any subject considered to be controversial or awkward. It was much more difficult to distribute hatred years ago to the masses, but today, people just have the capability to share anything and everything whether it's from a reliable source or not. As long as it's interesting enough to grab the attention of people, reliability doesn't seem to matter.

"It doesn't have to be true to be believed. Tell a lie often enough and people will believe it..." *– [Michael Jackson]*

This quote relates to so many things and is so true, we only need to hear or read about something once for it to become true, whether it is the truth or not, it doesn't matter, as long as it sounds plausible then people seem to believe it. Disability is no different, there is so much saying that 'disabled' people cannot do this or that,

The 'Disabled' Apartheid

when really, it's up to an individual 'disabled' person to decide whether they are capable to do certain things or not. It's definitely not up to society to decide whether 'disabled' people are capable or not. Able-bodied people are incapable of doing things, but you don't hear anything about able-bodied people unable to do certain things. It's all put on disability, and it isn't fair. People are just so reliant on media, and media has a responsibility to be truthful and fact based, but it isn't, and I think it's because modern culture is so fast paced, media has undoubtedly had to keep up with this lifestyle and match the rhythm of the twenty-first century. There are so many subjects that are constantly scrutinised in media everyday and disability, ironically, isn't left out from this scrutiny.

I think ableism comes from this lack of understanding. 'The Elephant Man' [1980] is a prime example of this. I know that the film actually takes a positive message of kindness, intelligence and sophistication despite the man's outward appearance, there are still undertones of ableism. The term 'Elephant Man' is offensive to start with.

The 'Disabled' Apartheid

The term is more well-known than the actual name of the person the term refers to.

Joseph Merrick, (sometimes referred to as John Merrick,) was a nineteenth century Englishman who was born with severe bodily deformities. I think to make it easier on social understandings back then, people referred to Joseph as 'The Elephant Man'.

To label someone an 'elephant man' is so far from political correctness that it's unbelievable. I understand that it was a 'different time' when Joseph Merrick was alive, the nineteenth century didn't have any legislation to protect the 'disabled' from this type of language and treatment, but, the film should have been named 'John Merrick' or even 'Joseph Merrick'. The thing is, in a perfect world, I feel that if the name of the film wasn't 'The Elephant Man', then it wouldn't have been as successful as it was. This isn't a perfect world unfortunately. Who cares about morals when stats and money are involved and ultimately take priority? Again, I understand that there wasn't much, (if any) protection for the 'disabled' back in nineteen eighty, but it should have been common sense that it was a problem to refer to someone as an 'elephant'. It's exploitation at it's best.

"I am not an elephant! I am not an animal! I am a human being! I am a man!" – [John Hurt's portrayal of Joseph Merrick – 'The Elephant Man' - 1980]

This quote from the film is so moving, but why it had to be included in a film actually titled 'The Elephant Man' is counterintuitive to me. I get that it's supposed to be a commentary on social views and beliefs from the nineteenth century, but society may not have realised it, I believe that the quote would've been much more impactful if the film actually highlighted the man and not the insensitive nickname of the past. I get the intension, but the execution could've been better. An opportunity to actually make people think about the person, instead of the offensive nickname was sadly missed. This is the problem, people don't have integrity when there is a promise of wealth. There doesn't seem to be any willingness to champion disability as 'normal' in media, there is an attempt, but it always has to be overshadowed by this constant need to point out the flaws before anything else. I mean 'disabled' athletes and comedians for example, are getting more exposure today, but it still needs to be worked on that disability is not something to fear, but to be treated as everything else in society. Mental health is much more open to conversation today so why can't disability have the same treatment? I don't know why, but there was a time that mental health was taboo, but people learned to talk about it openly and it's become somewhat of a thing of bravery to admit and share any issues with your mental health. It seems logical to me that disability should be apart of this, alongside mental health, as both disability and mental health go hand in hand. Maybe disability could just be mentioned in discussions about mental health, like a passing comment to begin with, but could be fed through more as time goes on. If it makes some people feel uncomfortable to talk about disability in a candid way, then maybe mixing subjects together could be the way to go, to start this much needed conversation.

It is this level of unknowingness that drives a wedge in-between society, letting people think it's

The 'Disabled' Apartheid

okay to treat 'disabled' people so disrespectfully just because it was 'okay' in the past to tease someone by their deformities or disability by blatantly calling them an offensive and hurtful nickname.

There is an obvious disconnect that is happening. Most people today are unable to separate the person from the disability. I wholeheartedly believe that it's because of films such as 'The Elephant Man' that has helped to segregate people further, by stereotyping those that society have been told are different and should be treated as different, maybe not intentionally, but they ultimately have been focusing on one thing, instead of looking at the whole person.

Social media is a modern extension of this disconnect. People believe that they can say or do as they please without any repercussions. They believe that just because they are behind a screen it's okay to 'make fun' and discriminate things such as disability. There doesn't seem to be any awareness there with people. People treat others today with disrespect and all because of the unrealistic thinking that they are 'safe' to say such harmful and truly disgusting comments towards another human being because they are sitting in front of some sort of hypothetical 'bulletproof' screen. Unsurprisingly and unfortunately, the 'disabled' get this bullying behaviour frequently. I don't know if it's because we're considered as 'easy targets' because of how we may look or act, or something else that isn't as easily explained, but it's irritating to say the least how much of it happens and how much nothing is done to help stop it.

"This is under-reported and under-prosecuted. The Home Office publication Hate Crime, England and Wales 2017/18 shows that there were 7,226 recorded disability hate crimes in 2017–18 while the Crime Survey for England and Wales estimates that there were 52,000 disability motivated hate crimes per year." – [Excerpt taken from 'Disabled online bullying' - Parliament.uk]

Fifty-two thousand hate crimes towards 'disabled' people per year. Just let that sink in. How these crimes go undetected and unpunished is beyond me. It seems to be that the authorities are turning

The 'Disabled' Apartheid

the other way when this is happening. It's as if to say, out of sight, out of mind, which is a dangerous attitude to have. Why doesn't the 'disabled' matter? Why are we always treated so terribly? Why is this allowed to happen? It doesn't make sense to me. 'Disabled' people use social media platforms as a way to talk to the outside world, and to learn that the 'disabled' are being bullied just for wanting to be apart of everyday life is just horrendous. It is a 'disabled' person's right to feel that they belong and feel independent. It's that sense of 'normality' that 'disabled' people crave, away from the everyday world of appointments and just the same mundane things day in, day out that most 'disabled' people have to face. Having social media can be a form of escapism for a 'disabled' person. It isn't fair that anyone who is considered 'different' by society, have to then deal with ignorant people who have absolutely no idea about disability. If the outside world is considered a place of silent judgement, then social media seems to be the place to voice that judgement. Social media platforms have a reputation for spreading the hatred that people in reality wouldn't dream of voicing in public. Social media gives a false sense of security, power and anonymity. It's those beliefs that drives ableism to it's highest level. It's so easy to deny a person's behaviour to other members of society from behind a screen, online, people can delete comments, but it's not so easy in reality. You cannot delete a comment in real life. That is why people seem to believe that they're invincible and unbelievably unbreakable online, because they are no clear consequences to a person's actions if they are sitting in front of some sort of screen.

Anyone can choose to be whoever they like online, and this is where trolling has become the most popular form of bullying. It's so easy today to become a bully, with all of the anonymity available to a person instantly. If you are in the actual outside world, less people will ultimately decide not to exhibit their personality for fear of repercussions of their actions. Reality never promotes anonymity. The online world does though, and there lies the problem. Online websites are a breeding ground for verbal abuse, especially social media platforms.

The 'Disabled' Apartheid

I don't know if you're aware, but I purposely made chapter three quite long to start the ball rolling on disability education. I'm not a teacher, I'm a graphic designer by trade, it shouldn't be up to me to educate others, people should realise the issues themselves and help to raise awareness of these issues, maybe then employers would be more understanding and more likely to hire 'disabled' people, maybe bullying behaviour would take a backseat, maybe disability could just be another standard part of life like other things are.

To be able to even consider this to be a potential possibility for disability equality, education is the best way to start. Yes, teaching can only do so much, and at the end of the day, it's up to the individual to be progressive in attitudes, we cannot force the subject of disability equality on anyone, (unfortunately), everyone has different opinions and beliefs, but if other demographics are finally being given a much needed spotlight, then it is only right that disability should be apart of the fold too. A bigger picture needs to be realised here.

Chapter 5
Taking Advantage of Disability

When you have a disability of any kind, it seems that people often have this preconceived idea that you're 'vulnerable' and 'easily led'. More often than not, people then take advantage of that notion that they have, and use it to either manipulate or promise things that they have absolutely no intention on delivering.

Most people see a 'disabled' person and immediately think that they aren't intelligent enough to understand the signs of control, because at the end of the day, it's all just a form of control, gas lighting if you will, but nobody sees it that way because of the constant disability labelling. If it was any other demographic being manipulated against, there would undoubtedly be uproar, and rightly so, but if you're 'disabled' and being manipulated, that's a whole different story. People don't seem to call it out so much if they see manipulation happening to a 'disabled' person because media has cemented in the minds of society, the false idea of disability equals

Taking Advantage of Disability

vulnerability, so people think that a manipulator is 'helping' a 'disabled' person, when in fact, they are hindering the 'disabled' person.

It's unfair how some people can have the audacity to treat another human being with such disrespect just because that person may just happen to have a disability of some kind. I really do believe honestly that the disability 'trademarks' help with this illusion of 'vulnerability', it's again going back to the Seven Second Rule. People see a 'disabled' person and immediately think that we can be manipulated to the point where they can start to control us by appealing to our 'naive' side. Media has had a part to play in this. The vast majority of articles online are all examples of fear mongering, stating the limitations of disability and that's it. It would be fine if there was a fifty, fifty approach to it, but all that I'm able to see are the problems. Nobody ever focuses on what disability actually means and represents. Disability really just means differently abled in my mind. Everyone is good at something. Not everyone can be good at everything, even able-bodied people. It's physically impossible, unless you are super human, (which I doubt very much anyone is, although I am aware of some who like to think they are.)

I'll admit, you are seeing a steady increase in disability in media on TV shows, comedians, TV presenters, sports people etc. which I'm so glad of, but as long as there is an online negative presence of disability, I feel that nothing will ever progress sadly. I understand that there needs to be articles with factual information about disability, but more often than not, the information written is mainly focused on that one small part of disability, and I believe that this is why disability has such a negative impact on society, and why people think it's okay to manipulate and take advantage of a 'disabled' person because of what's in the zeitgeist. The information currently, (especially online and in books), just constantly forces this false representation on people with a disability. The information out there is designed to focus on the 'vulnerabilities' of disability with very little argument showing the strengths of disability. It's absolutely no wonder why people think that a person with a disability can be taken advantage of and exploited for own personal gains.

Taking Advantage of Disability

"...people with special needs are more likely to suffer physical, mental and financial abuse than others." – [Special Needs Answers]

Constantly concentrating on those negatives, it's inevitable that people will start to accept the negativity of disability as cold, hard fact. The thing is, all of the negative press out there, gives manipulators ammunition to try and manipulate those who they believe are 'vulnerable'. Admittedly, manipulation can happen to anyone, anyone can be considered 'vulnerable' if they are in a difficult situation in their life, but more often than not, 'disabled' people and elderly people seem to bear the brunt of the manipulation. Most disabilities are visible, and elderly people, by social standards, are often considered 'fragile', so it makes sense that a manipulator would prey on these two demographics the most. It could be because 'disabled' people and elderly people are considered 'weak' by general society, so it's a lot easier to put manipulation into practice. I don't know, I'm just surmising, but it does seem a coincidence in my own personal opinion. Manipulators act on your insecurities, making you believe everything that they say. Personally, I think manipulation, looking at it now with fresh eyes, can be considered a vulnerability in itself. If people manipulate others to try and get what they want, then I don't think that they are happy themselves. Manipulation gives a sense of power and domination, something of which they may be lacking in their own lives, so they try to make others hang on every word that comes out of their mouths, to try and make themselves feel better by making others dote on them, and this is why certain demographics are often victims of this cruel trait. Exploitation is an extension of manipulation. Usually financial, but it can also be sexual exploitation.

"People with an illness, disability or health condition may be viewed as easy targets for exploitation because of their care and support needs and the impact of their condition on their ability to protect and defend themselves." – [Preventing Exploitation Toolkit]

Why some people should be seen as being 'easy targets' infuriates me to be honest. It's like people seek out the weakest in the food chain. How anyone can do that is just immoral. Nobody

Taking Advantage of Disability

should ever be treated as insignificant compared to another. Nobody. In my own personal opinion, (and experience,) the people who often use these types of tactics to manipulate, often feel insignificant and worthless in their own lives, so they manipulate for the power trip. That's my theory anyway, someone who is content and happy in life will always pass that onto others. I'm fully aware that people cannot be content and happy twenty-four seven, that's impossible and not to mention, unhealthy, no, what I mean is people who for the most part have a positive attitude to life, would ultimately treat others with respect and dignity. Of course, there are also other factors to take into consideration when you are theorising public behaviour, but this is just what I have personally found.

Manipulation could also be learnt behaviour from either family members, friends, co-workers, anyone. Someone may see another use manipulative tactics to get what they want, and decide to adopt that approach for themselves, just like 'following the crowd'. Traumatic events in a person's life may also lead to them becoming manipulators, as a coping mechanism, for example if someone was considered 'unpopular' in school for whatever reason, (like I was during high school,) this could trigger some sort of 'power', as it then let's that person who is doing the manipulation feel like they're in control over something, (or someone).

Manipulators, users, advantage takers, whatever you want to call them always come across as caring, trustworthy and attentive, but that's only to reel a person in, really, their main concern is themselves. Manipulators see 'disabled' people as an easy target. Never let them have the satisfaction of destroying you.

People may see disability as being an excellent alternative to their own lives. This is always going to be the reason why I'm sceptical of others, because some people see disability as an 'easy ride' (both literally and figuratively,) but it definitely isn't. If anything, 'disabled' people are constantly locked in this battle for justice and morals, but we rarely see any 'wins'. It's exhausting, and for people to then take advantage of the basic things that 'disabled' people need in order to enhance their life, by

Taking Advantage of Disability

claiming it for themselves when they are deemed able-bodied, is just unacceptable and it makes me sad for humanity in all honesty. How have we come to this? Where it seems morally acceptable to take from 'disabled' people? Just because it isn't physical, doesn't mean that the behaviour is any more acceptable. In a way, it's a crime, theft really, but because it's the 'powers that be' who ultimately make the decision. Disability doesn't ever get to have a say, we are just expected to 'shut up and put up' with the constant disrespect.

I've also recently heard about people who are now ordering Radar keys from the Internet. Radar keys are specially designed keys for a 'disabled' person to have access to a 'disabled' toilet when out. Only a 'disabled' person, support worker, or trusted family member or friend of the 'disabled' person should be the only ones to possess a Radar key. Now it seems that the public have become aware of these specialist keys and are now buying them from the Internet for their own personal convenience. Unless you are considered 'disabled' you should never consider buying one. Previously, the only way to get a Radar key was through your local council, but as they have decided not to provide them anymore, and they have now become available to buy online, anyone can take advantage.

When you think about it, when these keys were only available from your local council, people who are considered 'disabled', could of always had another key cut to give to anyone they like. Even then, there wasn't anything stopping able-bodied people from gaining access to these keys. The amount of 'disabled' toilets that I've found padlocked when I have been out for the day is utterly ridiculous. A Radar key wouldn't have been able to open the toilets with a padlock attached, and I always wondered why they were, now I know, to try and discourage able-bodied people using something that shouldn't be available to them in the first place. By doing that though, 'disabled' people are also being punished. It's our fundamental right to have access to a public toilet. Some 'disabled' people have bladder issues, so may require access frequently in case of emergency.

It has gone a bit further too. Absolutely anyone it seems can buy a Radar Key from a high street

Taking Advantage of Disability

store, such as a cobblers. There was a time where Radar Keys were only available from your local council and you needed documentation related to your disability as proof to obtain one, but because people can get them from places such as cobblers, that means that anyone can buy a Radar Key without question. It's wrong really, as I feel that this is yet another reason why 'disabled' facilities are padlocked after a certain time of day, because anyone is able to use a 'disabled' facility, regardless of ability. 'Disabled' facilities are just that, and are **essential** to 'disabled' people, but we are always being punished it seems because of the actions of society.

Everyone seems to be jumping on the bandwagon of disability, but only really to take advantage of our means of living, not because people want to treat 'disabled' people with the much needed respect we deserve. As I said, availability to the keys in the past could have been placed in the wrong hands with 'disabled' people getting their Radar Key cut to give to an able-bodied person, but it just seems to me that any 'disabled', person wouldn't let anyone take advantage of anything designed to help disability willingly. As these keys are available so easily today anyway, a lot of able-bodied people will just buy them from a store to use for 'convenience'.

This is just a theory that I cannot ignore, but in my opinion, 'disabled' people would never give an able-bodied person a key to what they may consider an 'easier and convenient life', unless the able-bodied person is a trusted family member, friend or support worker.

I actually questioned this during the survey, I asked:

"For convenience, do you ever use facilities designed for the disabled when out in public? (I.e. lifts, disabled toilets, car parking spaces?)" – [Question from the Survey]

The majority of the participants answered no to this question, but there are those who unfortunately said that they did. One answer stood out to me whilst I was reading through:

"On occasion I have used a disabled toilet when I have had a pram or two young children with me because public toilets are not family friendly. I have never parked in a disabled

parking bay or used a disabled lift." – [One Participant's answer to Able-bodied Survey]

I just can't comprehend this. Why aren't able-bodied public facilities built on a larger scale to accommodate people with young children, prams and buggies? Why does disability always have to suffer because of incompetence? Failing building larger facilities, building more family rooms could be the answer. Family rooms have extra basins, toilets and hand dryers designed especially for children, seats for children, extra space to accommodate prams and buggies inside a cubicle, automatic doors which open and close with an elbow button, amongst other facilities which makes it easier for families to use when needed. *[Information on family rooms taken from 'Danfo UK']*

The participant's response only confirms that either people are unaware of family rooms, there aren't enough available, or both.

Our lives aren't easy or convenient by any means, and for people to take advantage of our ways of living, more often than not for quickness, I really cannot understand it? I personally don't think anyone would be able to cope with and constantly fight the daily backlash, the sympathetic looks, the patronisation, the ignorance and just the blatant rudeness of others if the shoe was on the other foot. I wholeheartedly believe that people falsely think that disability equals stupidity. Yes, some may have a mental disability which may make these people seem a little more vulnerable, but other 'disabled' people don't. We need to start recognising the difference. We aren't 'stupid' or 'weak', if anything, we are stronger than most, for the simple reason that we have had to overcome so much, adapting to life, overcoming adversities, (or trying to), amongst other things that the general public aren't aware of. In many ways, I would wholeheartedly say that people with disabilities are probably more knowledgeable than you think. We've had to learn to live with something that can be considered a hindrance or inconvenience, all the time, trying to maintain a sense of independence for ourselves, and that in itself takes skill. It is wrong to assume that just because you're 'disabled' you are therefore unintelligent. If you believe that, you, yourself cannot be as intelligent as you may think that you are. Yes, it's a brutal way to get a point across, but it's true.

I truly believe that because of the false representation of disability in social culture, this false idea of being 'disabled' as an 'easy way of life' is ultimately an obvious repercussion of the poison that is ultimately put out there.

"...if it's told often enough, you start to believe it." - [Michael Jackson]

The trouble is, the information out there can be considered truthful to some extent as the majority of the information is fact based from medical science, but that's as far as the information goes. There isn't anything to say that disability is diverse by nature, so therefore people can have a disability but still carry out most day to day tasks depending on the condition of the disability and the severity. That is formative information right there. There, I'm not denying the fact that disability doesn't have it sets of risks depending on the condition and the severity, but nor am I outright dismissing any possible potential that a 'disabled' person may possess. It's an equal truth between the medical information and the individuality of a 'disabled' person. It's a balanced case. This is how all disabilities, (regardless of severity,) should always be written. Giving hope and positivity, instead of the constant doom and gloom disability information seems to have today. If disability was written like this, but individual to all conditions and severities, there is absolutely no doubt in my mind that people would think twice before treating 'disabled' people as they're gullible and can be taken advantage of just because, (most of the time) an unfounded statement is made, and that statement can, and unfortunately is, causing so much damage to the subject of disability. People tend to believe what they want, as long as it has some element of truth laced within the falseness, then people just accept it without question. The Internet has a responsibility to give truthful accounts and information on everything the public search for, even part truthful isn't good enough. A balance is hard to find though in a world so obsessed with appearance and media. Websites are often unaware of how society perceives the information they see and read. This is why a responsibility needs to be realised. It's quite obvious that it isn't

Taking Advantage of Disability

'disabled' people who are guilty of being gullible, but general society itself for believing everything they consume. I get that people trust things like the Internet for honest and truthful information, (especially media,) but it so isn't. People need to be more vigilant in their trust. Yes, that is a pessimistic outlook on the news outlet, but if all there is, is the constant negativity of disability, then it's only right in my own opinion to call out this as an issue. You cannot just write something that is only partly true, no matter how well it's written, it's unethical, immoral and ignorant. I would really like to believe that if everyone was vigilant to what they see or hear, especially when using the Internet, then websites that have a disability subject matter would only have one choice, to just write the truth, without any false information sprinkled in. You never truly know the damage that you maybe creating when you write misinformation. Nobody can actually write about disability in an honest way, unless you are considered 'disabled' yourself. It just doesn't seem right. A person who has a disability are the only ones who truly knows what it's like to be considered 'disabled'. That's logical. It's like asking a male to write about the difficulties of labour. It just doesn't sit right does it? Same issue with disabilities. A 'disabled' person knows their abilities and capabilities. Nobody else. For people to think that they can decide for another ('disabled' or not) is uncomfortable. You may think why all of this connects to the title of this chapter, but people decide whether they want to take advantage of those who they consider 'weaker' and more 'vulnerable'. After all, people decide their opinion of you in the first seven seconds of seeing you. It all connects.

Yes, my outlook of life can be considered cynical, but with all of the setbacks and negative experiences I've had to this point in my life. People have tried (and some unfortunately succeeded) in trying to take advantage of me, just because the saw that I was a nice, and trusting person with the added bonus of being in a wheelchair. Admittedly, I what was considered a shy child, I wasn't outspoken, but that was my personality, not my condition. Yes, in infant school and primary school, I had a number of friends both in and out of school, I wasn't shy in that regard, but I had manners, things that were

Taking Advantage of Disability

instilled in me from my parents, I never 'rocked the boat' when it came to authority, I absolutely hated how getting into trouble made me feel, so avoided it at all costs. That personality trait would ultimately become somewhat of a negative thing in itself as it allowed for people to take advantage of my good and trusting nature as the years went on. I've had to learn to be more guarded and more resilient of people. That maybe sad to you, but in my opinion, my personality before realising the cynicism was more sad, as I wasn't as strong mentally as I am now, therefore I ultimately was considered a 'pushover'. The cynicism makes me have a more positive outlook on life as strangely as it sounds. It's a statement that sounds counterintuitive, but it's true. In my own opinion, the more cynicism you have, the less you are considered 'vulnerable' as your attitude towards life may change for the better for you. Others may not like your new found confident attitude, but realistically, of course they wouldn't, after all, they won't have any control over you. What matters in this life is you, people always come, but they also go. The one person in this life that won't leave you, is you.

I'm not saying to be cynical of everyone in life for fear of being used or patronised, no, that's unhealthy. We are social creatures, we thrive when we are amongst others. You just have to look at the recent pandemic to confirm this. No, what I am saying is just be vigilant. Be vigilant to who you lower your walls to. I myself lowered the walls a bit too much at one stage in my life as I falsely believed that I was stronger mentally, I clearly wasn't, and I ultimately paid the price by unfortunately having a severe mental breakdown. It's okay to let people in, if they know you, the real you, but don't do it too often, because people will, and (in my experience) most do take advantage of those who are trusting and/or look a certain way, (i.e. 'disabled' or elderly.) I've been there once too often, so I know all too well about the repercussions of being taken advantage of. Never make the mistake that just because you are starting to feel better, always understand the starting part. That's the key thing. Starting doesn't mean that you are sorted so to speak. Be aware that you may still be in that depressive or anxious state, if something you consider good is finally happening in your life, your mind is just

Taking Advantage of Disability

responding to that. Mental health issues need to be continually worked on, you can't just rely on one experience to end your mental health issues, even though it's a nice thought, unfortunately, your mental health cannot just change for the better in one day. They can't be switched on or off whenever you want. No, mental health is a precious thing that we shouldn't take for granted. Looking after our mental health is a journey. I have now come to realise this myself. Looking after yourself and your mental health is a nonstop activity. If you are dedicated, your mental health will improve but remember, it's a marathon and not a sprint.

When you do eventually develop this new found sense of resilience properly, you often find that you lose 'friends'. I use 'friends' loosely in this capacity because if those who you consider 'friends' don't accept or support the new confident you, then they aren't your friends. A friend is someone who supports you no matter what. Who accepts you. Who encourages you to be the best person you can. If these 'friends' aren't prepared to do this for you, then you don't need then in your life.

Taking Advantage of Disability

We all need to be aware of being taken advantage of. You are at a greater disadvantage of this if you are considered 'vulnerable'. In short, categorise people by their actions, not by their words. If you feel that society is taking advantage of you, speak up! Tell them that even though you may look 'vulnerable', it doesn't mean that you are. Back yourself. Those in society who think it's are unintelligent and therefore easy to manipulate will be more respectful to you. We live in a world where confidence rules. You need to take advantage of this. A confident and resilient person is less likely to be taken advantage of. I've personally noticed this since I found my new confident and more resilient attitude towards life. Those who respect you, will never take advantage. You will never be taken advantage of again. To reiterate you may lose people along the way for whatever reason, but if you take on board the resilience and the confidence a person needs to be taken seriously in this life, you'll never lose the most important person. **Yourself**.

Chapter 6

Educating Disability

"Education is the most powerful weapon that you can use to change the world." - *[Nelson Mandela]*

The Need For Disability Education

I have said before that disability should be taught in schools, colleges and universities as black history now is. The results from my personal research seem to back this idea with all participants saying that disability should be apart of the curriculum, with one stating that disability education should be started in schools. In my own opinion, it should be made compulsory.

Think about it, if disability is taught in places of education, then, there is a chance, and I truly believe this, attitudes would change for the better. Children (and most adults, thanks to clickbait) are very impressionable and if we teach children and adults in education alike the normality of disability, and diversity in disability, not to discriminate, not to label, actually get into the reality of disability, not from media or hearsay, but actually learn first hand with others how normal we are, I know that the world for disability would be a better place instantly. There was one thing that really struck me when doing my own personal research through the surveys, and that was the amount of people who said that they would feel sorry if they saw a 'disabled' person, or think that the person needs assistance, the honesty is something that I wholeheartedly appreciate, but it's just telling how much we still have to learn.

I guess it is shocking to me to see it actually written down, in black and white, the first thoughts of people when they see a 'disabled' person. I always knew it was there, as I've sadly encountered the problem in my life, but I was never actually told that it's what some people think when seeing a 'disabled' person. Naively on my part, I guess I just put it down to my own paranoia. That the way I was treated and viewed was all in my mind. I guess that was my own way of coping with the blatant discrimination I've faced in my past. I wasn't prepared for such honesty, I think partly because I didn't want to believe that the world could be capable of thinking and acting in such a way. That answer caught me off guard if I'm completely honest. There isn't an easy way to say this, but that is ableism right there. I don't blame the person though, I blame culture. If you don't look a certain way to what people see in the media, it automatically seems to put you on the back burner of society. You're bottom of the food chain and you are either patronised, manipulated or discriminated against, or sometimes all three just because you happen to look a little different from the 'normal', 'acceptable' way people are supposed to look.

Recently, I had the honour of speaking with Brian Abram, a 'disabled children's book author. Brian, (who goes under the alias, *Granddad Wheels*, explained the reason why he decided to become an author of children's books which specialise in disability education.

"My Grandson Charles as only 9 months old when I was injured so he doesn't know me any other way. But when he was about 3 I began to worry that as got a bit older he might ask me why I was different to other people. Why I

didn't walk like everyone else. So I wrote a silly story about how I was attacked by a lion in the jungle. My wife thought it was funny and I just developed it from there into a full story which includes him pushing me into a skateboard park to give me an adventure. I found a local illustrator and together we self-published our first book as no publishers were interested." – [Brian Abram, (Granddad Wheels) author]

It is difficult to fathom as to why publishers weren't interested in Brian's books. After all, they are designed to teach children about disability, so I imagine that his books aren't too 'heavy' if that's what publishers were worried about? It sounds to me that his books are light-hearted, but with an important message at it's core. Brian, to his credit, is doing extremely well, as he does talks in schools about his books, and therefore, also trying to break the stigma of disability, one school at a time.

You may be thinking how has Brian become so knowledgeable about disability? I actually met Brian myself during a Jacksons concert in Halifax in June twenty-twenty-three. We were on the platform together. He said that he was in an accident, which caused him to be:

"T9 complete paraplegic. Many other injuries at the time of my accident on August 2013 including weakened arm, nerve damage and two broken hips that cannot be fixed...It's been 10 years now and as I am 66, the impacts have got worse with age. The two broken hips cause daily neuropathic pain that is only just bearable much of the time. The risk of skin breakdown and pressure sores together with fear of bladder and bowels accidents are constant worries, as they are for most people with a spinal cord injury. On a practical level, I have got used to being a full-time wheelchair user and despite a few everyday problems such as access difficulties, I am very much accepted this as the norm. " – [Brian Abram, (Granddad Wheels) author]

Going back, it was extremely interesting to learn why Brian became an author. I must say that I experienced what he imagined. Certain young children coming up to me and asking why I was in a wheelchair. My response was:

"It's only because my legs don't work like yours do, but that's okay, because I'm still me."

That was enough for any inquisitive child. I really do not mind inquisitiveness, as long as it's genuine.

"...when I used to support an amazing young lady who was very disabled, children would sometimes stare at her, and I would just say, "say hello [client's name]" even though she was none verbal, it seemed to break the ice, so to speak." – [Debbie Davies Bellis, support worker and social media participant]

Including the 'disabled' person in the process of 'normalising' disability, especially to children who are inquisitive, can be integral to show children how disability isn't a frightening thing. I completely understand to a young child that disability can be a daunting prospect, especially if said person is severely 'disabled', but including a 'disabled' person in the conversation or an interaction of some kind, will break down the barriers. Debbie's approach is fantastic, she encourages disability and society by 'breaking the ice', she merges the two. If there were more people like Debbie who encourages instead of heightens and discourages the subject, I do personally think that disability wouldn't be an issue.

Going back, Brian made something incredible out of what I imagine most people would consider 'the end'. He is making waves with his amazing books. This, in my view, is why disability education is **so important**. Brian is 'normalising' disability (for want of a better word) to the masses, which is absolutely fantastic! Brian is helping children to understand disability in a fun and positive way, I recently spoken to him through email:

"I have just passed the milestone of meeting more than 25,000 primary school kids who are all now better informed about disability and some of the issues we face." – [Brian Abram, (Granddad Wheels) author]

This is **definitely** the kind of exposure disability needs and deserves. That is **twenty-five thousand pupils** that Brian has spoken to. **Twenty-five thousand pupils** while now has a better understanding of disability because of people like Brian. This doesn't get broadcast on the news, really because disability is just seen as that still for many unfortunately, but if we all make noise on the subject, then there is still that beacon of hope that society will eventually change it's perception of disability into a more positive one.

Social Views On Disability Education

Of all the responses I had from my survey, there was one in particular which was surprisingly accurate and it just goes to show that there is some hope to salvage some sort of common sense:

"We shouldn't have to educate disabilities, people should be self aware and this should be through their upbringing. It's the narrow-minded that need educating." – [One Participant's answer to Able-bodied Survey]

This is exactly what I'm trying to say and make people realise, but unfortunately, it's a romanticised view, (and I hate to say it), but even though this participant speaks a lot of common sense, in reality, it's just isn't possible, and it isn't possible because, it isn't an ideal world. As it currently stands, people are partly unaware that they are being offensive, discriminative and basically ableist in their views and partly because the vast majority of society don't know the term 'ableism' and 'ableist'.

"...It's a time for education for non disabled people to see what we go through 12 months of the year, and to help disabled people connect and get changes made. It's a way of pointing out to businesses, such as what a top contributor mentioned, that we are not fire risks and worthy of their time to adapt so we can be included. That's what pride is about." – [Social media participant, Elle Williams]

It's not widely known because it isn't talked about enough in mainstream culture, I think that there's a combination of reasons for this, people are unaware of the term ableism, they don't like to think of themselves as discriminatory towards disability, or in fact, any demographic, people are unaware that they are in fact being ableist, or people just don't see there's an issue with being discriminative. Obviously, it goes without saying why this is a major issue. Nobody who is 'modern' today would ever dream of being racist, sexist or homophobic, it's just not done. We have learnt what is right and wrong in this respect, and I believe that it's because people have had time to become aware and adjust their ways of thinking.

I wasn't sure whether or not to include this next answer I received from a participant of my surveys for fear of any kind of backlash towards either myself or the participant, even though the surveys are anonymous, you just never know, but after long deliberations with myself, I came to the conclusion that it needed to be included, not for shock value or hate speech, or anything like that, I've decided to include it to hopefully show you how society actually thinks when it comes to disability. To try and raise awareness of this culture of negativity that people in my position face constantly. I'll admit, it took me by surprise when I initially read it:

"Do you mean education on disabilities in general because we already have that. If you mean for severe/debilitating disabilities, I wonder how you believe this would be done? There's already not enough time in schools for kids to get their work done adequately and too

much pressure on them to get the rest done at home, plus the added pressure of having to find casual or part time work outside of school. But this is also why we have carer positions; the people who want to educate themselves and help the disabled are already doing so." - [One Participant's answer to Able-bodied Survey]

I fully understand the concerns here, but sometimes we do need to look at and discuss the bigger picture. So many 'disabled' people feel pushed aside by society just by something like this sentence alone. I truly understand and appreciate the pressures children and adults, however this dismissive language is what I'm standing up for. I'm not going to completely dismiss the participant's response too much though as I've recently found out that the *Scouts* are educating disability, albeit in a general sense as the participant mentioned, but at least they are trying to be progressive and proactive in positively highlighting disability, more than what society is doing in my own personal opinion.

Educating disability in a general sense though isn't enough, and this is why I'm having trouble understanding the participant's response above to the survey, because general education just groups it together and I think it just stops any possible chance of making a positive difference. There are so many levels of disability, that if disability was just taught generally, nobody would be able to learn anything about the subject effectively.

Case in point, referring to the participant's carer positions comment, although are vital, can also harbour discrimination as they may only see the disability and not the person. Education doesn't teach humanity. I think that disability has a fundamental right to be taught in schools and I think there's a way to do it without additional pressure to children or adults. If disability was taught more in depth, if it is at all, then the participant wouldn't be so dismissive and understand that care work, is individual. It depends on the actual person whether they realise that there is a person behind the disability. Let me tell you, finding carers who understand this, in my opinion are few and far between. Luckily I now have a support worker who sees me first which is so fantastic and refreshing in Judi, she allows me to be me, my disability isn't the be all and end all with her, which I appreciate. Getting to this point however where I'm truly happy with my support wasn't plain sailing. There were support workers who's main concern was my disability and I felt as if I was secondary. It shouldn't be like this obviously, but this is the world we live in. So for someone to say that this is why we have carer positions, is just redundant in my own opinion.

There were lessons in high school when I attended called PSE (Personal, Social Education) solely for the purpose of teaching pupils about life. Recently, I was having a chat with Ceri, as she's a teacher in a high school and she said that PSE lessons are still very much in the school curriculum. In these lessons when I attended school, pupils were taught about a whole range of different subjects including, sex, puberty, bullying behaviour, getting a job, running a household on a budget, planning a family, drugs, contraception, cultural differences, basically everything and anything that the school board curriculum thought was necessary and needed for pupils to grow up streetwise, which was great, it definitely needs to be taught in schools, but the one subject was missing and crucial in today's world, especially with the things I've faced in my life is understanding and accepting disability. I think that there was (and still is in many ways) a need for disability education. Statements such as the one above made by a participant of the survey clearly shows that disability education doesn't go far enough. Furthermore, if disability education is taught in schools as this participant says it is, the actual reality of the subject must be limited, as if it was talked about in depth, there is absolutely no doubt in my mind that the participant's view on disability would change drastically. I get that everyone has a right to voice their opinion, I'm all for that, but an opinion should come from a place of understanding of the subject you are talking about, and not just by shutting down a discussion with a total disregard of the consequences of their arguments. Someone I know recently made a perfect point that demonstrates this. They've kindly given me permission to quote what they said, but I'm keeping the person's anonymity (but the anonymous person **is a teacher themselves**):

"Shouldn't we be encouraging and understanding of all disabilities whether severe

or not? And school and home is precisely the place to be teaching kids about how diverse our society is!!! Conversations about disability shouldn't even be a big deal. It doesn't take up much space in a teaching day to have a conversation. Also, there will undoubtedly be disabled children in most schools won't there? So, silence on the issue of equality is no good for them or their school experience ..." – *[Anonymous, in the teaching profession]*

Of course, there should be an open conversation in society to understand all disabilities. People should be at least willing to have a conversation. That should never come into question or cause issues for anyone in my opinion. We all need to express ourselves and be encouraging people. Hate only drives hate. Having constant dismissive attitudes only makes the ableist situation worse for both able-bodied people and 'disabled' people alike. People need to learn how to handle topics sensitively of course, but they should never be afraid to actually have the conversation. Reading between the lines of the comment above from one participant of my surveys, I can suggest that they maybe afraid themselves to open up to the idea of disability education, so that is why they've said what they have said. I could be completely wrong in my thoughts, and the participant themselves may not realise that they may feel like this, but to me, knowing how much people are so reluctant to talk about disability, this is what I personally take away. You learn a lot yourself when you are at the centre of it all. You have to learn to read between the lines of everything associated with disabilities.

As part of my reach out to social media and email, I asked the question to a few 'disabled' participants, and/or their families alongside disability charities and organisations on whether they think the education system would benefit from providing disability education. I will put each answer received below, to let you decide if education of disability is considered offensive to 'disabled' people, and to the families of 'disabled' people or not. The answers **do** speak for themselves though.

"Definitely! Maybe school kids spending some time in a wheelchair would be good education. If not, accompanying a wheelchair user as they

go out? I would be happy to do this." - *[Social media participant, Maddy C]*

"Yes very much, so when you leave school, you are going to meet people that are different as a true reflection of society." – *[Margaret Foster, email participant]*

"Yes physical and hidden but I don't think they will do it as they will argue kids have lots to learn already." – *[Anonymous social media participant]* (Argument made already).

"Definitely, it will give employees and employers, and students a better understanding of how to treat people who don't always have the same mobility of themselves." – *[Hayley Murphy, email participant]*

"Yes, I do if it's done in the right way." – *[Deborah Bayley, social media participant, mum and daughter]*

"Where would they fit it in secondary school?" – *[Anonymous social media participant]* (Covered already).

"Yes, this is something that children would benefit from. If the dialogue starts early then this creates a greater opportunity for becoming a natural language to be incorporated into their infrastructure." – [Jacqueline Whelan, Barrister]

"The Bobath Centre believes that disability awareness should be part of the curriculum in the education system, to educate children and normalise physical, sensory and psychological impairments. In that way, future generations will have a more inclusive society that embraces disabled people and recognises their unique challenges not understood by non-disabled people. We'd like all children with disabilities to be included in mainstream education and for school buildings to be physically accessible. We'd like history, literature and other subjects to include reference to people with disabilities and welcome the news that British Sign Language will be a GCSE." – [The National Bobath Cerebral Palsy Centre, London]

As you may see, 'disabled' people, their families, disability charities or organisations don't have any issues at all with disabilities being a part of the

Educating Disability

education system. If you think that some maybe questioning it, all that you have to try and understand is that it is a question, and a very good one, not because there is an uneasiness about the topic of disability education, but just because there's a question of how, given the time constraints of the education system, but I hope that I have answered this query with the PSE lessons argument.

Disability education for young children could also be a thing too. It actually is really, with the help of Brian Abram. There are toys out there that represent different disabilities, admittedly a certain brand of toy, and more representation from other companies could follow suit, but at least there is somewhat of a revolution happening. These certain toys could be used as teach aids to help young children understand better about disability. I will discuss this certain brand of toy later.

There definitely needs to be more awareness of BSL, and think it could be taught in schools, and for children to learn more about all disabilities, as sometimes things that they don't understand can be frightening.

I also asked if other places such as companies etc. would benefit from providing disability education. Again, participants from social media said:

"Definitely as lots of autistic people struggle at work." – [Anonymous social media participant]

"Yes if customer facing." – [Anonymous social media participant]

As you can see, a large number of 'disabled' people support the idea of disability education, both in the classroom and the workplace. You cannot hide behind the excuse anymore that it may cause some type of offense. Not providing disability education and training **is** the offense. Yes, you may say about the education system "budget" and "time constraints", but it is so obvious that these **aren't** an issue, like the anonymous teacher explains above, it doesn't take up much space in a teaching day to have a **conversation**. At the end of the day, that is all that's needed, to start a conversation, no matter

Educating Disability

how small, just something to get the ball rolling on disability equality, acceptance and inclusion.

PSE lessons are the perfect time for disability education to happen in schools, as it can fall under the category of the Social part of the lesson. I'm sure that the powers that be in the education system would have no problem in inviting speakers either with disabilities, or work in the disability profession to come into schools, colleges and universities to talk about disability. Maddy C herself said she would be more than happy to do this. There aren't any **physical** barriers stopping the suggestion. There are only **metaphorical** barriers. I believe that these metaphorical barriers are harder to overcome, which is absolutely heart-breaking. Excuse, after excuse, after excuse, that is all society seems to be nowadays. If we don't like the idea of something, we just 'justify' that thing not happening by saying "we can't do this because...", it's pathetic. Disability is a standard part of life, when are we ever going to see that?

Scouts UK **Paving the Way**

Recently, (as of writing this), both Rosie and Tommy (my niece and nephew) have joined *Cubs*, and I was thrilled to hear that they have to earn a *'Disability Awareness'* badge. When I heard this, I somewhat had a bit of a moment. I feel personally that 'disabled' discrimination has gone under the radar for so long, that to finally have something that encourages disability, is a step in the right direction. Yes, it is a small step, but a step forward all the same. I applaud and want to thank them for finally championing disability, (although championing disability shouldn't ever have to be a thing really, disability is apart of life, but unfortunately, here we are.) I feel like there is hope however, and where there's hope, there's potential change.

"As Scouts we believe in inclusion, which means everyone is welcome and nobody gets left out..." – [Scouts.org.uk]

The *Scouts* are paving the way in this regard and should be applauded for their efforts in trying to highlight disability as a standard part of life. Even the above quote on their website shows how

Educating Disability

forward-thinking they are, and dedicated to teach children about disability, and I'm quite surprised how much they try to teach children about the subject. You would think that because the focus is on children, then it would be a toned down version of the subject as it can be very heavy to talk about without the right information, but it really isn't. What I personally like is that *Scouts UK* seems to have made learning about different disabilities fun in many ways, not daunting. Taking away the heaviness and replacing it with fun tasks and activities, giving children the opportunity to actually see and learn what it's actually like to have some form of disability, and above all 'normalising' the subject, if there is such a thing?

"We cover all sorts of issues, physical disabilities, Autism awareness, and sign language to name a few." – [Scouts UK]

To earn a badge of this type, children can choose to focus on one thing from a list of four.

I've been told by *Scouts UK* that they cater to age, which **does** make a lot of sense. Some activities are for the younger members, and other activities are for the older members. I'm guessing the older the child, the more in depth the activities, but from research, I am pleased to learn that *Scouts UK* are not shying away from the subject of disability. It's refreshing, and hopeful.

I will add the activities for each group of children below, to make it easier to read and take in. All activity information is from *Scouts.org* with permission.

Beavers

1. **Disability awareness – do one of these:**

    a. Explain what a disability is.

    b. Find out about a Paralympian and their sport. Tell a story about their achievements.

    c. Visit an activity centre or playground for people with disabilities.

    d. Talk about how your meeting place could be made better so that everyone can take part.

    e. Make a poster that tells others about a disability. Choose something that's not mentioned later, in numbers 2, 3 or 4.

2. **Physical disability awareness – do one of these:**

    a. Show how to safely push a wheelchair.

    b. Talk about an aid that can help a disabled person. It could be a type of wheelchair, computer, grabber or rising chair.

3. **Deaf awareness – do one of these:**

    a. Learn how to fingerspell your name.

    b. Learn the Promise in British Sign Language.

    c. Explain what hearing dogs for deaf people do. Why are they helpful?

4. Sight awareness – do one of these:

a. Talk about what guide dogs for blind people do.

Cubs

1. Disability awareness

a. Explain what a disability is. What are the different types of disability?

b. Research a famous person with a disability.

c. Make a poster or write about their life and achievements.

d. Visit a local community building like a library, town hall or cinema. How accessible is it for someone with a disability?

e. Write down what you find out.

f. Show how you could help someone with a disability to make the Cub Promise.

g. Think of a different example to the ones in steps 2, 3 or 4.

Educating Disability

2. **Physical disability awareness**

    a. Find out about two different aids that can assist a disabled person. How do they help? You could find out about things like wheelchairs, computers, rising chairs or adapted cars.

    b. Find out about three ways to make it easier for a wheelchair user to use public places, like shops, parks, hospitals or libraries. How could your meeting place be made better for a wheelchair user?

3. **Deaf awareness**

    a. Learn the alphabet using fingerspelling. Show you understand a word communicated to you using fingerspelling.

    b. Learn a song in Makaton or British Sign Language.

    c. Explain what equipment a deaf person might use in the home.

> You might look at special features on things like fire alarms, telephones or TVs.
>
> d. Show how you would approach a deaf person and speak to them so they can lip-read.

Sight awareness

a. Describe two different ways a blind or visually impaired person can read. You could talk about how they would use computers, Braille or Moon.

b. Explain what guide dogs for blind people do. How are they trained?

c. Learn and read your name in Braille.

d. Show how to approach a blind or visually impaired person. How would you identify yourself?

The older the child, the more in-depth the activity.

There are also a number of other activities for autism, which children can take part in within *Scouts UK* under the category of 'Understanding Disability'. The category is sponsored by the *'National Autistic Society'*. What I would personally like to see is instead of the category being called *'Understanding Disability'*, I feel that it would be much better to rename it as *'Understanding Autism'*, therefore it would give other disability charities a chance to participate. As it stands now, I personally feel like the category is confusing and misleading for children, as they could interpret autism as disability in general. Children are very trustworthy and trust whatever they are told.

The actual activities are impressive in my own opinion. I'm not going to include the activities here, as there are quite a lot, but trust me, the amount of activities and to what level are genuinely incredible. You can see the activities for yourself on the *Scouts UK* website if so desired.

I must admit that, Jacqueline Whelan, Barrister said:

"I have seen a sea change regarding mental health, with less stigma than previously noted. That mental health is something talked about in schools. That BSL is being championed as a language to be taught on the national curriculum. That Makaton is something most children have been exposed to in their early years.

As a Barrister, there is a widening of knowledge and understanding regarding disability with training on diversity being on the agenda for each Chambers, with there being a designated officer whose role it is to ensure compliance of training.

Personally, when I started out looking to practise as a Barrister, I was fearful of potential Chambers knowing I had a child with a disability (I'm likely to have more time off for hospital appointments/school reviews etc.) now, I can be open about what I need from my Chambers without fear." – [Jacqueline Whelan, Barrister]

At first, regrettably, I didn't really believe Jacqueline with regards to *BSL*, mental health and *Makaton*. I think that it was due to my own negative experiences. This however, one's own negative experience should never cloud anyone's judgement on whether they believe things have improved or not. Experiences are individual. Not everyone is ever going to experience exactly the same. I'm just speaking from personal experience. Obviously, Jacqueline's experience is much more positive than mine is, which is absolutely incredible! I was amazed and overwhelmed to learn that mental health is now openly being talked about in schools, that *BSL* is being championed to be added to the school curriculum, I personally didn't know that *Makaton* is something children know from an early age. For Jacqueline to see this sea change speaks volumes in terms of how far we've come. Experiences like Jacqueline's gives me tremendous hope for the future of disability equality. It's slow, but it's a start.

This is going to break so many barriers if this continues, and just make the world a better place to be. I wasn't actually aware that things such as *BSL* is being championed to be added to the school curriculum, whether it has had any success, is a different story altogether.

It also hit me hard knowing that Jacqueline was fearful over fourteen years ago to say that she had a child with a disability . Thankfully, she's personally said to me that times have now changed in Chambers. The stigmatisation is virtually non-existent in her line of work today, which of course is a fantastic thing, as again it gives me hope that this will trickle down to mainstream culture.

Like I said in *CP Isn't Me*, there seems to always be this unproven notion that the word disability, means that there maybe continuous need for time off work for illness or appointments. I guess that a fear of being judged follows 'disabled' people and their families around, regardless of the circumstances. The stigma needs to stop as it puts into jeopardy the employment sector as a whole, thus creating more unnecessary unemployment, which then puts added strain on the economy and Government. This utterly ridiculous belief needs to end for the sake of society.

Remember the *Domino* effect?

Of course, education of disability cannot just start and end in the classroom, disability discrimination occurs wherever you go. The fact remains that either intentionally or unintentionally, whether people like to hear it or not, it definitely does happen and it happens all too often, as discussed already.

Educating Disability

Social services, workplaces, shops, cafés, accommodation, venues, you name it, they are all guilty. There's bound to be some type of discrimination lingering in the background. Going back to Kerry Evans, the DLO of Wrexham AFC, she said that when her disability progressed and she started to use a wheelchair, social services came in and (as they thought) made all of the adaptations necessary for Kerry to be able to live as independently as possible. She said that when her adaptations were 'completed', she was asked by the social worker to try them out and make a cup of tea. The long and short of it was, she couldn't. The adaptations made were unsuitable to her needs. She said this to the social worker that she couldn't make their request, and explained that the adaptations weren't suitable for her, of which the social worker asked why didn't she say something beforehand? Kerry said that she didn't, purely for the fact that she believed that social services knew what they were tasked to do. She trusted them really to make her life as easy as possible by putting the right things in place for her. After all, if you work in a specific sector, you should have at least some knowledge of your job, shouldn't you? In my mind, it seems a logical way to think. Society in general doesn't work on logic unfortunately. This is why society would benefit from asking people in the know about how to design things etc., that's intended to benefit a specific demographic. It sounds ridiculous, but unless we say what we need to make our lives easier, we aren't going to get it. People aren't mind readers, even though adaptations for disability should always be logical.

Kerry's experience, is just one example outside of my own personal experiences, of the outside world not understanding disability. If social services asked Kerry what adaptations she thought she needed at the time, then a total replacement of the adaptations wouldn't have been needed. Thankfully, Kerry now has the adaptations she needs, of which I'm thankful for, as I know how difficult it is to make anything accessible without either a long drawn-out fight for what is rightfully needed, or even for a chance of authorities actually listening to what exactly is needed. That's an uphill battle in itself, trying to be heard and respected. It's virtually impossible. You see, people think that they are qualified and know best just because they either, have a degree in social care, or have attended training days. You need to live it to be able to fully understand what it's like to be any kind of 'disabled' person (if there's ever such a thing). A piece of paper or certificate isn't going to do that. Proper lived experience is. Ask a 'disabled' person first what adaptations are needed, instead of always assuming. You wouldn't ask an able-bodied person to renovate a house without asking permission, involvement of said person throughout the process, or plans drawn up by that person. That wouldn't be right, and if I'm not mistaken, against the law. So why should people with disabilities always have to accept things that we hate, find inaccessible and inconvenient? That's discrimination in itself. Yes, you maybe thinking, Samantha, what about more severely 'disabled' people who can't make decisions? To that I say, in this case, the logical thing to do is to ask the families or support workers of that specific 'disabled' person. After all, these are the key people who maybe there to care for a person with a severe disability. They will know exactly what is needed in this case, as they would be the ones to use them whilst helping their loved one or client. This is what all 'disabled' people deserve. A little dignity and respect and the right to be able to live as independently as possible without having to justify ourselves or fight for it.

Social services cannot know every single person who has a disability of some form, they don't really know our needs, that's impossible and absolutely ridiculous if they think they do. We are individuals, separate from each other. Our lives are different in terms of ability, so our needs are also different. That should be on the main news as a breaking story. Somehow though, it seems like 'disabled' people are almost always dictated to. We are constantly told what is best for us by either a team of professionals or social services who really have absolutely no clue about what needs to be done, they are just going off by what they already know which really, isn't much. Now, I'm not just saying this to cause any harm or offense, my books aren't designed to offend, but to try and teach. I'm just saying the truth. Stating fact.

What's the saying? "If it ain't broke, don't fix it." This is the mantra that social services should be taught, not to replace equipment when a person reaches a certain age. The human race isn't the same. People can be short, tall, and weight can fluctuate. Even as an adult, you can still be small in stature and lightweight, or the opposite, small in stature but slightly heavier, slightly heavier and tall. There's no set level. What also gets me, (and I may have said this before) is that once a 'disabled' child reaches adulthood (eighteen years old) they are automatically taken from the healthcare system. Discarded. It's as if the healthcare system is saying that a 'disabled' person is able to look after themselves at the age of eighteen, that somehow, suddenly, by some miracle, we have the resources to help ourselves. Another news flash, we still need the healthcare system by our side just in case there is ever a change in our health or needs. It isn't right just to drop someone because they have reached adulthood, support should **always** be there regardless of the situation. That's common curtesy and human decency. A person's appearance shouldn't be punished. After our birthday, our needs aren't going to change overnight, or at a click of a finger, we don't have a magic wand. We will still require the same amount of help as we did before a milestone birthday. Maybe in time, our needs may change, in time, but not as soon as the clock strikes midnight. For any independence to take place, we need to learn skills needed to look after ourselves.

Nobody ever takes into consideration that everyone is built differently, with different skills and abilities. Some are quick learners, and some aren't, but that's okay. That also goes for 'disabled' people too, but this **isn't** a weakness or a strength. That is how the world operates.

You cannot have a 'one size fits all'. That doesn't sync with today's 'modern society'. More often than not, social services are providing inadequate support by always making the decisions, providing inadequate equipment just because something such as a piece of paper may say an adult who has a disability, may need a specific type of equipment, which could be too big or more difficult to use, when really their previous equipment still works fine. I get the Health and Safety side to everything and the liabilities of misusing equipment that is out of date, but wouldn't there be more risk to provide people with disabilities inadequate equipment? When it goes wrong, which it undoubtedly does, (look again at the case of Kerry Evans), it either costs the taxpayer more to rectify social services mistakes, or when an issue is brought to the attention of social services, it literally takes an age for anything to be redone. I've been there, I know what I'm talking about.

So, we've hopefully established that social services need a rethink on their approach of providing equipment for disability, and that the service desperately needs to take into consideration the biological circumstances of the human race. A 'disabled' person isn't any different in terms of growth. Stop treating us like we are. Re-educate yourselves in biology! This may seem harsh, but it needs saying. I for one am absolutely sick of being treated as a guinea pig, just seeing what may work and what won't. Spending hours upon hours with social services, as they try and figure out what is best for me, without actually asking me! If it wasn't so true, it would be funny. Second guessing isn't ever going to progress disability. Personally, I don't like to be 'seen' as being 'disabled'. I'm not ashamed of it, but I'm ashamed of the label of disability. That label causes so many unnecessary problems, that I personally try to minimise the label by trying to have equipment that is dainty and compact as much as I can.

If you listen to social services, and trust them completely, having absolutely no say whatsoever in equipment, there is no doubt in my mind that social services would have you in possession of the largest equipment possible, and therefore, the disability label will inevitably become larger as a result. Only you know you, nobody else. If you're uncomfortable with something that social services either suggests or provides you or a family member, speak up! Social services **don't** have all the answers, they are just going by what they've been taught to do in training. If it won't be beneficial, tell them, there are always alternatives to explore that may be more beneficial. Never be afraid to say no. Saying yes to everything won't get you anywhere in life, trust me, I know. I used to be a 'people pleaser', until I learned that it won't get you anywhere in life. I've started to become my true self with social services. I say how it is, and if I don't like something, I speak up. At

Educating Disability

the end of the day, social services don't care if you disagree with something, they are only there to earn money, truth be told. You make absolutely sure that you make them work to your needs.

Other Areas of Improvement

Society, as a whole, needs to learn about what it actually means to have a disability. Saying that though, disability does have a place in society today, but I really don't think that place is good. People still make comments, judge, patronise or discriminate against disability, that's a fact. There's no getting away from it. It's sadly always been apart of the mainstream. We need to practice what we preach. We need to start realising that disability isn't a disadvantage. That negative attitude towards disability is the biggest disadvantage and barrier.

I was curious to learn more about author Aideen Blackborough's book title, *'Does It Wet The Bed?'* I wanted to learn where that title came from. Aideen said it was:

"Based on an incident whilst travelling to Lourdes as a child, mum and I were due to stay

in a convent but one of the nuns directed this question to mum and she was referring to me. Needless to say, we found somewhere else to stay." – [Aideen Blackborough, Author, Disability Trainer and Speaker]

When I read this, I personally was in a state of confusion, disbelief and shock. How can **anyone** ever treat another **human being** with such disrespect, and so blatantly too? Yes, I get that they may not have understood disability, but to refer to Aideen as an "it"? Well, that's just plain ableism right there, not to mention asking someone such a personal question, directed towards another person rather than Aideen herself. I know that the other person was her mum, but still, I can imagine that it would have been embarrassing. If this would've happened to me, then I'd be embarrassed. This is what angers me really, and if it wasn't clear before, this is **exactly** why education of disability is so important today, to stop ignorance and offense. You cannot go around asking horrendous questions and expect to get a positive response. This just plays into the argument that society really doesn't know how to respond to disability. I said this in my previous book, so I won't explain fully here, but all I will say to reiterate my point is that, I was referred to as a "thing" when I was younger by a shop manager.

Both instances happened years ago admittedly, so you could make the famous excuse of "different times", but how long can that feeble excuse last? That excuse isn't good enough. People seem to rely on this excuse constantly, it's absolutely ridiculous. You probably think that nothing would happen as abhorrent as referring to 'disabled' people as objects today, maybe not as blatantly as years ago, but I personally feel that just because people aren't saying it, it doesn't mean that they aren't thinking it. Maybe we have become more 'accepting' on the outside, just to keep up appearances in a way. If demographics such as disability was accepted, Aideen, Kerry and myself probably wouldn't feel it necessary to try and change perceptions. Obviously, disability discrimination does still exist. Yes, this may sound cynical, and I absolutely hate cynicism, but I personally feel that it's the truth sadly, as do others.

"I don't think it's changed despite laws; discrimination against disabled people is still as common as it always was." – *[Aideen Blackborough, Author, Disability Trainer and Speaker]*

Obviously, society would benefit from a more hands-on approach to disability equality. Obviously the laws currently in place aren't enough. Aideen Blackborough sadly doesn't think anything has changed, and it hasn't in all honesty. There is so much more that could be done, if only Government would actually listen to 'disabled' people and take proper action to help us if we find ourselves discriminated against. Government need to learn skills to help stop disability discrimination. If Government isn't sure what qualifies as disability discrimination, then they should invite 'disabled' people to help setup steps to help end disability discrimination indefinitely. If 'disabled' people were allowed to be involved in creating a brand new system to end discrimination, then this would definitely create a stronger level of trust between 'disabled' people and Government. If stronger actions were put in place, then there maybe a small chance that society would rethink disability as a whole too. Government should take the lead in changing perceptions. It's like a *Domino* effect. Lead by example. I do wholeheartedly believe that 'disabled' people lost trust in their Government when the infamous surveys were introduced that were originally designed to determine the difference between real disability cases and people who weren't classed as 'disabled'. That system was corrupt in my own personal opinion. Again, I'm not going to discuss fully the problem with the surveys as I have already in *CP Isn't Me*, but I really do believe that any remaining trust or respect for Government, ended when those surveys began. Just the approach to those surveys alone, were just plain awful. We as 'disabled' people, were made to feel as if we were doing something wrong. We were interrogated. People rely on Government (rightly or wrongly) to be knowledgeable about different topics and demographics, and trust people in power to be able to make the right decisions to enhance the lives of **all** people in society. Those surveys, when they were put into practice, did the total opposite.

Government should always have integrity. That's the bottom line.

This is what I meant about education on disability. People **always assume** that you are talking about the school system when the topic of education is brought up. Yes, education from an early age on the subject of disability, is the best way to stop disability discrimination in the **future**, and it **is extremely important** to encourage the topic in schools and higher education, but what about the here and now? Disability discrimination still exists in the present, and it won't go away unless **everyone on the planet** is correctly taught what is acceptable behaviour and accepts disability as a standard part of life like anything else in society.

I asked Aideen Blackborough the question of does she, as a 'disabled' person feel like education on disability needs to be educated more, and/or expanded upon?

"Absolutely. We have the Equality Act but it's so often ignored and nothing is done unless an individual has the drive to take up a case. There's very little accountability and whenever I make a complaint, I get the standard response

of, "Our staff have been trained..." Training means very little when disability discrimination is still a common occurrence." - [Aideen Blackborough, Author, Disability Trainer and Speaker]

This is why I'm glad I decided to involve others with this book. Hopefully now you can see how other 'disabled' people feel. It's very straight to the point but also sadly very true. The *Disability Equality Act* is out there, that's true, but it's so blatantly obvious that society doesn't really follow it. Furthermore, you have to take into consideration whether this Act is still relevant to this new modern culture, or does it in fact need a reworking? Apparently, this is how the *Disability Equality Act of 2010* defines disability, according to the *Citizens Advice* website:

"The Equality Act says a disability is a physical or mental impairment which has a substantial and long-term adverse effect on your ability to carry out normal day- to-day activities." – *[Citizens Advice website]*

I think that this is **partly true**. A disability can be defined as either physical or mental. That's fact.

Where the definition falls apart is when it says it has a substantial and long-term adverse effect on your ability to carry out normal day-to-day activities. Some activities yes, but what I personally take from this is that the Act is implying 'disabled' people are unable to undertake all standard day-to-day activities. This **isn't true**. Again this is dangerous. It's just inevitably labelling and tarring **all people with disabilities** with the same brush. The quote just inevitably umbrellas disability. There's no room for individuality. As long as misleading quotes are out there, we cannot showcase our abilities. That's wrong and unfair on **so many** levels.

Kerry Evans, the DLO of Wrexham AFC, perfectly defined disability for the modern age. She basically said that *"everyone is good at something, able-bodied or not, but feels like there is a lack of equality for disabled people in general society." – [Paraphrase: Kerry Evans Disability Liaison Officer at Wrexham AFC]* This, undoubtedly speaks volumes. I'm also quite glad that someone else is saying exactly what I'm trying to say, fight for and make a reality. People need to realise this, and stop thinking that disability is a disadvantage or a weakness, this is where this lack of equality stems from that Kerry has mentioned. Ignorance isn't a cure for acceptance. Realisation is. Understanding is. Even intrigue is. If you're curious, ask, don't stare, or talk behind our backs. We would prefer inquisitiveness rather than the alternative. The alternative doesn't allow the human race to progress, (that word again), but rather regress. I for one, really don't think that the world today wants to regress. That doesn't match the 'modern society' image that we are so keen to promote. Now, maybe, this 'modern culture' is only a facade, something that society can hide behind, as already suggested, but I really don't want to accept that. I really want to believe that people are just genuinely unaware of their actions towards disability without realising any prejudices that they may be projecting. Again, yes this can be considered naive on my part. Denial if you will? I know that probably deep down there's a more complex reason, but I personally **choose** to believe my lack of education theory. That isn't denial or naivety, but security. Mental stability. If I just believed that lack of education was the issue, then I truly wouldn't be prepared for the potential reality. I'm aware that there maybe something more to it, but my mental state is too important to me to even entertain the idea of something more.

BSL (British Sign Language)

During my research, I stumbled across a page on the Government UK website that is solely dedicated to disability awareness, and I came across one statement that referred to deaf awareness. According to the *Gov.UK* website:

> *"...many deaf people whose first language is BSL consider themselves part of 'the deaf community' – they may describe themselves as 'Deaf', with a capital D, to emphasise their deaf identity." – [GOV.UK]*

If you weren't already aware, *BSL* is an abbreviation for *British Sign Language*. There's an estimated **"25,000 people who use British Sign Language as their main language across the UK." – [RNID.org.uk]**

This information from *RNID* is quite important and significant in a way, as it just goes to show how many people across the UK actually use *BSL* as their first language, their actual means of communicating with the outside world. It does obviously beg the question, in my mind at least, how many people in society outside the Deaf Community, actually knows *British Sign Language*? I mean actually knows how to use it to communicate with the Deaf Community, not just know the term?

"...sign language is a language that uses fingers and hands, gestures and facial expressions." – [Debbie Davies Bellis, support worker and social media participant]

I know through Rosie and Tommy that *Scouts UK* teach *BSL* as part of their *Disability Awareness* exercises, but apart from this, is *BSL* taught in other areas of society? Schools, workplaces etc., and if not, why not?

I felt it necessary to try to research *BSL* by actually asking for **real participants**, to explain their own personal experiences of *BSL*, both from a social standpoint and people who use *British Sign Language* on a daily basis to communicate.

"I was attending courses in Caia Park Partnership, one of them was BSL, I have a

friend who has a deaf son who got bullied, and I just wanted to be able to say hello to him when I saw them. I really enjoyed the course, passed stage 1, then enrolled on a night course at Yale [college, Wrexham, now Coleg Cambria] for stage 2...." – [Debbie Davies Bellis, support worker, and social media participant]

Unfortunately, any form of disability can be subjected to some form of bullying, including the Deaf Community, and it's a shame. Language is a wonderful thing, and the different ways of communicating should be celebrated and encouraged, not judged and ridiculed.

It is the lack of understanding that ultimately barricades society from actually seeing the **people behind the disability**, and of course it shouldn't be. This is why I find it absolutely necessary for the topic of disability to be taught. It's for humanity's sake more than anything. I was so pleased to find out that there are courses that teach *BSL*, however, I do think that this teaching of *BSL* could actually go a little further into mainstream education if Debbie's quote above is anything to go by. Learning *BSL* just because someone who is apart of the Deaf Community maybe being bullied, is an extremely awful reason to want to learn. Debbie Davies Bellis was so kind as to learn *BSL* to stop someone from feeling isolated, but I just personally think that it is a shame and a waste of a great opportunity to learn the language just to stop someone from feeling isolated. Pitying isn't a good reason really, but unfortunately, for reasons that I can't honestly personally understand, this is where we are. It just goes to show how the world operates.

"...I learnt that there are regional signs for most words. E.g. someone from Chester, could sign the word Chester, differently from people say from Liverpool, but the alphabet is always signed the same, so people can finger spell the word so they know what the word is....There is a BSL site where you can learn sign language with videos..." – [Debbie Davies Bellis, support worker and social media participant]

It is absolutely fascinating to learn from Debbie here that there are regional signs for most words in *BSL*. It's almost like accents, depending on where you live, a word can sound different in different regions. Having different ways of signing depending on where you live, 'normalises' *BSL*, and more importantly, 'normalises' the **person** using *BSL*. This is what I meant when I said that language is a wonderful thing, which should be celebrated and encouraged. Language is used to connect people, regardless of how it is presented. *BSL* is just another way to communicate with each other. That's it. That's all it is.

"I have looked for courses for BSL to refresh and learn more, but there doesn't seem to be any." – [Debbie Davies Bellis, support worker and social media participant]

An article from the *House of Commons Library* which was published back in two-thousand and eighteen, claims that *BSL* would be considered to be apart of the standard school curriculum and a part of GCSE examinations. Since then though, I personally assume no attempt to do this has been made. It can't have been if Debbie is unable to find any refresher courses on *BSL* for example. What hope is there for general disability education? Online videos, as Debbie has mentioned, just isn't enough. It isn't acceptable.

Educating Disability

With this approach to disability education, by rights, education in general should be presented in video format, and not readily available. This wouldn't be approved by Government, and rightly so, I'm just trying to prove a point. It really does annoy me that disability education isn't a priority. Education is education at the end of the day, it all counts for something. Regardless of subject matter, it's **all important**.

I mean, think about it, if disability was made apart of the standard school curriculum and GCSE's, wouldn't it be splashed all over the news? At the end of the day, like it or not, with society being so vain as it is today, especially with the rise of social media, I personally think that coverage of disability in any way would be welcomed, not as a genuine interest, but more like an ego thing, as if to then confirm in people's own minds that we are more aware an understanding, but of course, this would be without any input from actual society. I know I've said that disability in general doesn't get the coverage it so wholeheartedly deserves when it comes to the media, not by a long shot, but if it is something that is being made compulsory and could affect the futures of children, you would think that there would be some attempt made to cover such an important story and interest of it, as it could be considered a ground-breaking moment in not only general society, but the Deaf Community and disability as a whole. It turned out that my assumption was unfortunately correct.

"The Government does not currently plan to introduce BSL to the curriculum, although schools may choose to offer it themselves." – [House of Commons Library on BSL]

If so many people use *BSL* as their first language across the UK, and if Government acknowledges *BSL* as a way for the Deaf Community to communicate, then why shouldn't it be made a compulsory part of the school curriculum and by extension, examinations? There are multiple different languages that are already taught in schools, namely, Welsh, French, and German for example, so why can't *BSL* be considered? After all, *BSL* **is** a language. Years ago, Latin was even taught as a language in education. It is absolutely ridiculous to me how we can teach other languages, (which don't get me wrong, is absolutely fine, it's needed in order to make the world more inclusive, to be able to travel, for potential future job roles etc.,) but *BSL* seems to have fallen by the wayside. This is what I mean by ableism and ableist attitudes, denying extremely important topics in favour of others, in this case, language, just proves that we aren't as accepting and understanding as we like to think we are. The lack of *BSL* education is really down to the *UK* Government. Again, I can probably imagine that it's due to funding and time constraints put on teachers, but just because it seems daunting, it doesn't mean that it has to be. Just a suggestion here, but maybe incorporating *BSL* into a PSE lesson could be a starting point? As I've said, PSE lessons are designed **exactly** for this type of subject, and it doesn't have to cost the Earth to incorporate fundamental subjects that could actually be beneficial to, not only people now, but also to future generations. **These** are **exactly** the life skills that should be taught in schools in my own personal opinion. If funding is the issue, then teachers themselves could search for legitimate videos teaching *BSL* specifically for a PSE lesson (there are countless amounts of *TED*

Talks on the subject of *BSL* alone on the Internet). Both pupils and teachers could learn *BSL* together during the PSE lessons. That way, everyone is on the same page, and it could also be made fun somehow by making up games to remember, by maybe having competitions between the teachers and the pupils? Maybe, who remembers the most *BSL* from a video? I don't know, I'm just suggesting, but something **definitely** needs to happen. People just can't make excuses up anymore as to why disability is still treated so disrespectfully. PSE lessons happen once a fortnight and last one hour, replacing a usual lesson anyway, so plenty of time for teachers to plan ahead and search for any related information including articles and videos to *BSL*, and, the best bit would be, there would be no conflict in missing any scheduled lessons because PSE is a whole school compulsive. Nobody would be missing out and everyone could learn something invaluable. Win-win in my book, (literally). The Government should reconsider and make *BSL* a part of the school curriculum. It should never be left up to schools to decide themselves whether they will teach important subjects such as *BSL*, other subjects aren't decided by individual schools, the general curriculum is compulsory, why should disability education be treated any differently? It's discriminative, promotes ableism and further segregation. It's the job of Government to make decisions, not schools themselves. Going back to the participant's answer to my able-bodied survey, I just can't help but wonder whether if subjects such as *BSL* was made compulsory and not just a decision, I wonder if that particular participant's answer would be different?

I asked Debbie if, in her opinion, whether *BSL* is helpful to society, or if she thinks it's actually a barrier.

"I think it must be helpful, I personally don't think it is a barrier when out in public, if you see someone signing you know that at least one of those people are deaf, if you cannot sign, there is always other ways of communicating, such as writing." – [Debbie Davies Bellis, support worker and social media participant]

This is very interesting. To claim that *BSL* isn't a barrier when bullying behaviour occurs is counterintuitive to me. Writing can be a way to communicate with a person from the Deaf Community, especially with mobile phones, but really by writing, it just segregates further. Actually making the effort to learn *BSL* would be integral for encouraging disability equality and inclusion. I respect Debbie's suggestion and thoughts, and I'm definitely not dismissing her, I'm dismissing, and angry with *UK Government* for not providing disability education in the first place. I do wonder if it has ever been considered to be apart of the curriculum? If disability education was a thing, this chapter wouldn't exist. There wouldn't be a reason for it. This chapter would be redundant. Unfortunately for society though, this chapter does exist, it has to. My books exist. It shouldn't be up to me, or any other 'disabled' person to take on the role as teacher, we have the education system exactly for this reason.

Going back to the *Scouts* 'Disability Awareness' education, what I want to see is that example set by *Scouts* widened. If somewhere such as the *Scouts* can raise awareness and open up the conversation, why can't other places follow suit? We should have a better understanding of disability in general society, not run scared of the subject for fear of upsetting or offending anyone. I don't think people realise that by choosing to ignore the subject of disability, you are in fact causing more harm than good. People won't learn a thing if we just decide to ignore the subjects. It'll be a catch twenty-two situation, people won't want to learn for fear of offending or being ignorant, but it'll be that ignorance that will ultimately be offensive. We are getting there slowly with the rise of 'disabled' celebrities on television etc., which is fantastic, I've said this before, but I do think that there's a disconnect from what people see on television, to what and how people see things in reality.

Scouts do have a few minor issues with their teaching of disability awareness that they need to iron out, but at least they are trying to get the point across, trying to highlight and champion disability for what it **actually is**, compared to hearsay. To fully understand disability, you must be willing to learn about it first-hand without media influence and other sources deciding what you think. You have a brain, you have a voice. Take action and use them. I don't think it would hurt to get somewhere like the *Scouts* to go into PSE lessons in schools to teach about disability. The *Scouts* need more exposure to this venture of disability awareness of which they have undertaken. I think that pupils and teachers would benefit from such a thing. It'll be a missed opportunity if not.

For disability to benefit from being seen and treated as a standard part of life, I really do believe that education is the key, or at least something to start with. Unless we start to face up to it, and talk about disability in a frank and open manner, this discrimination will unfortunately continue to happen and get worse. I know that the topic of disability can be a daunting prospect. Where do you start right? I get it. There are so many layers of disability that it can be hard to determine which is the best method. I also know that people often steer clear of disability for fear of being offensive as established. I think that it was clear by one participant's answer to my able-bodied survey of which they showed concern over workload in education, but this current situation

Educating Disability

cannot continue. Something desperately needs to be done to change the idea of disability as a whole, and teaching children about the 'normality' of disability, will, I think be a clever move, as children are far more easy to teach, children soak information up like a sponge, and if it is the correct information being taught, then all the better. Disability education shouldn't be treated as this enormous task that needs to be undertaken. This isn't the attitude to have. I respect all points from my surveys that I carried out, and people are allowed to have their own opinion, but I personally feel that this constant dismissive attitude towards disability only segregates disability and society even more. There should be a window of opportunity for at least a small conversation to take place. It cannot be a one-sided approach anymore. A crucial dialogue needs to be opened between all demographics of society. The vast majority agree that disability education would be beneficial in this battle for equality, including the majority of 'disabled' people themselves. Enough with excuses. It's now time for action. We are learning about so many other important things, so why can't disability have it's place too? That's discrimination in itself. PSE lessons are the perfect time for disability education, schools can invite speakers to give talks, again, to reiterate, there are also countless amounts of *TED Talks* on the Internet that specialise in disability that are given by 'disabled' people themselves, if there's a fear of offending from the teachers. We need to start to take a leaf out of the *Scouts* book, yes, it isn't perfect, but at least they are trying to raise awareness. We need to stop being scared of the subject. Other demographics are now beginning to feel a part of society, demographics which in the past were too unfairly scrutinised against. These demographics said enough was enough and started their own campaign to be recognised for who they actually are. Like a revolution of sorts. It's now time for disability to make the same campaign. I don't think though that schools should just be to blame for this unfair dismissal of disability and should be the only ones to introduce methods of disability education as this won't challenge the public to see disability equality. This conversation should also be happening in staff training days, on social media, in the news, in TV programmes. I know it

Educating Disability

sounds like a bit of a silly thing, but soaps reach a nightly high viewing figure, and so I think that showing disability awareness in these types of programmes would in fact, be a great vehicle for change.

I don't know if you're aware, but I purposely made this particular chapter quite long, as a deliberate ploy to start the ball rolling on disability education. I'm not a teacher, I'm a graphic designer by trade, it shouldn't be up to me, or any other person with a form of disability for that matter, to educate others, people should realise the issues themselves and help to raise awareness of these issues, maybe then employers would be more understanding and more likely to hire 'disabled' people, maybe bullying behaviour would take a backseat, maybe disability could just be another standard part of life like other things are, just as the *World Health Organisation* claims. Maybe, one day. Unfortunately though, as much as I like to believe that disability is equal in the mind of society, the truth is, it's not, and I believe that if education became a part of the campaign for disability equality, then of course it would help. Not cramming every single piece of information into one lesson in one go, that is unachievable, but to separate the subject into different parts that people can easily understand, digest easily, and most importantly, use in their daily life. I truly believe that this would be beneficial in the long term. I long for a world where disability isn't ever an issue, to employers, and society in general. That is my dream. Of course, I'm definitely **not** tarring everyone with the same brush. I know that there are people who treat others with respect regardless of appearance. The actual problem is, finding those who don't have a preconceived idea of you. Non judgemental people **do** exist though. I know, I finally found them after years and years of searching. My family, friends, employer, support worker, clients, publisher. These are the people who treat me as a **human being**, not a charity. The equality I feel from these people is absolutely wonderful. I see now how much I'm loved, that is the most amazing feeling for me. It took years, and my first book to finally make that a realisation.

What I have now, I wholeheartedly believe that others in the same position as me, are entitled and deserve to be treated equally and with respect.

Educating Disability

Discrimination and prejudice of disability may start to decrease. Patronisation and empathy may stop. Just the whole approach to disability may change for the better. If more time and effort was put into the education of the subject, maybe then people wouldn't be so ignorant towards disability in terms of their views. I say maybe, as there isn't a one hundred percent guarantee that something may change for the better, (whatever the topic maybe), no matter how much we want it; but, what I am saying is, we won't know unless we **try**. That's the key word. **Try**.

Chapter 7
The Truth About Perfection

The human mind is a strange thing. One day, you can be on top of the world, enjoying every single thing life has to offer, and the next, you can be the lowest of the low.

More often than not, it's due to our life experiences, our interactions with others that determine how we think and act. One word or interaction may determine how we process the world, how we feel about ourselves, our complete outlook on life. There is one thing that can be blamed for how the world operates today, one catalyst that encompasses all of this negativity. Perfection.

Perfection doesn't exist, but somehow, the whole world runs on this idea of perfection. If you don't look or act a certain way to adhere to the ideals of perfection, you are automatically judged and labelled, it seems. I do personally think that it is due to the rise of social media and reality shows why this mentality exists. People watch TV or scroll

The Truth About Perfection

through social media and see celebrities and others looking 'perfect' and wish they could look like that. It's a dangerous game. What you see today in media, more often than not, isn't real. It's either staged or airbrushed. Nothing or nobody is perfect.

"There is nothing wrong with imperfections. When things aren't pristine, this is how we learn..." – [Mark Masters, Community Leader, 'You Are The Media']

Some people consider themselves to be perfectionists. A little control over your life is okay, but it becomes a problem when the perfectionism controls you. There is a danger that too much perfectionism will lend itself to self sabotage and mental health issues. Perfectionism is really just an extension of the idea of creating a 'perfect' existence, but that is just what it is if you strive to adhere to 'perfection', an existence, not a **life**. People who often identify themselves as 'perfectionists', are just chasing a dream that nobody is going to really make a reality. If you have a disability of some form, trying to adhere to 'perfection' from a social standpoint is impossible.

I am now going to add a few replies by a few different people from a post I added on social media, and asked about the idea of perfection. Every participant to the question have given permission to be credited. I will add the original question posed on social media for context.

QUESTION

"What does the word 'perfection' mean to you?"

REPLIES

"To me, it means achieving something to the best of My Ability. It may not be perfect, but it could be something, I'd put my heart and soul into. Then I would be satisfied, I had reached perfection." – [Karen Wright, support worker at Wrexham University and social media participant]

"Perfection to me is a feeling of content.. when I feel content with something or somewhere I would say that's perfection.. if that makes sense?" – [Elika Carrol, social media participant]

The Truth About Perfection

"Perfection to me is when your soul is happy." – [Jude Copnall, support worker at Bevris Support Ltd and social media participant]

"To me, perfection means to strive to attain the unattainable." – [Brian Maddocks, social media participant]

Perfection means different things to different people. It's individual. Your idea of perfect, isn't necessarily someone else's idea of perfect. It is a matter of individuality. Society comes in all shapes, sizes, ethnicities, abilities, genders, everything. Everyone is unique. You may think that you're perfect. Others may think that they're perfect, but honestly, we are all just trying to achieve the same goal. To be happy.

To some degree, the toys that children play with could do more to represent disability, to add the subject to this idea of perfection. There is at least one company which is starting to represent disability that I'm aware of. *Mattel.* So many more companies could follow suit though.

Disability Representation With Toys

When I was younger, *Barbie* dolls used to be my go-to toy, and my room was pink and filled with everything *Barbie*, like most girls my age. I had boxes and boxes filled with the different dolls, from *Princess Barbies* to *Veterinary Barbies*, but the one *Barbie* I never had was a *Barbie* that looked like me. Every doll was blonde, straight hair, slim, wore makeup. I had brunette hair that was very curly, wore glasses, splints on my legs to help to correct my feet, and a wheelchair user.

One Christmas, though, I remember receiving *'Share A Smile Becky'*. Branded as *'Barbie's friend'*, it was a doll from the same line as *Barbie*, but this doll was in a wheelchair. I was so excited when I saw the doll. Finally, a doll that looked like me. A wheelchair user. I felt as if I finally belonged. I used to play with this *Becky* doll constantly. Unsurprisingly, it became my favourite out of the hundreds I had. I could see myself in this doll. I didn't have to aspire to be anything because this doll represented me. I felt included.

"For me, dolls were always about the outfits. I used to make them clothes,... the Barbies they've [Mattel] released that are sitting in a

wheelchair, have really boring outfits in my opinion. When I started using a wheelchair, I started dressing more excitingly. I got rid of anything in my wardrobe that would not make ones eyes bleed. It was a really big deal for me to be seen as a person when I used my chair in public and giving people something else to stare at beyond the chair. I know I'm not alone in that notion. When I wrote to Mattel, I asked that they look into releasing a doll in their Barbie...range that was a wheelchair user. Because the outfits they were wearing, with the bright colours, sequins, fringe and fur, was closer to how I dress as a wheelchair user. Not just shorts and a shirt. I loved when they made the interior designer Barbie with the prosthetic leg,... it was great to have a doll with a career, who also has a disability. That for me, went beyond the gimmick of it all, having dolls who have careers, who also have disabilities, so disabled kids can see that the world sees them [disabled people] as more. Personally I'm a singer songwriter, I never see anyone do what I do, performing on stage with my guitar, in my wheelchair. And because I don't see that in the *world, I would easily think that's not possible. I know if I saw a doll that was a pop star, but she used a wheelchair, my future and plans would have felt a lot more possible and far less bizarre." – [Alice Trevor, singer/songwriter and social media participant]*

I'm ever so pleased to see that *Mattel* (the company behind *Barbie*) have now made their dolls in wheelchairs a thing, but Alice's comment speaks volumes. If *Mattel* made these *Barbies* initially with brighter clothing and gave them careers, then I believe that disability wouldn't seem so terrifying to those in society who still believes that disability isn't a part of the mainstream society, and **a lot more** 'disabled' people would see themselves more, and aspire to be seen as something more than 'disabled'. The *Barbie* with a prosthetic leg, has a career as an interior designer, putting much less focus on the disability, and championing the career. Like I've said, disability **is a very important topic** to highlight, but so are careers etc., the standards of everyday life. Showing children, both able-bodied and 'disabled' children alike, that it's possible to

The Truth About Perfection

have a disability **and** a career. I think that *Mattel* are now beginning to get the right balance.

Becky was ahead of her time in many ways, but she didn't really have a career, she was just branded as having a disability, and that was it. Yes, I know that I said that I didn't have to aspire to be anything when I received my *Becky* doll, but at that point in my life, I just identified myself as being in a wheelchair. I never knew that I could have a career, because my *Becky* doll didn't have a career. I didn't know that it was an option for me. Being a young child, I just looked at this doll, and saw myself in that period of time, I didn't really think about what I wanted to be as I grew up, because the opportunity to see it visually, never presented itself. I never knew when I was a child, that I could actually be something other than my disability. It's quite sad when you think about it, but that was just how the world operated when I was a child.

"There is no greater disability in society, than the inability to see a person as more." – [Robert M. Hensel]

There was another issue with the *Becky* doll when *Mattel* originally released it in nineteen-ninety-seven:

"Arguably one of Mattel's greatest failures concerned a wheelchair-using doll. This was Becky, a friend of Barbie's released in 1997. Unfortunately, someone had forgotten to check if the wheelchair fitted in the Barbie Dreamhouse, and thousands of girls were disappointed when it didn't." – [Dan Fitzpatrick, 'The Uncomfortable Reasons These Barbie Dolls Were Discontinued', The Atlantic Mirror]

This may not seem the biggest issue on the surface, but really, for a child, (especially a child with a disability themselves), who received the *Share A Smile Becky*, and excited to play with the doll, to then come face to face with a realistic issue that disability is discriminated against even with toys, (lack of accessibility wise), was such a disappointment, not only to the child, but *Mattel* and disability as a whole. Admittedly, I never had a *Barbie Dreamhouse* as a child, so I didn't experience this actual form of discrimination and

The Truth About Perfection

ableism myself, but if I had experienced this, I know for a fact the amount of sadness and upset I would feel, not being able to fit *Share A Smile Becky* in the lift. The frustration and confusion that would cause me at a young age, would be intense to say the least. Something that no **child** should have to question. With it being a lift of all things too, just makes the issue somehow worse. I have absolutely no idea why *Mattel* never rectified this issue? Admittedly, they should have tested for this to begin with, but not to even attempt to look into the issue, it's absolutely frustrating.

This would've gave the impression to 'disabled' children that they weren't important, worthy, or indeed, accepted by society to have the same level of accessibility and opportunities that others do. What kind of message is that to teach? Yes, this may have been a genuine unintentional mistake on *Mattel's* part, which (in general circumstances) **would be** acceptable. **Would be**, but because of the company's response, (or lack of response) to this issue to begin with, I'm not quite as forgiving as I would be if they had made a proper effort to rectify, once the concerns started to materialise.

"...The frame of the doll's chair did not fit into the house's front door, nor on the elevator in the house. Instead of modifying the dollhouse to accommodate Becky's wheelchair, Mattel discontinued the Becky line altogether." – ['Why Mattel's Inclusion Of Barbie Dolls With Disabilities Isn't Enough', Sarah Kim, Forbes.com]

For the wheelchair not even being able to fit in the *Dreamhouse's* **front door**, is a clear oversight, but an oversight that caused many young girls (with a disability or otherwise), feeling frustrated, disappointed, upset, confused, angry, perplexed, every negative emotion all because of an oversight that ended up impacting negatively on *Mattel's* sales and turnover. Sales and turnover isn't the main focus for customers, but they are to businesses, especially well established businesses such as *Mattel. Share A Smile Becky* was immediately pulled from shelves once this was realised. Instead of rectifying the issue, *Mattel* just decided to discontinue this version of *Share A Smile Becky.* You would've thought really, that big businesses such as *Mattel* would've looked at the most important thing and cost effective solution,

The Truth About Perfection

remodel *Barbie's Dreamhouse* to accommodate a wheelchair. Instead the company just decided to stop all sales fully. Why did the company feel that this was best? Best for whom? Certainly not customers and certainly not the company itself. Taking something away from a child that brings them joy is just cruel, (especially a 'disabled' child). By deciding to discontinue *Share A Smile Becky*, the company was inadvertently sending a message out to children of all abilities and demographics that disability should just be discontinued in a way, because a 'disabled' person cannot fit into our world. I get that this may not have been the intended message, but from where I'm sitting, this was indeed the message that was sent. It would be another two years before *Becky* reappeared onto shelves, this time with a whole new look and ambition thankfully as a Paralympian. Yes, it may have been a marketing ploy on *Mattel's* part at the time with the *1999 Special Olympics World Summer Games* (as it was known back then), after all, I would imagine that *Mattel* would have been eager to rectify their damaged reputation when it came to disability back then, (just to be clear, I have no evidence for this, I'm just going by my own assumption here), but in my eyes, I imagine that they had the *Becky* doll, and they **desperately** wanted, and **needed** to bring *Becky* back, but the company may have been worried about potential backlash if they did indeed relaunch *Share A Smile Becky* to the world, as it may have been a reminder of when *Mattel* failed disability. With the *Special Olympics* coming up, there is a reasonable chance that the company may have seen an opportunity and went with it. This would reinstate *Mattel's* reputation and reinstate public opinion .

Thankfully, companies, (especially *Mattel*), are **a lot more** conscientious and diverse today, especially when it comes to disability.

When it was my niece, Rosie's birthday one year, I bought her a wheelchair Barbie. She loved it, she said that it reminded her of me, which I loved. Yes, it was just a 'standard' Barbie who was sitting in a wheelchair, granted, but the fact remains that Rosie saw something that represented a part of who I was, her auntie Sam. She wasn't put off by it, but rather celebrated it, (at such a young age too!) That's what was important to me. Her

The Truth About Perfection

celebrating individuality, it warmed my heart. I just wanted to normalise disability for her and make her understand that despite having a disability, people are normal, and more importantly, disability is normal.

What is 'normal' though? I posed the question of 'normality' to Aideen Blackborough, her answer was very direct and to the point, which I appreciated:

"...what is normal? We're all different and I try to avoid the term in my work." – [Aideen Blackborough, Disability Trainer, Speaker and Author]

I agree. Really, 'normality' just plays into this unjustified idea of 'perfection'. Everyone has different ideas of 'normal' just like the misconception of 'perfection'. To be 'perfect', you have to be 'normal', that's the belief.

"It has meant different things at different times of my life. When I was younger, it was walking, for sure. It's what everyone wanted from me. Like the holy grail. Teenage and young adulthood was more me wanting to feel normal

in my own mind towards me. Now, it means a whole lot less. I have made a truce with myself and I have realised that 'normal' is relative." – [Richard Luke, Specialist Information Officer and Programme Lead, Scope]

"Normal, I think, varies for everyone. I want to look normal, like everyone else. I don't know what it is though!" – [Anonymous, social media participant]

It becomes a problem when people develop 'perfectionism' and they have a disability. Questions arise about the person's place in society, where they appear in the societal hierarchy, and indeed, whether they 'look normal'. It is wrong on so many levels how 'perfection' helps to create this delusional outlook. Some people expect things from you that aren't always achievable.

"I don't ever want to be 'normal' and disappear into obscurity." – [Lynne Davies Coulson, social media participant]

This **is** a **very good point**. 'Normality' **can**, and more often than not, **does** equal obscurity.

The Truth About Perfection

Obscurity Meaning:

"The state of being unknown, inconspicuous, or unimportant." – [OED]

If you try to 'fit in' (conform) to the idea of societal acceptance, you are in danger of losing **who you are**. Everyone will find **something** to criticise, no matter how we try to avoid it. There will **always be someone** who is always there to point out your flaws and faults, and that isn't me being negative, that's me being honest. Ultimately trying to please others won't make you happy in the long run.

For Richard, it was being expected to walk by society, putting added pressure on someone to do something that maybe more difficult to execute. This approach will harm those who aren't as strong minded as others. There is a danger that people will begin to hate themselves because they either look a certain way, or can't do as much as others, giving the false perception that they are insignificant to society.

Becoming a teenager or young adult puts more emphasis and added pressure on 'normality'. You start to see your 'faults' and imperfections a lot more. It's when we start to see more of the obsessive tendencies of image in society. It's good that Richard has realised that 'normality' is relative. It's subjective.

Imperfections just as Mark Masters says, help society learn, to learn about themselves, how to grow as a person, and become a little bit better than before, but without losing who we **actually are**.

"People are quick to tell others how to behave." – [Mark Masters, Community Leader, 'You Are The Media']

We live in a world where we look to others for approval. Like I say, it is due to the rise of social media and reality shows in my own personal opinion. Seeing images that aren't true to life, that don't properly represent society in **all of it's forms**, plays into my argument that society really is a dangerous place. By not celebrating diversity, we don't celebrate life itself. We have lost who we are. That is terrifying.

Mattel is using their platform for good, by highlighting and showcasing what little bit of diversity we have left, which I personally appreciate and applaud.

Left to Right: Share a Smile Becky Wheelchair Chelsea Wheelchair Barbies Downs Syndrome Barbie.

Mattel has even branched out with a Downs Syndrome *Barbie* doll (shown left), which is absolutely incredible! This just goes to show that there is a market for disability, and nobody should ever feel excluded or discriminated against just for having a disability.

Kandi Pickard, the President and CEO of *National Downs Syndrome Society* (USA) explained to the *Evening Standard*:

"This means so much for our community, who for the first time, can play with a Barbie doll that looks like them. This Barbie serves as a reminder that we should never underestimate the power of representation. It is a huge step forward for inclusion and a moment that we are celebrating." – [Kandi Pickard, NDSS President and CEO for The Evening Standard]

This is exactly my point! As these dolls grow in circulation around the world, children with varying types of disability can now play with a doll that looks like them. Something that represents them. This is a wonderful thing to have in existence today. The progress that has been made since I first received my *Becky* doll all of those years ago is absolutely outstanding in my own personal opinion. *Becky*, (to my knowledge) was the first ever doll from *Mattel* who was branded to have a disability, and it's just become more of a platform really to celebrate disability and diversity in all of it's forms. I recently posted on social media about the progression of these dolls and how wonderful it is to see disability starting to be recognised and brought to the forefront of society. I personally never knew the actual progression before researching for this chapter in particular, it was absolutely amazing to see for me. Knowing that large companies such as *Mattel* are doing this, highlighting disability in such a positive way, branching out by creating dolls with a variety of different disabilities and diversities, it just goes to show how much companies are dedicated to highlight important topics, (including disabilities), to a world where, really, whether people like to hear it or not, are obsessed with image. It's overwhelming, not just for me, but for other people who have a form of disability. It's hopeful.

"I would have loved this when I was younger, I used to wear callipers on my legs like this!!" – *[Natalie Copnall-Aspin, social media participant]*

This comment from Natalie, just goes to show how important these dolls are, and how much these dolls mean to 'disabled' people. The Downs Syndrome *Barbie* does have callipers (leg braces) on her legs, basically because:

"Some children with Downs Syndrome use orthotics to support their feet and ankles, and NDSS provided a box of orthotics to serve as real-life inspiration for the ones this Barbie Fashionista is wearing, matched to her outfit and the bright colors in her design." – *[Mattel.com]*

Mattel really is trying hard to highlight disability and other demographics today, and working with people and companies such as *NDSS* is absolutely amazing to see. Why *Mattel* is stepping up for disability, I personally think, that it's because of the 'inclusive world' that we like to uphold on the face of society. I believe that *Mattel* is just trying to bring an element of truth to this idealistic world. It's not enough for people to just say that they are

Paralympian Becky doll from 1999

inclusive, you have to show some willing to contribute to what the term **actually means** to be inclusive.

I would also just like to mention that the majority of these *Barbies* today come from their *Barbie Fashionista* range which is absolutely fantastic! Here, *Mattel* are trying to break the stigma of

The Truth About Perfection

disability by ultimately saying that even despite the disabilities, 'disabled' people **can be**, and more importantly **are** fashionable.

My *Becky* doll was even made into a Paralympian in nineteen-ninety-nine. The level of detail, care and consideration that *Mattel* are putting in to help celebrate the diversity of disability is absolutely outstanding, in my own personal opinion.

I still have my original *Becky* doll, all of these years later, as a reminder of when I finally felt included by society.

Years ago, children's perceptions of perfection wrongly came from dolls, (including *Barbies*). The design of the doll was pretty basic and superficial. Blonde hair, slim, makeup etc. Years ago, adverts on TV almost celebrated dolls that looked a certain way, giving children the false narrative that to be 'perfect', you needed to look like these dolls. The adverts themselves showed these dolls doing fun things. There was absolutely no diversity whatsoever. Yes, it was only a marketing ploy, designed to sell a product. No harm done right? Wrong. As an adult, you understand this,

The Truth About Perfection

the ploy to make money, but a child doesn't understand this. A child only perceives and believes what's in front of them, most children don't question why things are represented the way they are. Children take everything at face value, because children, (especially young children), trust the world around them.

"A child's innocence is the one gift, that once stolen, can never be replaced." – [Jaeda DeWalt]

You could argue that because of how the world is run today, the innocence of a child doesn't exist anymore, the way it once did. Yes, there is that argument, and a very good one to make at that, but I would counteract this by saying that children **are** born innocent. It's what children see and hear that ultimately make them less innocent. It's what children are subjected to and witness that ultimately shape a child's belief.

What I'm saying is that children don't actually question things with malice, but they may do, out of **inquisitiveness**. That's the difference. The amount of children who I've come across asking their parents why I'm in a wheelchair, is a lot to say the least, but I personally don't mind that, it's the **parent's reaction to that innocent question**, that I take issue with. The majority of adults who were asked this question by an innocent child, who is being inquisitive, eager to learn, quickly shutdown the child's question by saying basically not to look or ask questions like that. Now, I get that adults don't want to cause any offence, but what adults don't realise is that they, themselves are in fact being offensive by quickly shutting down inquisitiveness and innocence. By doing this, adults are automatically putting the false perception to children that disability is different, and should be treated as such. Do you get what I mean? I'd much rather adults come up to me with their children and ask **me directly**. By doing this, children would get the answer and they would treat disability as a standard part of life, as it should be. Having toy companies such as *Mattel* now showcasing disability in a positive light, is outstanding as the company is telling children, (and more importantly), teaching children about different disabilities and diversities.

"I would love children in wheelchairs or children with disabilities to be able to receive these

[disability Barbie dolls] for free. We need Action Man and Spider Man using mobility aids and wheelchairs too!" – [Hayley Wellerd, Occupational Therapist and mum of a 'disabled' daughter]

It would be absolutely amazing to have other toys representing disability. For 'disabled' children to receive these dolls for free, would be an excellent idea.

Having other toys like *Action Man* and *Spider Man*, (as mentioned), highlighting disability would be absolutely amazing. The disability subject would have more exposure if other companies followed suit. I'm not saying that male children cannot play with toys that are marketed for female children, not at all. Again, individuality should **always** be celebrated, whatever the demographic.

Wheelchair Ken doll

The Truth About Perfection

What I am trying to say, is that having male toys follow suit would have more of a potential progression towards disability representation, and therefore more of a chance of disability being considered a part of mainstream society.

There are 'disabled' *Ken* dolls in wheelchairs, granted, but these *Ken* dolls are from the *Barbie* range of dolls. As I've said, every child has the right to play with any toy they want, but the subject of disability needs, and **deserves** to be extended to other brands of toys, to fully get the desired impact of disability equality.

"They need to have a regular sized Barbie in a wheelchair too. I'd hate to think children were led into an eating disorder trying to look like these wheelchair Barbies!" – [Linda Smith, social media participant]

"...it's great that there are dolls with wheelchairs. But there are only those two variations, light skin light hair, dark skin dark hair. There is so much fabulous variety within the disabled community. And it's sad that wheelchair users just have that one look. There is a bit more variety in the dolls with prosthetic

legs, which is great, and there is also a doll with hearing aids." – [Alice Trevor, singer/songwriter and social media participant]

I wholeheartedly agreed with this quote from Alice initially. Agreed before I researched out of curiosity more than anything. However, this is **exactly** what I meant when I said that children take everything at face value. That is why it's so incredibly important to teach children the differences between people and the 'normalities' of the subject. *Mattel* **is** using their platform for good, which I personally appreciate.

Mattel clearly **has** progressed significantly with their representation, compared to how disability representation was when I was a child, which admittedly, was fantastic for the times as a child, but today, society is moving **so fast** compared to the nineteen-nineties and early two-thousands.

There **are** a number of different *Barbie* dolls with variations to them, which thankfully **are** available to buy, including, but not limited to:

- Freckles
- Curvy (plus sized)

The Truth About Perfection

• Skin tones

• Hairstyles

• Vitiligo – (a skin disorder that affects the pigmentation of the skin, although not considered a disability in the general sense, it is wonderful to see that other demographics are being represented. It's humbling)

• Plus many more

As some are shown above.

Really, if *Mattel* truly does want to make a full impact, then just by simply making ad campaigns for these dolls would make **all** the difference, and if they already do, showing these advertisements on a regular basis, would be a fantastic opportunity to desensitise disability in **all of it's forms** to children across the globe. Basically, these dolls do exist, so advertising these spectacular dolls more, showing that the dolls can also have fun, and **most** importantly, do the majority of things just like the other *Barbie* dolls children see, and giving the disability *Barbies* more exposure, and more of a platform, would be the next logical step forward in selling more of these particular dolls.

Barbie dolls with prosthetic legs

I didn't know that there are dolls with hearing aids and prosthetic legs. From research, I found out that the Hearing Aid *Barbie* in particular was endorsed by British Deaf actress, Rose Ayling-Ellis.

It's absolutely wonderful to know that these dolls are in circulation, and that 'disabled' celebrities are being involved with creating these dolls, and as a result, doing something to highlight disability in such a positive way. Personally, it makes me hopeful that humanity will finally accept disability and diversity for what it **actually** is, a standard part of life. Having the backing from 'disabled' celebrities immediately help the case.

The Truth About Perfection

The Downs Syndrome *Barbie* is endorsed by Ellie Goldstein, a model with Downs Syndrome.

It's heart-warming to learn that *Mattel* is working with 'disabled' celebrities to make sure that they're correctly representing the 'disabled' and diverse communities.

Maybe these dolls need more advertising? Just a suggestion. It does make me wonder if others have heard about these types of dolls? They do exist though, which I am extremely happy to see. I just wish that they were advertised a lot more, and that there was more of a variation of these dolls in appearance, as mentioned. Individuality is the key to the modern age today, most people are more accepting of individuality thanks to movements such as *Pride* and *Black Lives Matter*, but according to society, disability isn't allowed to have this same level of freedom or self-expression. It's so unfair. It's as if we aren't allowed to express ourselves because society isn't prepared to accept individuality of disability, let alone disability on it's own. *Disability Pride Month* **does** exist, granted, but again, it isn't as well publicised as the other movements. I sadly really do believe that it's because of the disability label attached to this particular movement as to why, it isn't as well publicised. Having companies such as *Mattel* in the disability equality corner, will help immensely to rectify this issue. We need and **deserve** other companies to take action. It cannot just be left to one company, regardless of how much of a 'household' name it may be. One company, however large, cannot be expected to change perceptions, change the world. No, it takes an army. I believe that if other companies helped in the fight for disability equality, then we would ultimately begin to see a positive change. Naive? Possibly. Impossible? No.

Personally, I have rebelled against this ridiculous belief. I have purple hair, I have four ear piercings with a chain ear cuff. I wear purple eyeshadow and purple eyeliner. Everything that goes against the grain, I do. I've purposely decided this. I am comfortable now with who I am, yes writing is helping, there's absolutely no question about that, but also because I have taken it upon myself to express my own individuality.

The Truth About Perfection

This is the twenty-first century. Isn't it about time that everything has a chance to be modernised? When I was younger, it was incredibly important and a positive experience (especially for me), to see disability starting to be recognised and represented by major companies, but society is moving on quick. Companies such as *Mattel* still do need to modernise their work strategies to include absolutely everyone in this modern age. Just sitting a *Barbie* in a wheelchair just isn't enough anymore, clearly. The level of detail and effort that is going into creating such dolls is a wonderful thing to see. However, more **definitely** could, and needs to be done to represent absolutely every single 'disabled' person, including individuality and uniqueness. Maybe having dolls with oxygen canisters to represent this demographic of people within the 'disabled' community? Or a *Barbie* with a cane, guide dog, and a *Braille* machine, to represent the visually impaired? I just wonder if *Mattel* has any future plans to release more *Barbie* dolls that are marketed to have other disabilities of some form? In my eyes, *Mattel* is just starting. There is a wide range of different disabilities across the globe, and in time, I would love to see other disabilities and diversities being properly and positively represented. A *Disability Pride Barbie* could be released in the month of July to coincide with *Disability Pride* Month, helping the event become more widely known to every person on the planet.

Now **is** the time.

Mattel (as do other companies), have a unique platform to highlight a number of different important subjects. The *Barbie* range is obviously beginning to take shape. *Mattel*, (whether they realise it or not – and I personally think that they do), **is** beginning to raise awareness of disability. I just hope that they continue to use this platform to speak out against disability discrimination.

Mattel is now beginning to rectify their perceptions on perfection from the past. Yes, there are still those *Barbies* that are still your typical *Barbie*. Slim, blonde, makeup, perfect hair, there will undoubtedly **always** be a market for the 'original', and that is absolutely okay. It's fine. *Barbie* is a global brand that is widely known for her blonde hair, slim waist and makeup etc. It would be odd, and discriminative in itself if *Mattel*

The Truth About Perfection

scrapped the 'original' altogether. That's the identity. The brand. If you lose the 'original', you've undoubtedly lost the brand. Everybody in the world recognises the 'original', and having that staple in the world, will allow *Mattel* to create other 'disabled' and diverse *Barbie* dolls. The 'original' is just the platform for the others to be recognised. To stand, or indeed sit next to the 'original', as a metaphorical voice as to celebrate how far *Mattel* has come in development.

Self Determination Amongst Social Ideals

People may look at you, and ridicule you no matter what you are doing. Some people will always find a way to find negatives for what you are trying to achieve. It doesn't matter if you are doing something selfless to help others, or just enjoying a nice day out, someone somewhere will always find a reason to belittle you, and say that you are just doing it for the glory or to be noticed. It's human nature. Yes, there are those who do just that, but not everyone.

Writing, I've come across people who have said negative things about me, and to me, basically saying that I'm not the same person that I was, that I have forgotten where I came from. Part of this is true. I'm **definitely** not the same person that I was, I'm a much happier, confident, and determined person than I was before I started writing. My headspace is a much nicer place to be, because I've gotten rid of things that just plagued and tormented me for years, and yes, I've had some incredible experiences and opportunities when promoting, from The Jacksons, and Lesley Griffiths MS, promoting *'CP Isn't Me'*, to being invited for an interview to talk about *'CP Isn't Me'*, at *Llangollen Eisteddfod*, and everything in-between. Experiences and opportunities that I will never forget, but I have also **never** forgotten who I am or indeed, where I came from. I have a fantastic family and wonderful friends who I can rely on and who support me. I'm a woman from Wrexham who is just sick and tired of the same old belief that disability isn't a part of everyday society. I'm sick of the way people treat disability, and I am only trying to speak on this. People may think or say that I'm just doing it for attention, but I'm really not. For anyone who knows me, the **REAL** me, you would know that public speaking and being thrown into the

The Truth About Perfection

limelight isn't a great thing for me. I would much rather stay in the background, but I have learned that staying quiet just lets the disability cycle continue, so I've had to learn to overcome my fears and anxieties (to a degree) in order to try to challenge perceptions.

In the beginning, admittedly, writing was a selfish thing, as I just wanted my feelings of negativity to stop, so I took a chance, I acted on what people were telling me for years. I didn't think that my writing would have had the impact it has, I never knew that something that I had written would be accepted the way it has. I am honoured and humbled though.

It's given me a platform. A platform to speak out against disability discrimination. I know how lucky I am to have been given this opportunity, so I definitely **am not** going to waste it.

Promotion is just the next step in getting something out there and known. Nobody would know anything without promotion. That's a fact. For people to call me out for promoting something that desperately needs to be said, is ridiculous really. Nobody actually knows the hard work that goes on behind the scenes to make sure that something gets the attention it deserves. The emailing, the negotiations that take place to make sure that something that's important, gets noticed. I'm not saying this to complain. I absolutely love what I do now, (I wouldn't have written this second book if that wasn't true.) I'm just saying to all those who have called me out, that promotion is hard work, but I do it because I love it. It's given me a sense of purpose, a sense of worth. Instead of worrying, I just put all of that energy into my writing. It's given me something to focus on, and if I change at least one person's perception of disability, then, it's all worthwhile.

When it comes down to it, what it really boils down to is jealousy. I hate to say it, but it's true. People like to say negative things about your successes just to make themselves feel better about their own lives. Social media is a great platform to create fake versions of lives, just to make you believe that others have a great (or perfect) life, doing, and just generally saying things that make them seem happy and fulfilled. It's just a big party on social media really. A pretence. A mask. It's just a small glimpse into

The Truth About Perfection

someone's life that, nine times out of ten, isn't the best. You are only seeing the 'highlights', what people **want** you to see. Not the full story.

Everything comes under this perfection umbrella, the desire to create fake lives, the want to look a certain way, the total disregard for anyone who doesn't look like your idea of perfect. For me, I **definitely** don't consider myself to be perfect, but what I do consider myself being is simply, happy and hard-working. When I set my mind to something, I make sure that I achieve it to **my** standards, not anyone else's. If I'm happy, then that's all that matters. I really couldn't care less now what people think about me. I've seen what I can achieve and I like it.

All that I'm trying to get across is that, you do you. Whatever makes you happy, you do. Forget everyone who says negative things, those people are only trying to make themselves feel better. I honestly think that the words 'perfect' and 'perfection' should be erased from the English Dictionary, as they don't exist, and those words are just there for people to create illusions. Something to chase and try and adhere to, but perfection doesn't mean a thing. Everyone is different and that's okay, nobody should ever be a replica. Individuality makes a society, it makes humanity. Let people say what they want, you can't win them all. What matters is if it makes you happy, go for it. Stop striving for something that nobody is going to achieve. It's not worth it, it's pointless. Stop trying to make others happy. Get up, get out, do things that you enjoy. If you like to do something, do it. Don't let anyone tell you that it's wrong to enjoy the little moments of happiness that you are entitled to. People have questioned me being a fan of Michael Jackson and The Jacksons in the past. Why? These certain people have said that I need other interests, but it's what makes me happy, it gives me a bit of escapism for when I feel a bit down. The music lifts me. I of course have other interests, writing being one now, but my music helps me get through the day. That will never change. Also, when life for me became difficult, my music helped me through. I had nothing to do for a long time, because sadly people prioritised my Cerebral Palsy before me. My music was, and still is in many ways, the only thing I have. A constant. Opportunities will come

The Truth About Perfection

and go, but as long as I have the one thing that I can rely on that makes me happy, guess what? I'm happy.

Chapter 8
Social Realisation of Disability vs What Still Needs to be Done

"Whilst recognising progress has been made in meeting the needs and aspirations of people with a disability, it is clear we still have a long way to go before all social barriers are removed and disabled people truly experience the same opportunities as everyone else... Inspirational figures like Samantha, who refuse to be defined by their disability, can act as role models by proving there is no limit to what you can achieve. It is, however, difficult for one individual or organisation to change everything and I firmly believe elected representatives and governments must lead by example. Encouraging public bodies, employers and organisations to take responsibility can create a more equal Wales for all, helping disabled people fulfil their potential and achieve their ambitions." – [Lesley Griffiths, Member of the Senedd for Wrexham]

What Still Needs to be Done

Lesley Griffiths MS is correct. Disability is starting to become somewhat apart of society, however, it is slow both in my own personal opinion and Lesley's, and I honestly believe that it is other people in society that need to share the responsibility. The thing is though, it's 'disabled' people who are always highlighting disability, whereas really, the whole world should take part in making disability a standard part of life. Like I said, it shouldn't be left to just 'disabled' people to highlight disability.

There's the fact that people are wrapped up in their own lives, continuing worries about the impact of the COVID-19 pandemic, and the recent cost of living has accelerated this need to think about number one, as it were, but these issues have also brought to light the very real knock-on effects these issues have had on disability.

"The COVID-19 pandemic had a profound effect on everyone, but particularly the lives of disabled people. Thankfully, we have emerged on the other side and many people's lives have returned to some sort of normality, largely thanks to the successful vaccination

programme. However, its vital we learn lessons and acknowledge the global pandemic has had a disproportionately damaging impact on disabled people's everyday lives. The aftermath has highlighted the inequalities that still exist and the barriers that need to be overcome to ensure people living with a disability lead the lives they want to lead. – [Lesley Griffiths, Member of the Senedd for Wrexham]

During the pandemic, we had a very different viewpoint on society. As our freedoms were taken away, we then became grateful for any sort of 'normality' that we could get. Being isolated from others in society actually gave us a selfless attitude. We didn't take anything for granted. Any sense of 'normality' was embraced and savoured. I can imagine that how society was during the pandemic was how society was during World War II for example. What I mean by this is the sense of camaraderie and support. The friendliness that came with not having much. The appreciation when people did get something. The little luxuries of life that people were so grateful for. The parallels between the two events are uncanny.

What Still Needs to be Done

Since then though, I do feel that we have returned to this selfish attitude once our freedom was returned back to us. Before, during the pandemic, people made time for others, whereas now, we have slipped back into this main character syndrome as explained previously. It's quite telling that for any humanity to happen, something like a global pandemic needs to occur. This definitely needs to be reversed. We've proved we can think of others, so we need to continue what we've started.

I get that society maybe worrying about their own lives in the aftermath of the pandemic, and how they will survive unscathed, but disability has more at stake in a way, and the constant battle for equality doesn't help. I do get that people may feel a bit uncomfortable with the topic, and also feel unknowledgeable to speak on behalf of disability, alongside worrying about their own issues in the wake of the COVID-19 pandemic. This is understandable, but again, this is exactly why education is key. Disability wouldn't seem so daunting or terrifying if education became a part of the mainstream. It wouldn't seem such a laborious task if disability education became a standard part of society. Education of disability would work wonders. As it currently stands, I think that people try to avoid the subject of disability as it does seem on the surface, a massive subject to manage, and people really don't have the time to spare to think about others in society, especially those who have an added condition such as a disability. I think that society leaves disability up to Government to ensure that it is funded, maintained and regulated, but as Lesley Griffiths MS has explained, the Welsh Government in particular can only do so much to ensure that disability has the correct support that they require, but both the UK Government and society as a whole can work together to make sure that disability isn't a subject that's forgotten, put on the back-burner. Government cannot just pass the buck and likewise, society just can't think that disability should be left up to Government to sort out. We need to work together as a collective to make sure that disability is highlighted in the most effective way possible.

"We'd like people with disabilities represented at all levels of government decision-making. All organisations should have clear inclusivity

targets, which are measured, audited and the results published. Disability discrimination should be as socially unacceptable as gender, race or religious discrimination. We would like to see free therapy (physio, OT and speech therapy) for everyone with CP that needs it, to reduce the pain, discomfort and fatigue they experience. We believe that if more people were aware about disability, the world would be a kinder place for people with disabilities. So we would like to see mandatory Disability Awareness training for statutory services (e.g. Police, NHS, Social Services, Social Care, Schools) and free Disability Awareness training for employers (paid by the Government)." – [The National Bobath Cerebral Palsy Centre, London]

The National Bobath Cerebral Palsy Centre paints a lovely, idealistic way of life. It sounds like a perfect and also a reasonable request, but I fear it wouldn't make the slightest bit of difference unfortunately. Everything free, and accessible to every 'disabled' person without consequence. Having **proper** training in statutory services. One can only dream of living in such a positive world.

It's a fairy-tale, a fairy-tale of which **desperately needs** to become true. If society is willing to change their views on disability, and if Government is willing to provide adequate training for statutory services, then this dream would undoubtedly become a reality.

As it currently stands, the reality of disability could improve greatly. If everything was to the acceptable standard, then my books would be irrelevant.

I asked *The National Bobath Cerebral Palsy Centre* to give their view on the state of disability equality through their own personal opinion:

"There has been some progress in making society more inclusive. However, there remain many prejudices, inconsistencies, administrative problems and practical/financial barriers, which negatively impact people with disabilities. At our charity, we have made a conscious effort to move away from the Medical Model of Disability (where the person is disabled) to the Social Model of Disability (where society can be constructed in a manner that disables the person). We have altered how we speak about

disabled and people with disabilities in our marketing and communications and in our therapy sessions. We also understand more about intersectionality now and how that relates to disability. For example, our Adult Meet-up service encourages discussions about disability alongside other topics including Men's and Women's Health, race issues, and accessibility in schools and workplace." – [Lorraine Kirby, Marketing and Communications Manager, National Bobath Cerebral Palsy Centre, London]

The National Bobath Cerebral Palsy Centre is leading the way in trying to change perceptions of disability. All of these added things, prejudice, inconsistencies, administrative issues, and financial and practical issues are just an added inconvenience that every 'disabled' person has to battle with every single day.

"We run monthly online sessions for adults living with CP. These often cover practical/ medical matters such as pain management or menopause, but we are broadening the scope to include topics such as relationships. We also

410

gather research via surveys, most recently on the experience of living with CP post pandemic, and the impact of the Cost of Living crisis. The topics covered are usually prompted by our service users. If it's something they would like to discuss, we do our best to provide a forum."
– [Lorraine Kirby, Marketing and Communications Manager, National Bobath Cerebral Palsy Centre, London]

It's just not the fact of having a disability, the added pressures that go on behind the scenes always have to be taken into account. The constant demands from local authorities who need to make sure that you still have a disability, by asking for your financial state, to determine whether you still need your benefits. The questionnaire the local authorities send you, with absolutely ridiculous questions, all just to make sure that you aren't claiming for something that you don't actually need is laughable at best. I feel like saying to authorities sometimes, *"I have a disability. I'm a wheelchair user. I undoubtedly will remain in this current state indefinitely, unless someone, somewhere will eventually find a cure for Cerebral Palsy – (which I very much doubt they*

What Still Needs to be Done

will)." Everything today is so unnecessarily intrusive, and it makes the 'disabled' person feel as if they're doing something wrong by claiming the things they need to live as independently as possible. *The National Bobath Cerebral Palsy Centre* is at least trying to make a conscious effort to improve disability relations and understanding. I think it's amazing how they're incorporating things such as menopause, race relations, men's and women's health, the COVID-19 pandemic, the cost of living crisis, and accessibility in schools and workplaces. I wonder if they have contemplated adding sexual orientation and gender into these sessions they have, as today, everything is amalgamated? Categorisation doesn't really exist anymore, so discussions about other topics and how they're related to disability is vital for actually understanding disability.

I really do believe that the presence of Paralympians, 'disabled' presenters etc., is helping disability to be 'normalised' **in a way**, but it still sadly **isn't** enough, as discriminatory language of disability still happens in the everyday. I still do believe it's that disconnect between a screen and reality as to why disability discrimination still exists in society. People seem to 'normalise' disability on screen, and I think it is due to the fact that there is somewhat of a separation. Media polishes this misrepresentation to a tee. Putting 'disabled' celebrities in the same vicinity as able-bodied celebrities, having them talk to each other equally, on a level playing field without difficulty, psychologically puts a sticking plaster over the actual reality of disability. Media tries to show the best of disability which on the surface, would appear progressive, but that perception of disability sadly doesn't show the harsh realities of the world, and there lies the issue. People, (especially today), I don't think, seem to grasp the concept that a 'disabled' person on screen, whether a Paralympian, presenter, actor or actress etc. is basically the same type of person that they may see in the street. There seems to be a disconnect. Yes, not all 'disabled' people are well-known, have high paying jobs, or can do the same things as somebody may see on TV. The whole world isn't like that, and neither are 'disabled' people, (hence why I'm arguing about equality). What I am saying is that the personality of a 'disabled' person is basically the same as those

What Still Needs to be Done

you associate with seeing on your TV. Even 'severely disabled' people have a personality. Just because they may not be able to do as much as others, does not mean that they are incapable or emotionless. People who have a 'severe disability' still have a personality. I personally believe that the word 'severe' is a negative prefix all of it's own. People don't know how to react to it, alongside the words, 'disability' and 'disabled'. Merging the two terms, would obviously create a preconceived idea of a person.

One participant, Christine Davies, a mother of a 'severely disabled' young person who has ***"Quadriplegic Cerebral Palsy" – [Christine Davies, social media participant and mum]***, kindly has given permission to talk about her son, Jake.

Quadriplegic CP basically is:

"...a form of cerebral palsy that affects both arms and legs and often the torso and face. Quadriplegia is the most severe of the three types of spastic cerebral palsy. It requires lifelong treatment and support." – [Cerebralpalsyguidance.com]

However, just because those are the 'facts' of the condition, that **DOES NOT** mean that people with this form of Cerebral Palsy, don't have a personality. Christine's son, who's name is Jake, although *"Non-verbal, a wheelchair user, and uses an Eye Gaze for communication"* – *[Christine Davies, social media participant and mum]*, he **does** have a personality. Just because the way Jake communicates is different, it really **doesn't** mean that **he, himself** is different. We often confuse 'severely disabled' people with lacking a personality, which is so wrong. Society often patronises 'severely disabled' people, because of the misconception that 'severely disabled' people are less intelligent than other people in society. People talk down to 'disabled' people in general yes, but also I believe that the more severe the disability, the more the patronisation somehow. Maybe it's the appearance? 'Severely disabled' people **appear** more 'vulnerable' in a way, but appearance **isn't the same** as personality. My support worker, Judi, is also Jake's support worker, so even though I don't know Jake personally, I feel that I do, if that makes sense?

What Still Needs to be Done

Again, I'm sadly not alone in this way of thinking. Others have said virtually the same thing. I was fired from my first proper graphic design job after graduation, that was only six years ago (at the time of writing this) in twenty-seventeen. Anyone can make the argument that society is progressing in their approach to topics that are/were deemed as 'difficult' to talk about in the past, but is it really? Is society leading the way in disability equality? The other incident that happened to me, which I spoke about in the beginning, about a disability equipment company rejecting me, was during the COVID-19 pandemic, not that long ago, maybe two or three years at the time of writing this at least? I can categorically confirm from those two experiences alone, that it's clear that society isn't doing anything to try and stop this old-fashioned way of thinking.

Why should it always be down to us to fight? It's not that hard is it? We just want to be treated exactly the same as everyone else in society. That's it. A disability is just an extension of a person, not the whole package.

What Still Needs to be Done

I understand that you may not know what an Eye Gaze is, so I've taken the liberty of providing information about the device:

"An eye gaze device is essentially a traditional tablet, however instead of using your hands or a mouse to navigate the screen, your eyes do the scrolling. Thanks to an inbuilt light sensor, the tablet monitors reflections from the pupils, tracking eye movements and converting them into mouse movements and co-ordinated commands. By looking anywhere on the screen, the user's eye controls the cursor, while blinking performs a click. The accessibility of eye gaze technology is much the same as any off the shelf computer, so it can accommodate for more sophisticated demands such as right, double and left clicks, which gives the user much more freedom. When paired with appropriate software, the synthesised voice will iterate words and sentences based on the input of the user. Akin to Grid Pads and Lightwriters, eye gaze machines also have internet and Bluetooth connectivity, allowing for the sending and receiving of emails, text messages and

What Still Needs to be Done

controlling the surrounding environment." – *[Thesequeltrust.org.uk]*

By explaining, I'm hoping to 'normalise' disability equipment so it's less unusual to society. You can argue that you don't see any difference between able-bodied and 'disabled' people, but it's obvious that society does have an issue with understanding that disability is a standard part of life, and disability equipment is there to assist a person with a disability, not create obstacles and barriers. Society needs to understand that by being the ones to create these barriers and obstacles, you are therefore denying disability equality.

Another participant, Deborah Bayley, kindly contributed by giving permission to speak about both her son, Ashley, who has *"Flaccid Cerebral Palsy, Hydrocephalus, a severe learning disability with Autistic tendencies and is sight & hearing impaired"* – *[Deborah Bayley, social media participant, mum and daughter]* and also her mother, Jean, who has Dementia.

Ashley

Deborah was extremely blunt with her thoughts on society, disability and how they connect with her son Ashley. Her comments are extremely harrowing.

Ashley is actually my second cousin, so I know him quite well I would say. In my opinion, (and I'm not just saying this because he's a relation), but he has a heart of gold and very innocent in his view of the world.

"As Ashley has a learning disability, thankfully 99% of the time he is unaware of negative or cruel opinions from the general public." – [Deborah Bayley, social media participant, mum and daughter]

That innocence should never be confused with vulnerability, which of course, society does constantly. In a way, not being able to realise the harsh, ableist realities of the world can be considered a benefit in my mind. Of course, not being fully aware of how the world operates is a difficult thing, I'm definitely **not** making light of Ashley's condition as this would just create more obstacles in the long run, and reverse my point. All I'm saying is that considering how negative the

What Still Needs to be Done

world is to difference, not being able to comprehend that negativity, is actually a blessing in many ways. As Deborah said, Ashley is unaware of the cruelty that surrounds disability every single day due to his condition. It is quite sad though that a parent or family member feels the need to have the same sense of relief, that their loved one is unaware of the world around them. How has it happened that family members of 'severely disabled' people feel relief that they aren't aware of society? What does this say about society? Society should be ashamed that they have created this barrier ridden, judgemental world where ableism rules with an iron fist. Delusion is actually the most consistent thing of society. It has to be, if they say they are more accepting and understanding, where at the same time, disability discrimination occurs wherever you go. That's a major inconsistency.

Ashley is a lovely person who just happens to have a disability that inhibits him to view the harsh realities of the world. Yes, he may have a learning disability, that's a fact, but his extremely sweet personality makes up for that tenfold. I asked Deborah to talk about any hobbies and interests

Ashley has, this is a means of providing context to Ashley as a **person, not a label**.

"Ashley loves dancing, performing and playing musical instruments and loves being in company and in social gatherings." – [Deborah Bayley, social media participant, mum and daughter]

The majority of Ashley's interests and hobbies are similar to others in society. He enjoys doing things that others in society enjoy. He shouldn't be then judged harshly for having a learning disability, Flaccid Cerebral Palsy, Hydrocephalus, sight and hearing impaired and has Autistic tendencies. Yes that list of conditions maybe daunting to begin with, but Ashley's condition or anyone else's potential condition should never be an issue for anyone else other than the one with a disability.

Jean

Deborah's mum, Jean, was *"memory monitored since June 2012..."* and had her *"...Mixed Dementia diagnosis September 2018"* – *[Deborah Bayley, social media participant, mum and daughter]*

What Still Needs to be Done

Somehow, there seems to always be a blurred line between disabilities in the traditional sense, and illnesses that aren't considered to be a 'true disability'.

As Jean is again, apart of my family, although not as close, my opinion of her is that she's a lovely lady with a great personality to match. She reminds me of my late nan, Mary in that way. Jean may have a form of dementia, her memory isn't as it once was granted, but every single time I've seen her and spoken to her, she's always had a smile on her face. Deborah did say though, *"she has times of being very depressed when she has episodes of being aware that she has forgot conversations, people, events. She gets very angry when she is convinced things have been altered by others (not remembering that she's done it herself). She gets very confused if there is a change to her daily routine/diary."* – *[Deborah Bayley, social media participant, mum and daughter]*

For anyone who are dismissive of mental conditions such as dementia, not being categorised as a form of disability, reread

Deborah's last quote. I can imagine the level of upset and frustration of something as serious as dementia would cause anyone. The stresses to the person who has the illness, alongside the loved ones who can't do anything to help, only sit on the side-lines and watch the deterioration happening right in front of them. That's heart-breaking for both sides.

It may surprise you to learn, that Jean is somewhat aware that she has dementia. I asked Deborah, *"does your mum see herself first, or her disability?"*

"Now I think she sees her disability first. She always used to say she has short term memory loss but now on occasion she says Dementia and gets angry and has very anxious moments of the fact she can't remember things. She also writes every tiny bit of information daily in her diary of what's she seen/said/done in that day. But often doesn't think to read it if she has a question about the day. – [Deborah Bayley, social media participant, mum and daughter]

This turns any preconceptions of dementia on it's head. Jean **is aware** that she has dementia and gets angry because her dementia really stops her from living a 'normal' life. Jean has basically had to adapt to her dementia, her 'new life' in a way. Writing things down daily I would say is a great way to keep her mind active. I know that Deborah's said that Jean may forget to read that diary if she wants to remember what she's done a particular day, but the point that she is writing everything down in a diary first of all, really does just quash any preconceptions of dementia.

Dementia **should never** be seen as a 'end of the line' diagnosis. As with Ashley, I asked Deborah to talk about any hobbies and interests Jean has.

"She loves watching the birds feeding in her back garden and watching the fish in her tank. She likes to do word search puzzles, reading magazines about the Royal Family and watching TV." – [Deborah Bayley, social media participant, mum and daughter]

As with Ashley, I asked Deborah this deliberately as to show that despite having dementia people can still live a life. This needs to be realised.

As with Ashley, I asked Deborah this deliberately as to show that despite having dementia people can still live a life. This needs to be realised.

However, it seems that dementia has escaped this misunderstanding, at least shockingly to employers.

"If your mental health condition means you are disabled you can get support at work from your employer. There are many different types of mental health condition which can lead to a disability, including: dementia." – [Gov.UK]

This is quite a ridiculous thing for me to read, understand and accept. It's ironic. Employees who may have a type of dementia can have employer support if they so wish. Not to trivialise dementia, but how is this fair to other disabilities? It doesn't make any sense? A disability is a disability, physical or mental, it doesn't matter. Dementia is a form of disability yes, but this isn't a great advert, if employers favour a disability over another. It's safe to say that UK Government is doing exactly this favouring, by encouraging employers to prioritise a single disability. All disabilities count. This is discrimination, and

What Still Needs to be Done

ableism right here, even towards the demographic. UK Government created this. Comparing disabilities in rank of superiority ultimately barricades disability and society further. This attitude does absolutely nothing to destigmatise disability and put equality to the forefront. It is awful, disrespectful, dire, and humiliating. How can we claim that we're 'modern', if picking and choosing a disability is a priority to UK Government, and by extension, employers? All it is achieving is favouritism. This **isn't** fair. This **isn't** a modern society, or a democracy for that matter.

Some may say that Kerry Evans, the *DLO* of *Wrexham AFC* is a pioneer in regards to this fight for disability equality, in many ways, I agree, but I believe that people often put 'disabled' people on a pedestal unnecessarily. I'm **not** saying that Kerry doesn't deserve recognition for her accomplishments, of course she does. What I'm trying to say is that society often praises a 'disabled' person more when they accomplish something that may seem 'impossible'. This is absolutely ridiculous really. We are constantly seen as being something of great delicacy, and to do something which goes against the grain of the idea of what it means to be 'disabled', is seen as 'extraordinary'.

Kerry has a disability, yes, it may seem difficult sometimes, but she doesn't let anything or anyone stop her from being the best at what she does. She shouldn't be praised for that, but for how she is putting disability on the map. Kerry is single-handedly changing the whole idea of disability with just her job alone. She's fought hard to get where she is, coming across obstacles that may have stopped another, able-bodied person, (job wise). She's pushed for disability equality and acceptance in many ways and she is starting to see the fruits of her labour come to fruition. In many ways, Kerry was lucky in my own personal opinion. Kerry *"...first started working at the Club when her husband volunteered for the Dragonheart radio show for Wrexham AFC." – [Paraphrase: Kerry Evans, the DLO of Wrexham AFC]* Originally, the Club took her on as a volunteer, but soon employed her full time. Of course, not everything she's accomplished whilst working for *Wrexham AFC* has been easy. Kerry has come under some backlash with some things she has fought hard for. The Club now has a 'quiet area' for those who need a quieter space to enjoy a match, for example, people with autism alongside other disabilities.

"The Racecourse Ground features an autism-friendly quiet zone, in section PG1 of the Macron Stand, as well as a waitress service, familiar-face stewards and a sensory room to ensure supporters with autism can attend and enjoy matches." – [Wrexham AFC receive Autism Friendly Award from National Autistic Society – Wrexhamafc.co.uk]

This area, surprisingly, did come under scrutiny when the concept of it was first conceived, Kerry admitted. Kerry, herself, was accused of being discriminatory, as the argument was made that she was basically separating people, and therefore labelling. This argument is ridiculous if I'm honest. This, (in my own opinion) just goes to show how little society understands disability and disability discrimination as a whole. Some 'disabled' people hate noise and rowdiness whether they have autism or not, (of which you can have a lot of at a football match especially). Having a 'quiet area' within the grounds is ingenious in my own personal opinion. The area is there **if** a person with autism, or just **if** a person with another form of disability needs a quieter space to enjoy a match. Kerry said to me that the area **isn't** mandatory. There **is a choice**. What people didn't really understand in the beginning was this 'quiet area' was, and **is, optional**. It's **not** mandatory. Nobody is going to make a 'disabled' person sit in the 'quiet area' against their will. For anyone to believe such nonsense is just plain ignorant.

I can maybe understand that it may have **seemed** like a separation to an outsider looking in, in the beginning, but let me ask you this, why would a 'disabled' person, like Kerry, be discriminatory, especially towards other 'disabled' people? It doesn't make any sense. Kerry knows about disability, she's living it, so she knows what's needed and what's not in her job as *Disability Liaison Officer at Wrexham AFC*. She is making sure that **all** disabilities are catered for within the Club.

Saying this, there is one thing that could be improved at *Wrexham AFC* disability wise, and

What Still Needs to be Done

that is allowing two carers within the wheelchair section of the Racecourse Ground if necessary. By rule, 'severely disabled' people require two carers on a daily basis. If a 'severely disabled' person is a fan of *Wrexham AFC* and wants to attend a match, realistically, they wouldn't be able to because their two carers wouldn't be allowed to sit in the same section, possibly putting a 'severely disabled' fan at risk, depending the severity of the disability. It is counterintuitive and ridiculous to deny a 'severely disabled' fan their rights just because the Club they support, stops a 'severely disabled' fan from having two dedicated carers. It doesn't make **any** sense, (to me at least). This is the only oversight that *Wrexham AFC* have undertaken in my own personal opinion. I do wonder how many 'disabled' *Wrexham AFC* fans have missed out on matches just because of this complete disregard? You aren't allowed two carers within the wheelchair section of the Racecourse Ground, and for there to be two carers, one carer would need to sit in another section, possibly at a fair distance from who they are supposed to be **sharing caring duties**. How is this fair? By denying two carers within the wheelchair section, *Wrexham AFC* are really just discriminating against a percentage of 'disabled' fans, which I personally imagine wouldn't be *Wrexham AFC's* intension. I urge Kerry Evans to look into this issue and try to come to a satisfactory solution before a real issue arises, and putting all Kerry's hard work and dedication in possible jeopardy. It would be a shame if this issue isn't dealt with properly. I want to see *Wrexham AFC* succeed in accessibility, and they **are** doing wonders with Kerry in charge, but it's just that small issue that could potentially escalate into a bigger issue down the line.

The Club has entrusted Kerry with providing sufficient accessibility, and easiness. I personally think that Kerry is doing great with the continuous battle for disability equality. *Wrexham AFC*, was, (in my opinion) extremely clever with fantastic foresight by hiring Kerry Evans full time as the *Disability Liaison Officer*. There is just that one issue that in my mind, is just putting emphasis on disability discrimination and ableism, however, *Wrexham AFC* **are** doing wonders for disability equality, but in my mind, this one thing is just stopping full, true disability equality to flourish.

What Still Needs to be Done

However, if other companies and places followed suit by hiring 'disabled' people for disability based jobs, I truly believe that the world would be better off. You may think that only hiring 'disabled' people in disability related jobs is discrimination in itself, and yes, of course it would be, I'm not scared to admit that as a fact, because it would be, there's absolutely no denying that. It of course depends on the type of job you are talking about. Aideen Blackborough agrees with this. I asked:

"Do you believe that every disabled person deserves a chance to showcase their abilities if able?" – [Question put to Aideen Blackborough, Disability Trainer, Speaker, and Author]

"Difficult question – for example, I believe disabled people should be protected from discrimination; however I don't think you should just be given opportunities because of your disability if that makes sense? If someone else is a better fit for an opportunity, they should get it. Hope that makes sense?" – [Aideen Blackborough, Disability Trainer, Speaker and Author]

I respect Aideen here, as I completely understand that there are jobs that some people physically cannot do in life, and you may need able-bodied people for certain jobs; but, for **all of those jobs that physically cannot be done by a 'disabled' person**, depending on the condition of their disability, there is absolutely no logical reason why a 'disabled' person cannot work **alongside** an able-bodied person, to explain how exactly accessibility for disability should be implemented. This is the ideal scenario for disability equality. Every company and outdoor space should cater for all disabilities, especially today, living in this 'modern' society, which we are so keen to claim. Nobody should ever be made to feel insignificant. This sadly is the case though. The amount of establishments that aren't 'disability friendly' in the twenty-first century is beyond a joke, and for those who 'claim' they are, the facilities are tiny, which is again, beyond a joke. It's like going from one extreme to another.

Again, Aideen Blackborough agrees, by referencing the *Disability Equality Act of 2010.*

What Still Needs to be Done

"Absolutely. We have the Equality Act but it's so often ignored and nothing is done unless an individual has the drive to take up a case. There's very little accountability and whenever I make a complaint, I get the standard response of, "Our staff have been trained..." Training means very little when disability discrimination is still a common occurrence." – [Aideen Blackborough, Disability Trainer, Speaker, and Author]

Training alone **isn't** enough. Training doesn't sort disability discrimination, **lived experience does**.

I hope I've given you food for thought? It's true, the *Disability Equality Act of 2010* **doesn't** go far enough. It's not just me saying it, other people are too. It **definitely** needs to be addressed and updated. So many issues are going under the radar. We have ramps on every bus now in the UK, but only **one** 'disabled' space. Dropped kerbs are designed for accessibility and more crucially, a person's **independence and their dignity**. So why, more often than not, do I find it difficult to find a dropped kerb on **either side of a road**? Why do vehicles find it acceptable to park on a dropped kerb? Yes, you may think that you are allowing space for other vehicles to pass, but what about a wheelchair, or even a pushchair for that matter? These are also vehicles, yes they maybe not driven on a road, but they still carry people around, just like a 'standard' vehicle. Why should it **always be our** access denied?

> *"...even if you have a disability or not everyone should be treated as an equal, everyone has something to offer and are an important member of society." – [Hayley Murphy, email participant]*

Disability equality is non-existent in today's times, there's absolutely no question about it for me. If equality for disability existed, then my mental health wouldn't have deteriorated significantly in the past, as I wouldn't have had any negative experiences in relation to equality. If equality for disability existed, my new experience as an author wouldn't be a thing. In a way, I'm the proof that disability equality really doesn't exist, and if it does, it **definitely** needs improvement as a lot of 'disabled' people, including myself, have not seen any trace of it. If it wasn't so laughable, it would

What Still Needs to be Done

be devastating. I for one, would love to be a fly on the wall when these 'training days for disability' are taking place. In my own opinion, the training doesn't go far enough. Whatever 'professionals' are teaching isn't worth it. Nothing is thought through properly. It may seem adequate on the surface, but I definitely don't want 'adequate', I want, (and deserve) efficiency, accessibility, dignity and respect, as do others who have a disability of some form.

Now, that isn't to say that all 'disabled' facilities are the same, of course not. I've seen a handful of 'disabled' facilities, (toilets) kitted out with space and equipment in, namely, *Wales Millennium Centre* in Cardiff. Their 'disabled' facilities in this particular venue are second to none in my own personal opinion. That is the problem though, there have been only a **handful** of 'disability friendly facilities' of which I have personally found **fully** accessible and acceptable.

The venue in question boasts:

"...height adjustable adult-sized hanging bench and a tracking hoist system. There is also a Changing Places toilet located on the ground

floor with a height adjustable adult-sized changing bench and a tracking hoist system. There is adequate space in the changing area for the person who needs it and up to two carers, a centrally placed toilet with room either side. There is a left transfer accessible unisex toilet within the gender-neutral toilets inside Cabaret, which is located on the ground floor on the south side of the building. This venue has its own external entrance. Tracking hoist system. There is adequate space in the changing area for the person who needs it and up to two carers, a centrally placed toilet with room either side. There is a left transfer accessible unisex toilet within the gender-neutral toilets inside Cabaret, which is located on the ground floor on the south side of the building. This venue has its own external entrance." – [Wales Millennium Centre, Cardiff]

It was so refreshing to go into a venue and see a facility that was actually accessible. It is sad though that I felt pleasantly surprised. I feel like a broken record but there should **never** be any issue with providing accessibility.

The *Senedd* Commission employee was recently kind enough to also participate in this book, by

What Still Needs to be Done

answering questions related to accessibility at the *Senedd*. They said that *"...the Senedd estate is fully accessible." – [Senedd Commission employee, the Senedd]* which is great. I must say that when I was invited to see the first book, *CP Isn't Me* on display in the *Senedd* Shop, the building was indeed fully accessible, with regards to the areas I had the pleasure and honour to be invited to. Even though I was invited, and saw for myself, I wanted to ask the *Senedd* Commission employee themselves about accessibility to give them the opportunity to explain the facilities, as I think it's better coming from someone who actually works in the *Senedd*, rather than it just being my own recollection, of which isn't a one hundred percent guarantee.

"The design of this building has been described as exemplar in the media. The following enhancements have been included in the design to ensure the building meets its target of being exemplar in terms of accessibility in the public areas..." [Senedd.Wales]

The full list below of accessible features are taken from *Senedd.Wales.*

- *Additional lift installed at front of the building for public access to the entrance;*

- *Enlarged public lift within the building;*

- *Installation of fire evacuation lifts at the rear of the building;*

- *There are public lavatories in the Neuadd and a Changing Places facility is provided with an adult changing bed and hoist;*

- *Provision of a parent and child room;*

- *Hearing induction loops installed throughout the building;*

- *Fully accessible reception desk in terms of staff and visitors;*

- *Provision for 3 spaces for wheelchair users in the committee room galleries with an additional 2 if required;*

- *Provision for 9 dedicated spaces for wheelchair users in the debating chamber gallery and seating can be removed for additional spaces if required;*

- *12 parking bays are provided alongside the Senedd Building for disabled people;*

- *Covered walkways from the parking bays for disabled people to the lifts at the front of the building;*

- *Signage in Welsh, English and both forms of Braille;*

- *Provision of tactile markers to the exterior plinths;*

- *Operational plans for the utilisation of the building.*

[Information taken from *Senedd.Wales*]

This is the standard that all venues should have in place. I'm extremely happy to learn that the *Senedd* has a *Changing Places UK Toilet* for a start. Signage in *Braille* is another thing that the *Senedd* should be applauded for. A simple addition, but an effective one for the inclusion of disability. I'm not sure whether or not if other venues has *Braille* signage, but again, it should be by standard. Even having nine dedicated spaces within the *Chamber Gallery* and if needed, more seats can be removed on request, which is absolutely fantastic. Including disability in places such as a *Chamber Gallery*, giving 'disabled' people the opportunity to participate in debates etc., if desired, is a massive step forward in the right direction. 'Normalising' disability is truly important, and the *Senedd* are 'normalising' the subject in spades.

"To 'Provide good access for people with disabilities' was one part of the architect's original design brief. We review these features regularly and consider improvements following feedback." – [Senedd Commission employee, the Senedd]

It's absolutely fantastic to learn that the *Senedd* regularly reviews facilities and features, always looking to see how these things can be improved following feedback. Other venues can learn **a lot** from the *Senedd's* practices and adopt them for themselves. It would be a fantastic opportunity for other venues to join in with this much needed equality and inclusion fight.

What Still Needs to be Done

The *Senedd* Commission employee was also kind enough to add a quote from Ivan Harbour, architect and *RSHP* Partner leading the *Senedd* project.

"In a parliament, business frequently happens "behind closed doors". In the design of the Senedd, as a modern democracy, we removed those doors to make the work of the Senedd visible." – [Ivan Harbour, Architect and RSHP Partner leading the Senedd project]

Basically what I personally take away from this quote is that, Ivan removed the standard obstacles of a building in order to make it more accessible to all.

"This quote from the architect summarises what the Senedd building aims to be. A place which is open and accessible for the public, for it to be a place that is functional for as many people as possible." – [Senedd Commission employee, the Senedd]

I asked if the *Senedd* plans to improve accessibility a bit more in the future:

"We have recently made some adaptations to the outside spaces to make certain areas less slippery in the rain by replacing some of the slate. Small changes like this are regularly happening. They can make a big difference over time however, in making the spaces more approachable. We're likely to see radical change in how digital devices can support, including providing opportunities for us to make the spaces more accessible in the future. This could be by developing our own app for visitors to interact with staff during their visit, or that the devices that people have with them will have additional accessible features, such as the development of built-in features like text-to-speech from photos. The latter being more likely I believe, and we need to be ready to adopt those features when available; therefore it is important to spend time on the learning and development of the team."
– [Senedd Commission employee, the Senedd]

It's absolutely wonderful to know the *Senedd* are constantly looking at ways to improve accessibility and are willing to learn about new

What Still Needs to be Done

developments in technology, to potentially adopt for their own venue. This is what venues across the world should take notice of and put it into practice, not just say that they will, but actually take measures to incorporate these things themselves. This is what is needed and required for inclusion and equality. It's not enough just to claim to be inclusive and equal, we actually need to do something to make that claim a reality.

Of course, not all buildings and venues can be accessible (mainly old and listed buildings).

"Tŷ Hywel and Pierhead are older buildings, particularly Pierhead, and therefore have had some adaptions over time. Parts of the Pierhead are not accessible/usable for the public or staff, and others opened by the installation of a lift." – [Senedd Commission employee, the Senedd]

It is a little more accepting to know that a building such as the *Pierhead* in Cardiff, is inaccessible to the public as a whole. If you have a disability of some form, you know that venues such as the *Pierhead*, is inaccessible for all, not just one demographic. Therefore, we're all in the same boat so to speak. It's therefore a level playing field for equality and inclusion if that makes sense? It's not acceptable to have a building or venue that is only accessible for those who are able-bodied. Either, adapt buildings and venues fully, or close them off to the public altogether. There should never be any 'grey area' when it comes to this. It's either all or nothing. (Excluding listed buildings of course).

The disability facility company, *Closomat Ltd.* are a supplier to *Changing Places UK*, which admittedly, does make a lot of sense that the two companies would indeed collaborate.

"Closomat Ltd are the UK's leading supplier of Changing Places toilets. Bigger than a standard 'Doc M' disabled toilet, these 'ultra-accessible' toilet rooms allow disabled people and their carers to use the loo or be changed in a safe and hopefully clean space. Equipped with a hoist, adult-sized changing bench, height adjustable wash hand basin, privacy screen and all the usual grab rails. The standard also recommends a wash and dry toilet to be included to further enhance the rooms inclusivity." – [Robin Tuffley, Closomat Ltd.]

What Still Needs to be Done

It is absolutely fantastic that these facilities actually exist, but more does need to be done to have these facilities installed in more public places. As it stands currently, 'disabled' people just have to accept the hand society has dealt. It's the attitude of "put up or shut up", that is absolutely disgusting. We are in the twenty-first century and still disability is being treated as an inconvenience. The ironic thing is, disability wouldn't be an inconvenience if our needs were actually met. Accessibility seems to be an afterthought.

This is just my experience, I cannot speak for other's experience, this is just what I have found, but I do **think** that if I had issues with space, there is absolutely no doubt in my mind that others have sadly experienced the same, especially people who are considered to be 'severely disabled'. It would be anion impossible for 'severely disabled' people to use, let alone access. It's just unacceptable.

Changing Places UK built this facility in the *Wales Millennium Centre*, a campaign that raises awareness and fights for the right of actual 'disabled' facilities.

What Still Needs to be Done

There are other venues in society that have excellent facilities for 'disabled' people, namely I'm thinking of a hotel chain, and one hotel chain in particular which we as a family always use, just for this reason. However, more public venues and places **must** adapt to accommodate disability.

I am so honoured to have Jill Clark, campaigner for *Changing Places UK* and blogger involved in this book. She said:

"...Standard accessible toilets do not meet the needs of all people with a disability. Over ¼ million people in the UK with a disability need extra equipment and space to allow them to use the toilets safely and comfortably. These needs are met by Changing Places Toilets...I started my campaign 8 years ago, because I was limited where to go, because I require a hoist to go to the toilet." – [Jill Clark, Campaigner, Changing Places UK and Blogger]

I somewhat ran into the same issue as Jill here, not exactly the same, but similar. When I was going through the process of trying to get two support workers to be able to go out further afield, not that I need two support workers really,

What Still Needs to be Done

(only for personal care – using a toilet), because of health and safety reasons, I was told that I would have needed to use a hoist when out with the support workers. The issue is, 'disabled' facilities traditionally only have the basics, (grab rails). Hoists and other disability equipment in a 'disabled' facility is near enough non-existent. I say near enough as there are those facilities which do provide disability equipment, (*Changing Places UK Toilets*) *but* they are few and far between.

Mum explained this when we were in the process of getting two support workers. The response was basically, to find out the locations in the UK where hoists are in place in 'disabled' facilities. This obviously isn't practical. There was absolutely no way that I was going to painstakingly find out every single 'disabled' facility in the UK which possessed a hoist. That was a ridiculous suggestion to make, and just goes to show the total disregard of disability in it's purest form. Needless to say, we never progressed any further with this.

Fully accessible facilities that are fully equipped with equipment to accommodate **all** disabilities is the standard that all 'disabled' people deserve, yet most 'disabled' facilities are tiny in my view, as you saw in chapter three.

That image is just one example of many. When I attended the *Disability Pride Parade* in Chester, I used a 'disabled' facility in a restaurant. To put it bluntly, I thought of Jill and the *Changing Places UK* campaign, as it just reinforced in my mind the need for these particular facilities across the UK. I

 knew that you probably wouldn't believe what I'm about to say, so I had taken the liberty of taking photographic evidence to backup my findings.

First of all, the standard accessibility issue in terms of space, which unfortunately I always expect, but there was something I didn't expect, which caught me off guard, and admittedly I did laugh at what I saw. The total ineptitude of who designed this particular 'disabled' facility is beyond me.

What Still Needs to be Done

Why is the soap dispenser high on the wall? Realistically, people in wheelchairs would never be able to reach this particular soap dispenser. The only way, (possibly), this dispenser could potentially be used, is if another person was assisting the said person with a disability. However, **not all 'disabled' people require assistance when using a facility**. If a 'disabled' person uses this particular facility and are a wheelchair user, hypothetically, the person would have to ask another person to help them to do a menial everyday task, taking away dignity, privacy, independence and pride. The pride issue really struck a chord with me that day, especially since I went to Chester to participate in the *Disability Pride Parade*.

There is absolutely no thought for the feelings of disability here. You may think that I'm just making something out of nothing, but unless you have lived through disability discrimination, you **cannot** pass comment. If you have lived through disability discrimination, you know **exactly** my issue here.

Furthermore, having standard hand-wash with a pump design isn't really accessible to all disabilities. Not all people with a disability have upper body strength and so may find it difficult to use a hand-wash of this nature. Having a sensor based hand-wash would be the ideal solution, where a 'disabled' person would just put their hands under and hand-wash would automatically be dispensed. A simple change, but an effective one.

According to *Changing Places UK*:

"Only 15 cinemas in the UK have Changing Places Toilets." – [Changing Places UK]

Also:

"Only 19 pubs and restaurants in the UK have Changing Places Toilets." – [Changing Places UK]

As of twenty-twenty-two, according to the *Film Distributors Association*, there are **"1,087 cinemas in the UK" – [Film Distributors Association]** and undoubtedly more as of writing this.

What Still Needs to be Done

According to *Statista.com*, there are *"approximately 46,800 pubs in the UK."* – *[Statista.com]*

There are also *"...42,477 Full-Service Restaurants businesses in the UK as of 2023"* – *[ibisworld.com]*

Admittedly, the *House of Commons Library* stated:

The number of pubs has been decreasing steadily for several decades. From 2000 to 2019, pub numbers have declined by 13,600, or 22%. More recently, 2010 to 2020 saw pub numbers fall by 15%. Recent Office for National Statistics (ONS) data indicated that the number of pubs in the UK decreased in the year to March 2020, although not all areas of the UK saw a fall. From 2019 to 2020, London had 1.1% increase in the number of pubs. Yorkshire and the Humber and Wales also saw increases in the number of pubs." – *[House of Commons Library]*

Numbers may have decreased over the years in regards to the total of pubs in the UK, but that

does not excuse the fact that only **nineteen** pubs and restaurants in the UK have proper 'disabled' facilities. Remember, *Changing Places UK* said that there are nineteen *Changing Places Toilets* in pubs **and** restaurants in the UK in total, meaning that there are fewer of these fully accessible facilities in pubs. It is truly and utterly disgusting.

It wouldn't be so bad if public spaces started small by maybe introducing *Closomat* toilets into 'disabled' facilities. Yes, it would be a small step, but that is better than no step at all.

Closomat Ltd. manufactures toilets that have a wash and dry system installed. I contacted the company with the goal of finding out more information on the specific equipment. I am ever so honoured to have a representative agree to speak on the company's behalf.

"In 1962, Robert Willan founded Closomat in the UK, becoming a wash and dry toilet pioneer. He knew that this innovative product had the potential to change the lives of countless individuals who were living with disabilities. Since these humble beginnings, Closomat has grown to become the leading

What Still Needs to be Done

brand in the UK, providing dignity, independence and control for the last 60+ years." – [Robin Tuffley, Closomat Ltd.]

I personally have one of these specialist toilets at home, so I personally know the benefits that these toilets provide for people with disabilities. These toilets give 'disabled' people independence, ease of use and comfort.

"More often than not, the inclusion of a wash and dry toilet is the difference between living independently or relying on carers. At Closomat we believe that everyone deserves the right to live as independently and in control as possible. A Closomat wash and dry toilet goes way beyond 'hands free toileting'. Making use of numerous accessories, the Closomat Vita range can be personalised to each user's preference, now and in the future. We achieve this by having a dedicated team of support staff and service engineers on hand to service, maintain and adapt our toilets for continuity of use." – [Robin Tuffley, Closomat Ltd.]

Knowing that *Closomat Ltd.* is dedicated to promoting independence, is absolutely fantastic! Usually, disability equipment ultimately decreases independence, (however much companies will state otherwise). Disability equipment really just enhances the misconceptions of 'vulnerability'. It's just an added barrier that 'disabled' people always, unfairly have to fight against. Usually equipment just confirms that 'disabled' people are weak. That we need equipment in order to live a fulfilled life. The reality is, equipment is needed to assist and enhance us to live, not give us a life. This is the mistake society often makes.

"At Closomat we're all about making things easier for the people who use our toilets, so that's why there are just two products in our range. Both wash and dry, and both can be personalised to individual requirements. The only choice to make is whether you want a wall mounted toilet or a floor mounted one. We know that everyone is different, even if they have the same disability or condition. That's why we ensure our products are customisable in thousands of ways. From different heights, integrated support arms and soft seats. As our

What Still Needs to be Done

customers' needs change over time, the toilet can be adapted to accommodate those changes. Our in-house service team will visit their home and adapt the toilet." [Robin Tuffley, Closomat Ltd.]

Also, knowing that *Closomat Ltd.* tries to take away the notion of vulnerability by giving us some sense of independence back, is absolutely wonderful to say the least. They know about different needs and are accommodating towards disability in all of it's forms. Other companies (disability specialist or not) should always be aware of different disabilities, the needs of the differences, and the willingness to accommodate those needs without difficulties.

It gives me a sense of hope however, that disability discrimination maybe extinguished for good in time. For this to happen though, we need more companies to take the same mantra as *Closomat Ltd.* This company is a trailblazer in disability equality in my own opinion, with this refreshing attitude towards disability independence.

"The vast majority of Closomat wash and dry toilets are specified and supplied for installation within domestic settings. However we will install a Closomat toilet wherever they are required. As the specification of a wash and dry toilet is often Occupational Therapy lead, it is their remit to review the disabled person's activity analysis as well as their 'occupation' and if that involves going to school, college or work, then there's no reason why their personal hygiene needs shouldn't be met." – [Robin Tuffley, Closomat Ltd.]

A *Closomat* toilet was installed in my primary school, specifically for the 'disabled' pupils, so I know for a fact that these toilets can be installed in public places. Society definitely need to install *Changing Places UK Toilets*. Whether it's because of financial constraints, but really, why should that even be an issue? Why does disability always have to compromise with inadequate facilities just to adhere to the overall majority of society? This is just confirmation, (to me at least), that society priorities able-bodied people instead of society as a whole. This is what Government should do, but instead it feels like favouritism in a way.

What Still Needs to be Done

It's not just *Changing Places UK* and *Closomat Ltd.* that are committed to improving accessibility for disability thankfully. One company in particular, *Haycomp Pty Ltd.* based in Australia, have created a specialised lift for airlines specifically designed to transfer passengers from a wheelchair for example, to the airplane seat with ease.

"As an Australian manufacturer of patient lifters, we were contacted by Qantas to see if we could develop a lifter that would work in an aircraft." – [Representative, Haycomp Pty Ltd.]

It's fantastic to know that airline companies are starting to become more aware of the accessibility needs of all disabilities. This to me, gives me a sense of satisfaction to know that disability is finally starting to be recognised.

When I went to Paris when I was twelve, it was completely different accessibility wise, Ian had to actually carry me onto the plane, which wasn't ideal really. Don't get me wrong, I love Ian, he's my brother, but having to be carried onto an aeroplane especially at twelve, isn't the best to promote independence if you have a disability of some form. That's why it's fantastic to know that airlines have finally got the memo and decided to accommodate disability. When I went, it was just shambolic in the airport, as they lost my wheelchair, so I had to be pushed around in an *Evac Chair*, which if you don't know what it is, it's extremely uncomfortable and really just screams disability. Just a reminder, I really don't mind having a disability, I just hate what disability represents to society.

"The GLOBEX STANDARD PLUS EVACUATION CHAIR enables one person to evacuate a mobility impaired person safely and easily downstairs in the event of an emergency, or when lifts cannot be used in the same way as our standard evacuation chair with the added benefit of having a carry facility for going up stairs and over." [Information from Globex Evacuation Solutions Brochure]

 This is what it says in the brochure for *Globex Evacuation Solutions*, the company behind the *Evac Chair*. It is great that there is a company that is dedicated to promoting

What Still Needs to be Done

disability safety in emergencies, but in my opinion, they are missing one crucial feature, comfort and wellbeing.

You mainly see these evacuation chairs (left) in hotels, but there were a couple in my high school, and every time there was a fire drill, I had to sit in this *Evac Chair* to get down the stairs. Now, I don't know whether the chairs have been redesigned since I used them, but if not, they **definitely** need to. You could feel every bump as you were taken down the stairs. It was so uncomfortable. To this day, I cannot stand the sight of the chair. You may think that this is an overreaction, but put yourself in the shoes of a person with a disability, how would you feel if your only option for safety was to sit in a chair that doesn't actually entertain the idea of comfort? Bear in mind that these chairs are designed to assist 'disabled' people get to safety during emergencies. There didn't seem to be any thought for the actual wellbeing of a person with a disability. With this disregard of wellbeing, this may cause a number of added issues for a 'disabled' person. Again, the concept was there, of which I'm thankful, but the actual end product wasn't very effective or efficient.

"...we demonstrate the equipment to be used, but unfortunately not all our products are comfortable, but they are only for use in the event of an emergency for short periods of time, and not built for comfort. In some cases, cushions and additional supporting straps have been provided." – [Darren Franks, Globex Evacuation Solutions]

Realistically, providing cushions to **all** *Evac Chairs* would be more beneficial. I appreciate the argument that this equipment is only to be used for short periods during emergencies, but this **really isn't** the best reasoning to have, or in fact believe. Take into account the fact that these chairs are, more often than not, supplied to hotels, (which can have **a lot** of stairs, depending on the location of the accessible hotel room). If a person with a disability has to use an *Evac Chair* due to an emergency during their stay, and their accessible hotel room is located near (if not on) the top floor, (especially if the hotel in question has a lot of floors), that **wouldn't** be a short

What Still Needs to be Done

period of time. This is what I don't personally understand? Unless these companies actually are prepared to try the equipment out for themselves, and feel **every single step, every single bit of discomfort** that an *Evac Chair* provides, these companies do not have the right to speak about the benefits of such a chair without listing the negative side also. I get that it's bad for business to list the negatives of equipment, (especially equipment that is designed to aid disability in emergencies), but when you have a business that is crucial for disability safety, companies **must** be prepared to list the negatives of said equipment also, just to let 'disabled' people know the potential flaws, just to make 'disabled' people aware. We are driven by money though, and negatives don't drum up business. No business equals no money.

Having a disability myself, I know the importance of promoting comfort to equipment. Why should it always have to be a choice between comfort and functionality? Why can't it be both? Disability is always treated as an afterthought it seems, all that we should do is just comply, and be grateful? Why? Why does disability always have to compromise like I've said? General society would voice their opinions and concerns to something that may be considered a disadvantage, so really, disability **should**, and **deserves** exactly the same level of opportunities and respect. Opportunities to voice the negative experiences that disability faces constantly, and the respect when we do. We either are patronised or we are automatically made to feel insignificant by society. This is absolutely awful. Society and companies need to understand the importance of allowing other demographics have a voice. Enough with this delusional outlook on disability that society blatantly shows without shame. Disability is part of being human, it's not an inconvenience or an alien concept. Yes, disability maybe an alternative way to live, but that's exactly what it is, a life. The sooner society realises this, the better. Maybe companies who specialise in providing disability equipment would be more understanding of the need for efficiency **and** comfort. It shouldn't **ever** be a question of choice.

"At first glance accessibility has improved, but in real terms very little progress has been made. Many adaptations have been done FOR

What Still Needs to be Done

disabled people instead of WITH disabled people and it shows. For example; A university near me recently built a new student building, advertising its up-to-date and inclusive design.. which sounded great until it was opened and we were invited in. I could access the corridors and main communal areas great but my wheelchair didn't even fit into the study rooms. I had a meeting sitting in the hallway as a result. Had they actually consulted with wheelchair users this could have been avoided." – [Sarah Smith, social media participant]

It's obvious that society could do better, but for whatever reason, there still seems to be a disconnect for society understanding what it **actually means** to be accessible. This is what I mean by allowing 'disabled' people to help design accessible facilities. It's not enough just to claim, there needs to be some **real** action behind the words. That's the most important thing. Making 'disabled' people sit in areas that aren't appropriate just because of insufficient accessibility is absolutely disgraceful. We **always** seem to be penalised and unfairly treated just because we have a disability. This is discrimination, and ableism in it's truest form. This is why I've decided to write these books, to do what I can to try and shake up the public perceptions of disability.

"...we usually have trouble when attending hospital appointments (we are in the UK). My husband uses a mobility scooter, and there is simply no room for such a patient to wait with everyone else. He has been asked to sit out in the corridor on more than one occasion, and has been treated as a nuisance. This can also constitute a fire hazard, should an emergency happen. It is however totally inexcusable in a new building." [Maja Tompkins, social media participant]

With respect, companies, venues, businesses, public spaces etc. don't have a clue about accessibility, unless the person in charge has a disability of some form themselves. It's completely understandable that accessibility is an issue when you take into consideration this as fact. The general public cannot understand proper accessibility without proper insight and oversee

What Still Needs to be Done

from 'disabled' people. This however, should **never** be an excuse for laziness. That may seem harsh to call lack of accessibility lazy, but I personally don't really care. Accessibility should **never** be an issue to anyone in society. That is a democracy. It's so obvious that society isn't doing anything to try and prove the democracy status, really it's just the 'buzz word' without any actual meaning.

I recently, (as of writing), was invited to be a guest on a podcast, specialising in disability advocacy and equality, alongside my publisher, Allan to speak about my first book, *CP Isn't Me* and the need for disability equality in general. I was contacted by Krystal Schulze, the co-host of the podcast, *M4G Advocacy Media* in Texas, USA, asking if I would like to appear. Before the initial reach out by Krystal, I didn't know that the podcast existed, which says a lot about the current state of disability as a whole.

"We decided together after dealing with many of our own challenges, both personal and dealing with the public, that a platform for others to share their experiences was needed.

We are dedicated to helping others understand and appreciate themselves, as well as other people. We want to encourage them to not let others dictate who or what you are. We also want educate on the different diversities of the disability world, how you can show better inclusion and empower everyone to have equal humility. Our hope is that others will also be encouraged and help us through collaboration to share and be a light of help and love!" – [M4G Advocacy Media, Krystal Schulze & Mark Desa].

This is **exactly** what the world needs. People with disabilities need to have a voice, a platform. It's telling the reason why Krystal and Mark decided to create this podcast. Krystal and Mark's collective experience demonstrates the need for disability education, but it does seem that it is solely left up to the disability community to make this subject apart of the mainstream conversation. Society as a whole doesn't seem to entertain the idea of helping to promote disability equality, maybe because of the fear factor of it, or maybe because it doesn't concern the overall majority? Whatever the reason, disability equality is run by

What Still Needs to be Done

'disabled' people only. For any change to happen, there needs to be solidarity in this uphill battle for equality. We are trying, and little by little we are seeing small changes, but there's no 'I' in team.

M4G Advocacy Media is co-hosted by Mark Desa and Krystal Schulze. Krystal explained to me:

"...we had decided from the beginning we do everything 50-50, so we are both each other's co-host. It's really important to us go forward being an example of showing others that disabled or not, no one is less, we just bring different abilities. Regardless of your ability or position in your job or just dealing with people personally, everyone deserves the same respect and appreciation." – [Krystal Schulze, M4G Advocacy Media]

This is extremely important to note. By doing this, Mark and Krystal are subconsciously sending the message to society that regardless of ability, both co-hosts are equal, and therefore, sends out the message that everyone in society is equal regardless of your ability or background. This message is vital for actually having the potential to change perceptions, not only for disability, but people who would be considered inadequate by society. Mark and Krystal purposely made this decision. There is a social hierarchy whatever your background. Their approach to referring to themselves as co-hosts rather than saying one is the main host, rightly demolishes that ridiculous hierarchy.

M4G Advocacy Media is a platform to highlight disability in a positive way without it being too much. It's conversational, which is a better approach. Conversation gets to the heart of important topics, rather than a question and answer based scenario. It's easier to retain important information, and it's more likely to stick in people's minds if it's done in a laid back approach. This is what I mean when talking about education. Disability education should use this method, it would be extremely effective. People don't learn the truth if it's question and answer, they only pick up the facts. Questions are controlled, whereas, the flow, the art of conversation is natural. Krystal and Mark's approach is necessary to get the desired impact and results.

What Still Needs to be Done

The Societal Problem With Advocacy and Activism

"...Advocacy is so important and the issues will be better understood if we all work together!" – [Krystal Schulze, M4G Advocacy Media]

When we were guests on *M4G Advocacy Media*, Krystal said something that has resonated with me, and it maybe one of many reasons as to why disability equality is left on the back-burner, so to speak. She basically said that the term 'advocacy' could have a negative prefix to it, almost as if people think we are complaining if we advocate for change. I get that logic. What do you think of when you hear the terms 'advocate' and 'advocacy'? They're associated with standing up for what is right. Greta Thunberg, Narges Mohammadi and Malala Yousafzai are advocates and activists in their respective fields. Greta for climate change, Narges for human rights in Iran, and Malala for education, (specifically for girls in education), all of which are extremely important issues. Advocacy and activism though, does seem to have this unjustified reputation for complaining for the sake of complaining.

People by rule, don't like to be told what to do, how to act, or how to behave. By rule, people don't like to be told that their views on certain subjects may need to change, to meet with today's 'modern' way of life. It's just how the majority of society is, (not the whole of society, but a selected majority). Greta, Narges and Malala are all trying to advocate for change, albeit in very different areas, but they are trying.

"Everyone has some form of inner rebel that likes to question or do the opposite of what we're told." Experts call this feeling or need to rebel psychological reactance. It's your brain's reaction when you feel a threat to your freedom or think your choices are being limited." – ['You're Not the Boss of Me! Why We Don't Like Being Told What to Do', ClevelandClinic.org]

Backstories

Greta Thunberg

Greta Thunberg for instance, the backlash she has faced by a lot of people has been perplexing. She began her climate change campaign at the age of

What Still Needs to be Done

fifteen in two-thousand and eighteen. Her journey as an activist has seen Greta address, and call out world leaders on the subject of climate change. Her dedication holds no bounds. Yet, I do personally think starting her journey as an activist at the age of fifteen, ultimately gave her a disadvantage from the viewpoint of society, as I believe that society saw her as this 'girl' at first, who was just passionate about her advocacy subject. As time went on, I believe that society started to feel fed up with her constant battles to reverse climate change. I personally think that people became annoyed by her continuous, tireless and commendable effort to highlight the important, and very real issues that climate change is creating. Greta was mocked. People realistically aren't going to want to listen to a teenager, (which of course is absolutely disgraceful, it doesn't matter the age of a person, if they have a reasonable argument that is of public interest, then of course society **should** listen and show respect whilst listening). People don't like to be told what to do, how to act, think or feel, especially by a child. Adults are the masters, the leaders, children are the followers by rule. Anything that disturbs the natural order, we always find a way to retaliate. In Greta's case, unfortunately the act of retaliation was mocking. This doesn't matter in the slightest, but Greta is Autistic, bullying (because that's what it was), bullying an Autistic child, really does just show society's viewpoint and character when it comes to disability, challenges, and just generally the overall consensus on things like climate change.

You've seen it with the COVID-19 pandemic, some people broke lockdown rules, (as an example), because simply some people didn't agree with the way in which Government was handling the situation, and some questioned the authenticity of the pandemic altogether. This *'psychological reactance'* definitely occurred during the period of the pandemic. The term can also be used when on the subject of advocacy and activism. Politicians get the brunt of the defiance, but so do activists and advocates. Case in point, Greta Thunberg. We live in a society of defiance, deviance, blaming, finger pointing. How is this a democracy? How is this modern? If society has a *'psychological reactance'* problem when our beliefs are challenged, then of course society can't claim to be a democracy or modern. The two cancel each other out. To claim modernism and democracy driven, society needs to accept and, most importantly, **respect** advocacy and activism. You may not agree, everyone is entitled to their opinions, but that's no reason to disrespect advocacy and activism. Listen to a point, it's up to you whether you agree or not. All advocates and activists are saying is, to give important subject matters a chance. This is what a democracy is. This is what modernism is.

Narges Mohammadi

Iranian Human Rights activist, and *Noble Laureate* for the *Peace Prize*, Narges Mohammadi, was jailed whilst trying to fight for human rights in her country. This is unbelievable to learn. Why imprison a human who is trying to campaign for human rights? She actually won the *Peace Prize* in twenty-twenty-three whilst in jail. To me, this says a lot, how society remains conflicted. How it's the people of high standing, aiming for the exact same outcome as an advocate or activist, giving the reward. Whereas, it should be the general public who should be backing the advocates and activists, yet they are in fact the ones to punish them. Countries such as Pakistan and Iran still live in this past world where basic human rights are taken away, and if anyone tries to stand up for what is right, then those people are punished in the most barbaric ways. Narges has been arrested on numerous occasions with her continuous battle for human rights in Iran. She was first arrested in twenty-twenty, and has been released, then rearrested ever since, all for the exact same reason, standing up and speaking out for basic human rights.

Human rights are a standard part of life that we as a first world country take for granted. Narges unbelievably saw a sentence of ten years and nine months in total, on charges of actions against national security and propaganda against the state. Narges Mohammadi is an activist fighting for equality and because she voices her opinion, she is punished for speaking out? That isn't how the twenty-first century should work. You would think Narges experience is vital for a welcomed positive change, not incarceration. I personally cannot get that logic? How can poorer countries approve of treating someone inhumane,

What Still Needs to be Done

especially when that person is trying to improve the country? I cannot understand the logic. It is a complete mystery.

Malala Yousafzai

Malala Yousafzai, is a woman from Pakistan advocating for the right for girls in the country to receive twelve years free education. Pakistan was taken over by extremists who banned many things, including girls education. Malala spoke out rightly against this abhorrent ban, and as a result of her activism and vocalisation, she was made a target. She was shot in the head in twenty-twelve after a masked gunman boarded her school bus, which then put her in a coma.

This didn't deter her though, this incident made Malala more determined to speak out, as to give a message to the extremists that she would not be silenced. When Malala eventually regained consciousness, she made it her mission to change ideas on girls education. Girls education is a standard part of life regardless of which country you live. Denying such a vital part of life is utterly unbelievable. This why people advocate for change, to try to put an end to things like this.

What Still Needs to be Done

Banning the right to free education for girls? It doesn't make any logical sense. Advocating shouldn't be ignored. The whole reason for advocacy and activism is to speak out for what is right, to ultimately break the stigma around a subject and change it for the better.

Greta, Narges and Malala are trying to change the planet, to try and make the world a much more happy and harmonious place to be. So much destruction happens today, we need advocates and activists to remind us of what's important, to drive towards the positives, instead of always veering off course to the negatives.

Disability Relations

You maybe thinking, "what's the connection? Why did Samantha write about Greta Thunberg, Narges Mohammadi and Malala Yousafzai? How does these separate women relate to disability?" Two words, advocacy and activism. It really doesn't matter the subject, advocacy and activism can be achieved through a whole host of different subjects. Climate change, the right to girls education and human rights are all vital to allow a society to succeed. Disability rights needs and

What Still Needs to be Done

deserves to be added to this. Disability rights are human rights at the end of the day, only slightly different, but means exactly the same overall.

Disability advocacy and activism is just as important as the topics covered by Greta Thunberg, Narges Mohammadi and Malala Yousafzai. On the subject of disability advocacy, people like Krystal Schulze, Mark Desa of *M4G Advocacy Media* and myself for example, need the backing from absolutely **everyone in society** to help make a difference, a **proper** difference. It cannot just be left up to us any longer, please share some of the load that society has placed upon us. We need to work together, as Krystal Schulze has said, then, and only then is a possibility for great change.

The Need For Disability Podcasts

M4G Advocacy Media's tagline is:

"Educating, empowering, and encouraging people with all abilities, their families, and friends. Creating a better understanding and building healthier relationships. Together we

can all make a difference." - [M4G Advocacy Media, Krystal Schulze & Mark Desa]

There is a *BBC* podcast, *AccessAll,* that's available in the UK which is a weekly podcast that discusses disability and mental health through news, life stories etc., which is available globally. These podcasts are crucial to start the conversion, unless we keep talking, any potential interest will slow down to a complete stop. These podcasts are great for highlighting disability and mental health for that matter, but I can't help but wonder how many listeners these types of shows get? It's no secret that the subject is daunting to begin with, and I wonder because of this, whether these podcasts are successful? Yes they're crucial, yes they're important, but I do personally wonder if these podcasts get the listenership they wholeheartedly deserve? As it's such a niche topic, and it only affects a certain percentage of society, unfortunately, and it's a sad thing), realistically I do personally feel that these types of shows will not get the coverage they deserve. It's wrong of course, but there is a possibility of low listenership because of this.

What Still Needs to be Done

I do think that disability podcasts, especially *AccessAll* by the *BBC* are really missing out on a golden opportunity. *AccessAll* is hosted weekly by presenter, Nicky Fox. Nicky has a disability and a wheelchair, so a perfect host right, you would at least imagine, which is fantastic, I'm guessing that the *BBC* thought it necessary to hire a 'disabled' presenter to present the podcast. Ingenious and obvious. This is fantastic for 'disabled' people, but I'm guessing the *BBC* intends to reach a wider range of listeners across society, otherwise what's the point? The trouble is, with this approach, the *BBC* are in fact doing the complete opposite. Yes, being identifiable is important as it builds bonds, builds familiarity, builds reassurance, but only to that one demographic the subject matter is being broadcast to. To really try to make a full and proper difference, you must show other demographics within your platforms to give the message that the subject matter is a standard part of life. I personally think that *AccessAll* has opened up a dialogue, granted, but it's a dialogue that is probably only listened to by 'disabled' people. To really see a difference *AccessAll* should by rights have other demographics either co-hosting or as guests. This would really make a positive difference.

The tireless effort that go into making these types of podcasts, alongside podcasts as a whole really does deserve to be rewarded. It does take a lot of time to record, edit, just produce one episode of a podcast. People in society really do need to take notice, recognise podcasts with extremely important subject matters such as disability equality. It may sound boring, but trust me, these disability podcasts educate, fascinate and make logical sense in equal measure. Disability podcasts may educate you in a way to stop you from being unnecessarily, and/or unintentionally ableist. You maybe thinking of course, I would say that, promoting disability equality in all of it's forms, but I'm not a teacher, neither are the majority of some 'disabled' people. I'm just suggesting that social cues may in fact be a learning curve. By listening to important podcasts that offer genuine stories on the subject. Everything could potentially become easier to handle. Gone would be the day when you would have to watch what you say and do, as everybody would indeed know that subjects such as disability is a standard part of life,

What Still Needs to be Done

regardless of condition. Listening to an important and vital podcast would work wonders for a society who is terrified to have an opinion, yet somehow feeds on the fact of public image. A disability podcast would ease the pressure of some people for fear they may come into contact with a 'disabled' person during the course of the day.

Disabled Facilities – Asking For Help

Going back, I really do just wish that society would accept they need help and ask people in the know about how to design 'disabled' access facilities. It makes so much sense. Listening to podcasts based on disability would help people understand what is needed, instead of always second guessing. I personally do think that pride barriers any opportunity to ask for help with designing these types of facilities. Having pride in your life is usually a good thing, but when it comes to shaping society for the better, this should **never** be a reason for inadequate accessibility. There's actually no viable reason for inadequate accessibility.

"I think it very much depends on where you are. I live in Australia and we're way behind the eight ball in terms of accessibility. I was amazed at how good the UK (and from what I'm hearing, most of Europe) is in comparison. The thing that I think is the most significant for me in both the UK and Australia is the complete lack of comprehension by councils/planners/people in general that a sharp ramp from a pavement to a road with a lip at the bottom is a death trap for wheelchair users as are narrow pavements with a camber slanted towards the road. It doesn't matter how engaged people are, how many accessible public areas such as parks, museums, shops etc are, how helpful rail staff are. If we can't safely wheel along a street we're still isolated and the issue is literally everywhere." – [Hari Candlin, social media participant]

I wholeheartedly agree with Hari here, it is incomprehensible to me that Hari said that they are basically impressed with how the UK and Europe are accommodating to accessibility compared to where they live in Australia. It does concern me to think that a country such as

What Still Needs to be Done

Australia, doesn't have adequate accessibility. I know for a fact that disability accessibility could be made better in the UK, as do others. I'm not too sure about Europe really without doing research, but I personally would say that accessibility could always improve, regardless of how much society likes to claim that accessibility is second to none for 'disabled' people.

Disability 'Achievements'

Wrexham AFC are taking the lead in providing the resources needed to ensure that there is accessibility for disability in their Club. I recently had the privilege of being invited to attend one of Kerry Evans', *Quiet Walkabouts* where she takes potential new fans around the Club, showing and talking about the accessibility that the Club now has. Again, I believe that *Wrexham AFC* were extremely forward-thinking by hiring a person with a disability to run the disability section of the football club. You could argue that because we live in the twenty-first century, that it's a complete no-brainer to hire someone with lived experience into a job role that would be a benefit in the long run. After all, it's just good business sense. Yet,

What Still Needs to be Done

you unfortunately don't really see this come to fruition in any other part of life. I assume that some people have common sense, and hire a 'disabled' person in a disability job role, but I am yet to actually see it for myself in other areas of life. (Excluding my job as a freelance graphic designer in the motorsport industry, of course).

This is why it is a great thing that *Wrexham AFC* have become somewhat of a leader, (and may I say, a pioneer), in this case. By hiring Kerry Evans as the *DLO*, *Wrexham AFC* are really the front-runners in providing disability equality for all.

On the *Quiet Walkabout* I attended, Kerry went into great detail as to what the Club offers, of which I personally applaud. Believe me, when I say that the Club, with Kerry in charge have exceeded my expectations and have gone above and beyond to make sure that they meet the needs of all disabilities. For more information on the specifics, you will have to contact Kerry Evans directly or view the *Wrexham AFC* website itself. It is truly incredible though, just the level of detail that the Club offers.

What Still Needs to be Done

Hats off to both Kerry and the Club for making disability equality a thing within football. We shouldn't have to congratulate somewhere that is just doing what should already be in place however, regardless of how ground-breaking the facilities are, but it does give me hope that other venues will look to *Wrexham AFC* for inspiration for how to better equip their venues. Kerry has said that she always welcomes feedback and suggestions on how to improve the accessibility of the Club. The Club is constantly improving to accommodate more disabilities as time goes on. You can say how awe-inspiring the Club is by continually progressing with accessibility, but in all honesty, it shouldn't be awe-inspiring. It shouldn't be awe-inspiring because simply again, this is the standard that all public venues and places should be striving for. *Wrexham AFC* are really just the leaders that everyone should follow. Simple as that.

Kerry has said that *Wrexham AFC* are the only football club who provides walkabouts to potential new 'disabled' members as of writing this, which just backs up my argument that

What Still Needs to be Done

Wrexham AFC are really the front-runners in providing disability equality within football.

The Club has done so much for disability equality in football that their autism-friendly award was renewed in May twenty-twenty-three, to recognise the fantastic work that *Wrexham AFC* are undertaking.

"Wrexham AFC are proud to have received an Autism Friendly Award from the National Autistic Society, recognising our continued work to support and include autistic people and their families." – [COMMUNITY | Wrexham AFC receive Autism Friendly Award from National Autistic Society – By Colin Henrys]

This just goes to show how serious the Club is to provide adequate resources to 'disabled' fans. The award just cements how important it is to *Wrexham AFC* to accommodate all fans, regardless of ability. This **should always** be the case for **all** public venues and places in general. I am aware that I sound like a broken record by constantly reiterating that other places and venues should follow suit, but it really **is** important. The more you say something, the higher the chances of getting the results you want an deserve.

"The Football Club are delighted to have recently renewed our Autism Friendly award with the National Autistic Society. We first gained our award in 2018 and were very proud to be the first Club in Wales to obtain such an award, and the first business in Wrexham. We are fully committed to continuing our partnership with the National Autistic Society to offer the very best match-day experience for fans attending Wrexham AFC." – [Kerry Evans, Disability Liaison Officer at Wrexham AFC Interview, COMMUNITY | Wrexham AFC receive Autism Friendly Award from National Autistic Society – By Colin Henrys]

I **cannot** stress this enough, it is absolutely wonderful to know that *Wrexham AFC* are committed to keeping the resources needed for disability. It does help to have a 'disabled' person in the driving seat making accessibility possible. I really don't like to put unnecessary emphasis on the disability subject, as society is so negatively obsessed with the topic, but if this doesn't go to prove the need for 'disabled' people working within disability related jobs, I really don't know what is. Kerry Evans being the *DLO* of *Wrexham AFC* is the perfect scenario for disability equality.

Being a *DLO* however, doesn't mean that Kerry knows everything about all disabilities, this is why it is so refreshing to know that Kerry encourages suggestions on how to improve the accessibility of the Club. The Club is always willing and ready to improve, which is absolutely fantastic! More often than not, venues and places just do the bear minimum to say that they have 'disabled' access, when really, all that these places have done is installed a couple of ramps, and to my mind, have just placed a disability sticker on a public toilet just to keep up with modern practices. Modern practices though, really do not have a clue on how to provide proper accessibility for 'disabled' people. It's really just a 'tick box' exercise in my own opinion.

Ramps? *Tick

Grab rails? *Tick

Lack of space? *Tick

What Still Needs to be Done

Inadequate support? *Tick

You only have to go back to the quotes from *Changing Places UK* the absolute shocking statistics in regards to how many of these types of facilities are installed in public places and venues for example, and this unfortunately is just the tip of the iceberg.

At least with *Wrexham AFC* actually employing Kerry Evans as the *DLO* and not just keeping her as voluntary, it sends an important message that 'disabled' people are worth the money in many ways. Kerry has done so much for the Club. I personally think without her input, *Wrexham AFC* wouldn't really be in the position they find themselves in today, accessibility wise. I am sure that the Club are grateful to Kerry for all she has brought, and continues to bring to the venue.

"The Football Club became the first in Wales – and indeed the first business in Wrexham – to receive the award, when we were first recognised in 2018. The award has now been renewed, with the latest acknowledgement focusing on key areas including how to provide customer services, information and

environments, which are accessible and inclusive for autistic people." – [COMMUNITY | Wrexham AFC receive Autism Friendly Award from National Autistic Society – By Colin Henrys]

As I've said, *Wrexham AFC* is the standard that all other venues and places should look to, to improve accessibility at least across the UK, if not the world. Their success with access is all because of a person with a disability. I know that I keep saying this, but I feel that it's extremely important to drum it into you that Kerry alone is proof that a person with a disability **can** be successful and do amazing things for their employers, quashing the myth outright that 'disabled' people don't have a place in the world of employment.

I wanted to actually find out if other venues and places have at least the same level of access as *Wrexham AFC* has. I contacted a number of different football clubs across the UK, and I'm pleased to say that *Liverpool FC* has granted me permission to quote what is on their website, of which I'm truly grateful.

What Still Needs to be Done

"We recognise that disabled supporters may need assistance to fully enjoy the experience at Anfield Stadium and offer a variety of reasonable adjustments based on individual needs, not their disability. This guide has been designed to ensure that you have all the information you need to help you plan your journey to Anfield." – [Liverpool FC Accessibility Guide]

From what I've read from their website, this is true, the Club, (like *Wrexham AFC*) do provide a lot of accessible features within their Club.

"There are 7 accessible entrances into Anfield Stadium" – [Liverpoolfc.com, 'Stadium Facilities and Access']

There is a table on the *Liverpool FC* website full of the number of wheelchair spaces within the stadium, alongside the number of elevated platforms of which I will briefly add below. All of the information is directly from *Liverpool FC's* website.

Number of Wheelchair Spaces

What Still Needs to be Done

- One hundred and eleven wheelchair spaces in the Main Stand, with a mixture of pitch side and elevated viewing platforms

- Forty wheelchair spaces in the Sir Kenny Dalglish Stand, with elevated viewing platforms

- Fifty two wheelchair spaces in the KOP Stand, with pitch side viewing

- Thirty six wheelchair spaces in the Anfield Road Stand, with pitch side viewing

- Up to twenty four wheelchair spaces in the Away Supporters Stand, with pitch side viewing

This is fantastic to know that *Liverpool FC* is extremely accommodating towards supporters in wheelchairs. It just goes to show how important it is to the Club to accommodate as many supporters in wheelchairs as possible. This is all we want. Inclusion, and both *Wrexham AFC* and *Liverpool FC* are providing this in spades between them.

What Still Needs to be Done

Other things that *Liverpool FC* provide are hospitality in both the Main Stand and the Kenny Dalglish Stand, their museum tours are fully accessible. Audio Loops, Induction Loops, and a Sensory Room. The Club also has low counter facilities, Seat Serve or waiter service, (whichever the supporter prefers). Match day programmes are also available in a different format if required. The Club also provides large print menus for those who require them.

"These menus are printed in black size 16 font and are presented on a yellow background. Just ask a member of the catering team at the kiosk or in the hospitality lounge for a copy on the day of the game." – [Liverpoolfc.com, 'Stadium Facilities and Access']

There are also **two** *Changing Places UK Toilets*, **not one, but two** within the stadium, which when I found this out, I actually smiled. As I've said, the inclusion of these facilities in particular are monumentally important for disability equality. Having places such as football clubs does give me a sense of hope that other venues will follow suit, (including *Wrexham AFC*).

What Still Needs to be Done

Going back, *Wrexham AFC* have recently installed Stoma Friendly accessible facilities.

"A stoma is an opening on the surface of the abdomen which has been surgically created to divert the flow of faeces or urine. People who have had stoma surgery are sometimes known as 'ostomates'. – [ColostomyUK.org]

Again, installing facilities specifically for supporters with stomas within *Wrexham AFC* is just another step forward for disability equality and inclusion.

"For people living with a stoma, a lack of suitable toilet facilities can be a huge barrier to doing many of the things most of us take for granted, like attending a football match, so we hope this announcement will encourage ostomates in Wrexham, North Wales, and beyond to attend a game at the STōK Cae Ras." – *[Giovanni Cinque, Marketing & Campaigns Manager at Colostomy UK, Wrexham AFC, 'COMMUNITY | STōK Cae Ras now Stoma Friendly']*

What Still Needs to be Done

It's great to know that *Wrexham AFC* have taken the initiative and installed the first ever Stoma Friendly accessible facility within their Club. It's a real honour to know that I live somewhere where the local football club are breaking down barriers for disability.

"This is a very important initiative which is very close to my own heart, as I also have stomas and therefore a good understanding of how this will help fans with hidden disabilities. It's yet another important initiative for us, as we continue to push inclusivity at the Club." – [Kerry Evans, Disability Liaison Officer at Wrexham AFC, 'COMMUNITY | STōK Cae Ras now Stoma Friendly']

Hidden disabilities, such as stomas, tend not to get the same respect as physical disabilities. It's all down to the visual. Like I've said, as long as the 'props' are there, it's easier to identify and differentiate between an able-bodied person and a 'disabled' person. Hidden disabilities are just treated like a thing of controversy. You almost aren't 'worthy enough' to be given that demeaning label of disability. Like it's a 'right of passage' and an 'honour' to have this label thrust upon you.

I just hope that other Clubs and venues follow the examples of both *Wrexham AFC* and *Liverpool FC*, and make **proper accessibility** a thing. If *Wrexham AFC* now provide Stoma Friendly accessible facilities and *Liverpool FC* provide *Changing Places UK Toilets*, what's stopping *Wrexham AFC* installing a *Changing Places UK Toilet*, and *Liverpool FC* installing a Stoma Friendly facility in the future? If these football clubs can install such facilities, then surely there's absolutely no reason whatsoever other public venues can install facilities of this nature. It's important for disability equality and inclusion. I understand that funding and planning are involved with installing such facilities, but it **is** possible. Never say never.

Accessible Accommodation

Recently, (as of writing this), I took a short weekend break away to Stratford-upon-Avon to see the sights and to finish this book. My parents and myself stayed in a lovely accommodation in

What Still Needs to be Done

Coughton, Warwickshire called *Windmill Barns Holiday Lets*.

Admittedly, I have stayed in 'accessible accommodation' before whilst on holiday/trips, but **never** to this outstanding standard before. Really this accommodation shouldn't be described as 'outstanding' as all accessible accommodation **should** have facilities worthy of that title in the first place. It's a no brained. Sadly though, 'accessible accommodation' isn't to this level of detail.

This accommodation is second to none in regards to outstanding 'disabled' facilities including:

- A through-floor *Wessex* Lift

- Open-plan

- Hoists

What Still Needs to be Done

- Equipment, i.e. shower chairs

- Profile beds

- Wet rooms

- No steps on entrance or exit to accommodation

- Hot tub

- Low kitchen facilities

- Option for physiotherapy equipment

The owners of the accommodation have a 'disabled' daughter themselves, so know full well what maybe required. Yes, every disability is different, but everything listed above is just the standard that all accommodations should aspire to. All accommodations should have 'disabled' friendly facilities, maybe not everything listed, but at least some.

What Still Needs to be Done

"Our wheelchair-friendly cottages offer superb facilities for disabled visitors and their families, and provide the perfect rental accommodation for accessible holiday makers looking to access the Cotswolds and the Warwickshire countryside. Superb disabled access & facilities - accessible hot tubs - 2 and 3 bed options, sleeping up to 6 persons per cottage. Wheelchair lifts, tracked hoists, profiling beds and wet room bathing are available in all our cottages." – [Windmill Barns Holiday Lets]

Windmill Barns Holiday Lets cover all of the bases when it comes to accessible accommodation. When I stayed at the accommodation, it was home from home. Usually when I go on holiday, mum and dad always have to pack the 'essentials'.

When I say 'essentials', what I actually mean is the things that others don't take into consideration. The things that allow me to love as 'normally' and independently as possible. This is what **all** 'disabled' people deserve, the chance to get away from time to time, knowing that their every need is catered for without any hassle.

This is what I mean when I say that society should ask people with disabilities how to properly design accessible facilities. *Windmill Barns Holiday Lets* know the basics of what is needed to properly advertise themselves as being accessible. They even put 'extras' in the accommodations to make them a bit more special and luxurious with hot tubs. Just because you may have a disability of some form, doesn't mean you don't deserve a  bit of luxury when you go away. I'm not saying that the extras are essential, they just give a lovely added touch. Really all accommodations that claim to be fully accessible, should provide hoists, open-plan wet rooms, and open plan accommodation as standard. Just claiming that your accommodation is fully accessible, doesn't make it so.

What Still Needs to be Done

Not a Fully Accessible Life

Saying all that, there is a real, important reason as to why I'm writing in the first place. I'm trying to change perceptions on disability, of which I personally feel has been making great strides in the right direction of late, but there's still so much more that can be done to improve attitudes. Case in point, (as of writing), my recent trip to Llandudno.

I visited Llandudno on this particular day, and decided to go take a look at the Tram Stop for the future.

My mum went and asked if there was space to accommodate a wheelchair on one of the trams, and the staff member said basically that they take wheelchairs, but I would have to move out of my wheelchair, walk onto the tram, and sit on the seat. Obviously I can't walk on my own. They did offer assistance, but I suspected they wouldn't have had adequate training in assisting a 'disabled' person.

To top it off, a passer by also asked on my behalf, and the staff member said, and I quote:

"I've already answered this question. There's no room to keep a person in a wheelchair, as there's too many seats on the Tram. We can't have a motorised wheelchair on board for health and safety. For any disabled person to access the Tram, they need to take a few steps to get to the Tram and we fold a manual wheelchair and put it at the back of the Tram for the journey."

Mum said that I wasn't in my powered wheelchair, which was true, I was in my manual chair, as it's much easier to manage around somewhere like Llandudno for me personally. The staff's solution to this was absolutely shocking to say the least!

What was their solution? Order a taxi, it's cheaper!

This is laughable! I have a *Motability* car, so if I wanted, dad could drive that journey, but really, I wanted the experience!

The staff member said so blatantly otherwise that I would have to get out of my chair and walk onto the Tram.

I understand health and safety, what I take issue with is the staff member's dismissive attitude to

What Still Needs to be Done

Llandudno Tramway

the question, as if I was just a 'thing', I'm not a 'thing', I'm a woman in my early 30's who has a form of Cerebral Palsy. Disability shouldn't be treated like this ever.

There was a wheelchair access sign (pictured right) with an arrow directing you up this hill, and turn left to the Tram. Two issues with this:

We would've had to endure a steep hill only to be met with a dismissive attitude.

Realistically, the sign **should** say *'Some mobility required, no wheelchair access to the Tram.'* The sign is extremely misleading and needs redesigning. Furthermore the attitude of the Tram Stop needs altering.

This attitude just encourages the struggle for equality and inclusion that disability fights for everyday.

This is the real reason for these books, to try to highlight the issues that go under the radar in the hopes that society will eventually see the error of their ways, and try to change perceptions before those perceptions negatively overtake all of the efforts the 'disabled' people fight for day in, day out. There's a real fear on my part that if we don't try to do something about this negative attitude, society will just become worse and worse, until disability is totally beaten down into submission, and we sadly accept what is written about us. If this negativity continues, we, as a society, a collective, stands to envelope real fear towards disability, feeding the negativity until it's overconsuming. It's absolutely terrifying. We shouldn't have to accept negativity **ever**. Society isn't a Utopia, it can't be, if we still have experiences like this. It is unfair that disability is

What Still Needs to be Done

treated as an everyday inconvenience and afterthought.

Disability is part of being human. We aren't objects. We're human, just like everyone else. Dome may need a little more assistance than others, but to deny equality and inclusion solely based on that assistance, is just pure evil and unjust.

Another experience I had was at Llangollen Railway, (a couple of months back as of writing), I was with Judi, mum, and mum's friend June, and we decided to go to Llangollen and go on a steam train, again for the experience. If you read *CP Isn't Me*, you will know what I experienced when I boarded the steam train as a child, we were put in the luggage compartment. That isn't the best, but I can understand why to a degree.

Those steam trains in Llangollen are years old, dating as far back as the mid nineteen hundreds, so of course disability wasn't taken into consideration, as disability was catastrophically treated as being something of which was debilitating. The realisation of the treatment of disability during the nineteen-thirties **did start** to get better, but that isn't really saying much, considering how disability was treated before the nineteen-thirties. This change in attitude towards disability was in it's infancy during this period admittedly. Word of this change wasn't going to reach far and wide overnight, and this is my logic for the Inaccessibility on these steam trains in the nineteen-thirties, but I digress. I just wanted to give you a potential reason as to why these steam trains weren't accessible during this time.

The steam trains weren't built with disabilities in mind back then, and Llangollen Railway almost prides itself on the steam trains being original. They blatantly advertise it really, it's their gimmick in a way. I fully understand that the Railway wants to preserve a little bit of history, especially today with society being so technology obsessed. Surprisingly though, the lack of accessibility on these steam trains, although abhorrent, isn't the main issue I have. It was what happened at the destination which I take issue with.

When we boarded the steam train, mum and June went in the carriage, but because I'm in a wheelchair, and the steam trains are old, I sat, with

What Still Needs to be Done

Judi in the luggage compartment. Not ideal granted, but it is what it is, those trains in particular cannot be redesigned. It was when we arrived at our destination, I wasn't so forgiving. Bear in mind that we only had **forty minutes** at the destination before we had to head back to Llangollen on the train. When we made our way onto the platform , we headed for the lift and the stairs, only to be greeted with the conductor saying that the lift was broken. **The only lift that exited that station**. I'm not going to say how much it cost us to board the steam train, but what I will say is that it was expensive. Too expensive for the experience and treatment we received.

When you have a disability, you rely on things, and expect those things to work when needed. I understand that technology isn't fool-proof, that there will be mechanical faults and breakdowns from time to time, that's fine, but that conductor said that the lift had broken the day before. If I worked at that railway, or anywhere with 'disabled' facilities for that matter, I would absolutely make sure that equipment to aid disability was repaired ASAP. Of course, I have a disability, so of course I would make sure all accessibility was fully working,

What Still Needs to be Done

I'm not oblivious to that. What I just cannot understand is the lack of common sense. I suppose if it doesn't affect the person directly, then of course, important issues like equality and accessibility sadly **is** going to remain on the back-burner. The selfishness of society really does shine through when things like this happen.

I was offered to be carried down the steps. If you know me, you'll know that I hate causing a scene, and that admittedly is all to do with how society perceives disability. Usually, if a member of the public sees a 'disabled' person receiving help, (especially help which maybe considered out of the ordinary), this will only further segregate disability as the public will see the 'vulnerabilities', only confirming what is falsely taught.

After declining that offer of being carried down the steps, we were then offered a free drink for our trouble. It just isn't good enough. To pay an extortionate amount of money to board the steam train, to be met with a free drink? It's just absolutely unacceptable to say the least. Being offered to be carried down the steps by two people who I would imagine hasn't had any

What Still Needs to be Done

training in that, is a health and safety risk if you take away the ridiculousness of the offer. We had to sit on the platform for forty minutes whilst others went and explored. Our original plan was to go and get refreshments whilst we were there in a little café and admire our surroundings, as it would've been a different experience, instead, we sat on the platform for those forty minutes waiting to board the train again. I must say that there was a member of staff who was very apologetic, and they said that they'd raised the lift breakdown issue the day before, but that issue was dismissed. I guess nobody anticipated a 'disabled' person wanting to use it. It's disgusting. The amount of annoyance I felt that day was immeasurable. I know I have a disability, and so do others who see me whilst I'm out in public, don't enhance the fact by taking away our independence, it's cruel and uncalled for. It was humiliating to say the least, others were looking at that situation, and I bet they never saw a woman in her early thirties who has a degree and what is to be considered successful in employment. No, I can imagine they just saw a 'disabled' person that day, struggling with discrimination. How is that fair?

What Still Needs to be Done

Let disability have the same level of opportunities as everyone else in society, Beit employment, or social. At the end of the day, that's all we ask and deserve. It's simple, but it really sounds impossible if experiences such as Llandudno Tram Stop and Llangollen Railway is anything to go by.

UK Government Input – 'Disability Action Plan'

Since writing, I recently found out that the current UK Government is putting together a 'Disability Action Plan', headed by the current UK Parliament *Minister for Disabled People, Health and Work*, Tom Pursglove MP.

"Here in Wales, I truly believe positive actions are happening. Although the Welsh Government has limits to its powers, it is determined to make progress and tackle the systematic issues. In July 2021, the Welsh Government launched the Disability Rights Taskforce, which aims to remove the inequalities experienced by disabled people in society, beyond the COVID-19 pandemic. By working collaboratively with individuals, disabled people's organisations and other relevant bodies, the Taskforce is studying a

wide range of priority issues facing disabled people, such as COVID recovery, health and social services, facilitating independent living, education, housing, employment and transport. The Taskforce's work will lead to a co-produced, cross-governmental 'Disability Rights Action Plan', which will start being drafted in early 2024. Promoting and embedding the Social Model of Disability, in both Welsh Government and public bodies across Wales, is also a firm commitment of the current Welsh Government. Real transformation can only begin when those who make decisions and develop policy understand their role in removing the barriers that restrict people." – [Lesley Griffiths, Member of the Senedd for Wrexham]

The plan was for 'disabled' people, alongside disability organisations to speak out on what could be improved for 'disabled' people to live as independently as possible. Unfortunately I found out about this plan on the fourteenth of October twenty-twenty-three, a full eight days late from when it closed for contributions on sixth October twenty-twenty-three. It definitely wasn't well advertised, I didn't see this until I viewed one of my social media platforms. I wonder if this was a feature on the news? If it was, it **definitely** needed more coverage. How are things going to improve if you don't advertise your campaign well?

If I'd have known of such a plan, I **definitely** would've had my say, as so much still needs to be done. It's stated on the Government website that they will consider all points in Autumn of twenty-twenty-three and write up a report on what they are going to do, once they've read through everything.

It's Autumn of twenty-twenty-three now as of writing, so I wonder what improvements will be made if any? Costings always have to be carefully considered before any 'action' can take place. I wonder if Government will acknowledge what is said, and actually do the things that 'disabled' people and disability organisations are asking for? I hope this isn't just another popularity ploy or gimmick to get the public on side. I hope there's some weight to this initiative. Like I said, actions speak louder than words. Government cannot just play the disability card when it suits them. Disability is real, therefore, so should any attempt

What Still Needs to be Done

of improvement. Disability isn't a 'buzz word', disability is real, people with disabilities are real. We need to be taken seriously and have promises made to us kept. It does seem as if Government does forget about disability until it suits. This needs to stop. We aren't just a demographic, we are also part of a democracy. It's about time Government realises this and helps to integrate us into society, not treat us like a statistic that's easily forgotten. This is why I hope that Government actually does something when they've read through all of the responses. Improvements desperately need to be made.

I will keep an eye on how this 'Disability Action Plan' progresses and probably give my opinion in the next book.

It'll be very interesting to see what happens.

Chapter 9
Disability vs Employability

Somehow, the subject of employment becomes somewhat of a taboo in many ways, when it is coupled with disability. In my last book, I said that the research suggested that the reason why employers tend to favour able-bodied people rather than a 'disabled' person when it comes to employment, is simply because, they may think for whatever reason, 'disabled' employees may leave employment due to health issues, or may need time off for appointments etc.

Appointments maybe a factor, but realistically, everybody has appointments at some point in their lives, regardless of ability. It's true, appointments aren't anything new, so why does disability always have to take the brunt? Other employees who are able-bodied are allowed to take scheduled time off for appointments. Why should disability be treated any differently?

Disability vs Employability

Well, I do have a theory, and this is my personal take on it, it may not be true, but it is a very good observation, if I do say so myself.

Basically, I personally believe it's that disability label.

The Problem With The Disability Label

You may have noticed so far that whenever I said the word 'disabled', I added quotation marks. That **wasn't, and isn't** a mistake. The word should be abolished in my own opinion. It's too negative, and puts an unfounded emphasis on something that has absolutely no bearing whatsoever on a **person**. The word 'disabled' and even 'disability' seems to always bear the brunt of how society perceives and treats difference. It's the pinnacle for allowing others to be inappropriate. Inappropriate in the way of how a human being treats another human being. Somehow people's behaviour around disability, (I sometimes feel) gives an able-bodied person somewhat of a superiority complex. As if to say, *"I'm better than you, because I don't have anything to stop me, unlike you."* That's how it sometimes feels to me anyway. Don't get me wrong, there are those who treat everyone exactly the same, of which I'm thankful for, and grateful to in equal measure, but unfortunately, these people are few and far between still to this day. Also, it is sad that I'm thankful and grateful for being treated as an equal. To me, it definitely does seem that we are in a bygone era with this ridiculous attitude.

I despair.

We are often seen as 'vulnerable' and 'naive' to society, just like puppies or kittens almost. It's like as if we can't do things for ourselves or even set boundaries for people to adhere to. We are 'disabled' people, so we shouldn't have any say or rights, people can do what they want because they feel as if they're 'helping' by always intruding. The trouble is, that that 'help' that people in society is so quick to thrust upon us, isn't always necessary. Sometimes it is, (when we ask), but not always. It seems that any moral compass or logic goes straight out of the window. Hasn't it ever occurred to you that if we look capable, more than likely we are? Just 'helping' to look as though you're the 'good Samaritan' isn't helping anyone, least of all a 'disabled' person. It's an ego thing, a

Disability vs Employability

superiority complex that the whole world isn't immune to. Really, it's to give the person a sense of achievement and pride to think that they actually 'helped' someone in need. Unless we ask for help, don't offer. By just doing something for someone without asking automatically takes away a person's independence and sense of self worth. With how the world is today with the rise of social media etc., we often like to have our fifteen minutes of fame, and what's the best way to be noticed? Offering help to those who you may deem worthy enough to receive help. It's offensive. Like I said, 'disabled' people can't say these things usually, otherwise if we do, we are often patronised for doing so. We can't set boundaries for ourselves because we are then seen as 'a trooper' for 'wanting to try and be independent'. This ridiculous mentality of always wanting to be a hero in society, needs to stop now, as it's damaging humanity, plain and simple.

I said last time that I definitely don't have a problem with having a disability. It's just the way it is. I'm not angry, bitter or sad, I can't afford to be. There's no point anyway. Feeling sorry for myself isn't going to change anything. I mean, when I was younger, I used to say to mum occasionally that *"I wish I could walk"*, I think it was seeing others my age, running around, having fun, and I wanted a bit of that. Those feelings would pass though, and I'd go back to my reality again. A reality of fun, laughter and adventure with my family and friends. I mean, those feelings never really bothered me, just occasionally, my mind would go to 'that place'. I'd always snap out of it though. It was as I grew, more and more issues seemed to materialise, (especially with society and my own mental health struggles as a direct result of the constant discrimination). I lost a job, because I was a 'disabled' woman, and I was totally disrespected at another, as previously described earlier. This is what I'm saying. Disability is treated differently in every corner, (whether you want to believe it or not), discrimination of disability regrettably does still happen, and never is it more of an issue today than in the employment sector.

This is why I despise that label. It always puts us at an automatic disadvantage. It really doesn't matter what we achieve or how we see ourselves,

Disability vs Employability

that label says that we can't. We really don't have a say. The label speaks for us it seems.

The Disadvantage of the *Disability Equality Act of 2010*

Recently, (as of writing this chapter), I was kindly invited to *1st Enable Ltd.* Summer Ball to promote *CP Isn't Me*. Whilst I was there, I had a very insightful chat with Jeff Dawson, where he spoke to me about something which I never took into consideration. He said, (in his own personal opinion), that the *Disability Equality Act of 2010* itself, could be a reason as to why employers tend to favour able-bodied people when hiring.

It is abhorrent, but I can well believe Jeff's theory here. The *Disability Equality Act of 2010* is designed to basically give 'disabled' people a level of protection in a way, against disability discrimination, but because of the amount of regulations and legislation within the Act, it could put potential employers off from employing a 'disabled' person. I hate to say it, but able-bodied people don't really have any added laws, other then the usual *Health and Safety at Work Act of 1974*. A potential 'disabled' employee has the added *Disability Equality Act of 2010* in the mix. So to save any potential issues arising from hiring a 'disabled' person, hiring an able-bodied person, maybe the best choice for the employer. The easier choice. The better option. The *Health and Safety at Work Act of 1974* obviously has been in circulation longer than the *Disability Equality Act of 2010*, so employers have had more time to adjust and comply to the Health and Safety Act without any real issue I suppose, whereas, the *Disability Equality Act of 2010*, is relatively new in comparison, but this **does not** justify or give any excuse for the blatant disability discrimination. It is now twenty twenty-twenty-three, as of writing this, so by rule, **all** employers should be made to improve their work environments and strategies to meet the needs of 'disabled' employees. Yet, because of either an unwillingness to learn, or total ignorance, potential 'disabled' employees get hit the hardest.

It's ironic that something that is designed to protect disability, in fact, could potentially be doing more harm than good. Without it though, disability is just left without any safety net. Without it, society would be able to just do what

Disability vs Employability

they want, without taking into consideration the risks their actions could potentially cause to 'disabled' people. Jeff also mentioned that hiring able-bodied people are **also** quite risky, as able-bodied people obviously also have risks when hiring. The difference is, those risks to able-bodied people are insignificant compared to risks with 'disabled' people. The disability label strikes again! Risks are risks, regardless of which demographic you talk about. Yet, disability is almost always treated much more provenance? It's devastating to say the least.

All we want is a little bit of equality and the same opportunities as everyone else. Yes, going back to Aideen Blackborough's comment:

"...I believe disabled people should be protected from discrimination; however I don't think you should just be given opportunities because of your disability...If someone else is a better fit for an opportunity, they should get it...?" – [Aideen Blackborough, Disability Trainer, Speaker and Author]

This is a very insightful comment, and it is true, just because you maybe a 'disabled' person, it doesn't mean that a job that a 'disabled' person is under qualified for, should be offered just because of a disability. That behaviour just harbours further misrepresentation. Feeling sorry for a 'disabled' person **isn't** what we want or deserve. We aren't prepared to accept that. True equality means being honest and having integrity. Disability shouldn't be an excuse for others to feel better by giving us opportunities that aren't suited to us. It just gives another way to patronise.

However, our disabilities don't define us, and if we do have the knowledge and qualifications needed for a certain job, there's absolutely no reason whatsoever why we cannot be considered for employment. It's just a case of knowing the difference and being honest with the 'disabled' person as to why they haven't been considered for the job. Not because of the disability, but the actual qualification and experience side of the job. If a 'disabled' person is in fact qualified for a job they've applied for, there's absolutely no reason whatsoever why employers won't consider the person. Yes, the *Disability Equality Act of 2010* maybe a factor, but this should **never** be a reason for inadequate equality.

Disability vs Employability

National Disability Employment Awareness Month – America

I have just found out that the month of October is National Disability Employment Awareness Month in America. This definitely needs to be brought to global attention.

Too many disabled people living in the UK miss out on employment opportunities due to the fact that they're disabled. I know I have. I've experienced this first-hand unfortunately, and that, (coupled with the personal injury matters in my life) destroyed me as a person, my confidence, my self-belief and my happiness. Life shouldn't make you feel worthless. Opportunities should be given no matter how you look.

No-one is good at everything, but everyone is good at something.

If you have a disability of some form, but are capable and willing, then you should be given the same equal opportunity to showcase your skills. That's the bottom line.

Disability vs Employability

I urge *UK Government* and *The Senedd* alike to consider introducing this as a possible national day of awareness.

Not hiring a person just because they may have a disability of some form isn't a good reason. All people have potential regardless of ability. Disability should never become a barrier in any respect including access to work.

The Cost of Mental Health Deterioration

There is a problem with the rise of mental health issues as it is. Denying employment to individuals with disabilities is just adding to the issue unnecessarily. If this ignorance continues with employment and disability, it wouldn't be too farfetched to say that society would end up worse off, with rising unemployment and mental health issues. Government needs to start looking into welcoming Disability Employment Awareness Month as an annual event . By doing this, maybe employers won't be as reluctant when viewing potential 'disabled' candidates. It's time to think about the economy, and hiring potential 'disabled' people who have the correct skillset, attitude and willingness to work hard, can only be a good thing for everyone.

Disability and Employment – A Match Made in Heaven

Hayley Murphy, secretary of *MDM Designs Ltd.*, gave a very clear answer to the question if, as a company, do they support equal opportunities for everyone regardless of ability?

"Yes. Every disabled person has loads to offer, they are clever, smart and knowledgeable, and are an asset to any company, just need to be given the chance." – [Hayley Murphy, email participant]

This is all we want and deserve, a chance to showcase our capabilities. *MDM Designs* gave me a chance to showcase my capabilities when nobody else would. Hiring me to work as a freelance graphic designer in their company since two-thousand and seventeen. I just wish all companies would realise the importance and benefits of hiring 'disabled' people, rather than just always focusing on and finding ridiculous excuses for avoiding the subject. Disability isn't controversial, it's the public who make disability controversial. I'm sure companies just create more obstacles in order to avoid hiring 'disabled' people. The public makes the very simple subject awkward and out of place, not disability itself. Also, of course, this can go to the other extreme, as always where companies advertise themselves as being 'disability positive', and use this as a label, a gimmick to show off and have a positive reputation in society. In reality however, more often than not, this is just a pretence. Said companies who promote this type of thing, often really don't care about the individual in question. I can say this because I know. I've had this experience many times unfortunately. Namely, my first and my second graphic design job after leaving university and graduating, which I detail in my first book. This sadly is the way of the world. 'Disabled' people need to be wary of this. Society can either take advantage, or ignore the person entirely. There isn't a middle ground. Society can promise the world, creating a fantasy world to entice the person, for free advertising, free publicity, which of course, companies such as this

Disability vs Employability

have absolutely no intention of delivering. This is a major red flag.

I also asked Hayley:

"What would you say to other companies who don't support equal opportunities for everyone regardless of ability?"

"Treat a disabled person the same as an able person, just because they may have a disability it doesn't mean the can't do the job, that's discrimination." – [Hayley Murphy, email participant]

Employers need to realise this. My previous research for *CP Isn't Me* actually said that there are many misconceptions relating to disability employment including, taking frequent time off for appointments or illness. In reality, 'disabled' people actually are the most hard working as they feel they need to prove themselves. Of course, they don't. Nobody should have to prove themselves with anything, let alone employment. Allowing any human to prove their capabilities is inhumane and quite frankly, disturbing.

Fully Accessible Employment

All workplaces **should** be **fully accessible** as standard. It should **never** be an issue. This shouldn't have to be said, it is the twenty-first century after all. As I keep saying we like to claim that we live in this modern, inclusive world, but when you delve a bit deeper, it's clear that we're not. Not even close. To be modern and inclusive, we must look at all areas of life and adapt to accommodate those areas. It feels, to me at least, that it's always the other way around. Disability has to always adapt to society. We always have to be what society tells us to be.

Finding employment if you have a disability, shouldn't be a barrier, yet another unnecessary obstacle. Employability should be available to all. Yet, I do somewhat understand why employers may opt for the 'easier option'. I may not agree with it, but I can possibly understand it. As I'm not aware of the full Act, (I just know the basics), I researched the UK Government website for some clarification on the actual law on employment.

"The Equality Act 2010 protects you and covers areas including:

Disability vs Employability

Application forms, interview arrangements aptitude or proficiency tests, job offers, terms of employment, including pay, promotion, transfer and training opportunities, dismissal or redundancy, discipline and grievances." – ['Disability Rights: Employment', GOV.UK]

Gov.UK also goes on to say about possible adjustments to a working environment to accommodate disability, recruitment information, and redundancy and retirement information.

"An employer has to make 'reasonable adjustments' to avoid you being put at a disadvantage compared to non-disabled people in the workplace. For example, adjusting your working hours or providing you with a special piece of equipment to help you do the job." – ['Disability Rights: Employment', GOV.UK]

It's true, an employer has to make reasonable adjustments based on a 'disabled' employees needs, but nowhere does it say what those reasonable adjustments are. It literally has this one sentence on the subject of adjustments. Maybe, if some of the potential adjustments were actually listed on the UK Government website, then

maybe the anxiety of disability for employers may not seem as bad? I don't know, I'm just surmising. Realistically, it could go entirely in the opposite direction and put even more pressure on employers, but we won't know unless we try.

I get that every 'disabled' person has a number of different needs, depending on their form of disability, and the UK Government website cannot list all adjustments, **but**, they can **at least** list the basics. I've decided to take it upon myself to list the accessibility that should be in place in workplaces across the world by standard, but really, this is the job of Government. I **shouldn't** have to explain, as these things are a necessity in today's 'modern' times, and **should be** put in place by rule.

- Accessible facilities (preferably *Changing Places UK Toilets* and *Stoma Friendly* accessible facilities if possible), but really, just the basic accessibility facilities will suffice to begin with)

- Height adjustable desks

Disability vs Employability

- Disability friendly equipment (*Braille,* specialist computer equipment, etc.)

- Space to accommodate a wheelchair/ walking frame around the **whole** building

- A large number of **adequate** accessible parking spaces

- Widened doors

- Automatic doors

- Ramps

- Remote controlled blinds/lights

- Lifts

- Shelter by 'disabled' parking spaces

- **Adequate** evacuation procedures

This list maybe scary for employers to read, but this is the reality, the standard that we all deserve and expect when applying for a job. Depending on the disability, there maybe more adaptations needed. It is an overwhelming prospect for any employer admittedly. I understand that there is a wariness of hiring a 'disabled' person, with all of the regulations that employers would have to put in place properly, (not cut corners). In this regard, there's an argument for not hiring potential 'disabled' employees, but it is **definitely not** the ideal scenario for creating this 'modern, inclusive society' that we somehow like to promote.

"More employers need to recognise the benefits of using positive action to increase the number of female, disabled and ethnic minority apprentices in Britain and help address the barriers these groups face in wider employment, according to the national equality body." – ['Employers fear using positive action to close disability, ethnicity and gender pay gaps', Equality and Human Rights Commission

Understanding the benefits of hiring a 'disabled' person should be a no-brainer. Most employers have somewhat been brainwashed into believing the misconceptions of difference, especially when it comes to the subject of disability, with regards to illness or leaving employment, and countless other misconceptions which are so blatantly out there for everyone to see. Jeff Dawson's own theory does hold some weight to the potential

Disability vs Employability

ableist attitudes that employers have seemed to adopt.

Jeff's theory of there being too much litigation and 'red tape' involved with hiring potential 'disabled' employees, more than likely could be down to the cost. Adaptations aren't cheap by any stretch of the imagination, believe me, I know, so if a potential 'disabled' employee requests adaptations in order to make their working life easier to manage, so they can be more productive and efficient in their job role, this could give an employer means to not entertain the idea of hiring, or indeed, instead, actually firing that employee, (in an employer's mind), if there are a number of adaptations required. Of course the company finances need to be taken into account when reviewing such physical changes. Employers need to weigh up if the business will bankrupt itself if too much is done, (especially if the company is small, and the building is old). I do understand that, but I feel that employers cannot see the positives of making suitable and necessary changes to improve a working environment. I'm not saying adaptations need to be state of the art, not by any means, but an employer should do

everything in their power to make sure that their 'disabled' employee's needs are met to the standard of the *Disability Equality Act of 2010*. It's basic human rights, and this Act is really just an extension of the *Health and Safety at Work Act of 1974*, just adding suitable adaptations to make 'disabled' employees feel safe and equal. The *Disability Equality Act of 2010* is really just our version of the *Health and Safety at Work Act of 1974* if you really think about it.

Why shouldn't our needs be met? If we are qualified for the job we're applying for, we have as much right to employment as the next able-bodied, qualified person. Adaptations should **never** be a barrier, a reason for unemployment, of course, adaptations should be the opposite. Adaptations are there to help, not hinder at the end of the day.

Everything surrounding the words 'disabled' and 'disability' are treated as a frightening concept. Like I've said, it's that fear of inadvertently offending, or harming that gives disability a 'scary' reputation. The prefix of the terms are negative. People focus too much on the words, the prefixes,

Disability vs Employability

not the person. It is the media that feeds into it really, yes it has become better overtime, but that still isn't saying a great deal. It's like putting a sticking plaster over a gaping wound or a broken limb. Media is trying hard to reverse the damage they've caused over the years by painting disability as being this 'vulnerability' that everyone should take notice of, but it is too little, too late, in my own opinion anyway. Media's attempts to rectify disability really isn't doing much if employers are still reluctant to hire potential 'disabled' employees, from what is still out there on the Internet for example. There's still a barrier. On the Internet, looking at articles and research papers on disability, the ultimate take away is that we cannot do or achieve anything. The Internet just gives us this unfounded and unjustified reputation of being the weakest link, and because it's been ingrained in society for years and years, people believe it. Although speaking on a different subject entirely, Michael Jackson once said something that has stuck with me for years, especially being both a witness and the target of discrimination and ableism. I have said it above, but I will reiterate it as I feel this quote in particular is integral for getting my point across.

"It doesn't have to be true to be believed. Tell a lie often enough and people will believe it..."
– [Michael Jackson]

What is currently out there online about disability could just be considered lies, or at the **very least**, not the **full truth**. You shouldn't believe everything you read or hear, as more often than not it is just sensationalism.

Employers really should have more sense when it comes to disability. Employers aren't stupid, they should be able to know the difference between reality and fantasy. Employers should have the knowledge to differentiate between the truth and fiction. At least you would expect them to?

It is a terrifying prospect to learn that employers aren't immune to believing nonsensical stories, after all, what is currently out there could be considered stories where they are just **based** on true events, just like a film, which is absolutely heart-breaking. We **shouldn't** be treated like this

ever. Respect unfortunately doesn't exist when it comes to the subject of disability.

However, thanks to *Scope*, I have learned about something called *Access to Work Grants*.

"Access to Work grants can help pay for adjustments at work and for specialist assessments. These are Government grants but it's your responsibility to apply for them. You have a right to apply for this support. You can apply for Access to Work online or by phone. If you do not know what adjustments you need, an Access to Work assessment can help. This is not the same as an occupational health assessment." – [Scope]

This really just eliminates my cost theory when it comes to potential 'disabled' employees. It just puts more emphasis as to why the mistreatment of potential 'disabled' employees needs to end for good. With this grant, employers don't need to fear any costs, as this grant was specifically created to help with costs and accessibility in the workplace in general. In other words, there's support out there for employers to manage costs when it comes to disability accessibility. In my mind at least, there's absolutely no excuse for this disregard of human rights – (yes, disability rights **are** human rights). It's just wrong how many employers are willing to disregard a potential 'disabled' employee. There **is** support out there. Employers need to start realising this, and working with UK Government to modernise accessibility. Employers are only shooting themselves in the foot by not considering disability as a viable option when hiring.

"You do not need to get disability benefits to apply for Access to Work. Any benefits you get will not affect your application. If you get Universal Credit, Jobseeker's Allowance or Income Support and work for more than 1 hour a week, you are eligible for Access to Work." – [Scope]

It is quite confusing as to why employers tend not to hire a 'disabled' person, when there's support out there in the shape of grants that are put in place by UK Government specifically to help. The only thing that I can think of as to why employers shy away from hiring 'disabled' people is simply they're scared to. Yes, maybe on a practical level

Disability vs Employability

with regards to all the 'red tape' and litigations that come with disabilities, but maybe also on a personal level. Society has this strange relationship with disability. We are too 'vulnerable' to function as an active member of society, yet we are 'courageous' and 'strong'. We are 'inspirational'. It's counterintuitive. How can we be two opposite things at once? It's impossible.

The experience I had in one of my past jobs, (which I wrote in *CP Isn't Me*, confirms the personal fear theory. I understand that there maybe some initial concern when hiring a 'disabled' employee, as employers maybe worried about potential issues with either overworking or the litigation side of things, but once a 'disabled' person 'proves themselves' for said jobs, any doubts or fears should disappear. The reality of 'proving ourselves' is barbaric and definitely **not** in keeping with the 'modern times.' Of course, it could just be fear of disability as to why employers tend not to employ 'disabled' people. It's not right of course, but this could be a potential reason. I know for a fact that fear of disability tainted my own personal experiences with employability. With all of the political correctness today, it does seem out of place that fear could in fact be a driving factor, but here we are.

"Since 2013, the earliest comparable year, up to the start of the pandemic (March 2020) the general trend in disability employment has been positive. There has been strong growth in the number and rate of disabled people in employment and a narrowing of the gap between the rate of disabled and non-disabled people in employment (the disability employment gap)." – ['Official Statistics Employment of disabled people 2022', Published 26 January 2023, Gov.UK]

This is all well and good on the surface, but dig a little deeper, and I can **guarantee** you that not all 'disabled' people have experienced this positivity when it comes to employment. UK Government are really just highlighting the uncommon positives. This **definitely isn't the reality**. It maybe against the law to discriminate against disability, but it absolutely happens.

Disability vs Employability

"The UK's new disability minister has admitted the government "has scope to do better" when it comes to getting disabled people into work."

— ['Minister for Disabled People on employment: 'We can do better', By Keiligh Baker, 2 December 2022, BBC News]

This is **definitely** true. Employability for disability hasn't improved, or even come close to improvement. There's **definitely** still an issue, and for news outlets to report on the discrimination of disability in employment, just goes to prove that it definitely hasn't bettered. For the article to report on the Minister for Disabled People, actually admitting that employability needs to be improved for disability, just goes to show that it still happens, even after UK Government said that disability employment has improved. Clearly it hasn't, if the Minister for Disabled People is even admitting to the actual fact. I wonder if any actual research went into the claim on the UK Government website, or was it just to plaster over the issue, in the hopes that people won't notice, question or find out later on down the line? It's absolutely offensive to learn that UK Government are trying to sweeten the reality of disability, by only explaining the bare minimum. Employability for disability sadly remains a problem. I know this for a fact.

Having UK Government say the opposite to the **actual reality** of disability employment, just discriminates against disability further. UK Government isn't taking the real issue of disability employment seriously, and that in itself, **is a problem**. If UK Government isn't taking the real issue of disability unemployment seriously, then we have absolutely no hope of having any proper respect that we wholeheartedly deserve.

There maybe 'disabled' celebrities coming more to the forefront in recent years in the media, which again is fantastic, but discrimination does still happen in the 'real world'. Employment takes the brunt of the unjustified discrimination. I personally don't think that society really makes that connection between 'disabled' celebrities and 'everyday disabled' people. They can't, if disability discrimination is still occurring. The lines are blurred. There is a disconnect. This is what needs to be addressed. People tend to fictionalise what they see in the media, compared to what they

Disability vs Employability

actually see in reality. Admittedly, I'm only surmising here, but if you take into account the continuous battle for disability equality, my assumption for this disconnect becomes more plausible, in my own personal opinion anyway. I've tried to research this, but was unable to find anything related to my assumption. I would love to know if this theory is correct or not, but it is an interesting thing to actually think about in any case. Psychology, sociology and anything else to do with social behaviours are interesting, especially when talking about how these connect to topics like disability.

Going back, it is wonderful to know and actually see that the issues are beginning to be recognised and somewhat rectified slowly in media, as somewhat of an apology in a way, but so much more **needs** to be done to really get to the heart of the situation. Addressing disability discrimination properly, not just saying it for popularity. For any **real change to happen**, we need society to understand and mean it. To **want to change**. To be determined to achieve equality. Only then, do we have any **real** hope for what we are striving for. For anything to be successful, you must put the work in.

Employers need to recognise the error of their ways, (sooner rather than later), and be prepared to hire potential 'disabled' employees if they are qualified for the job. The employment sector is being constantly hit hard by all of the financial constraints nowadays, with things like the high cost of living, the pandemic etc. So employers could really benefit from hiring 'disabled' people if qualified. Fear shouldn't be an obstacle. The financial reasoning doesn't exist, as I've proved with the *Access to Work* grants that are available. Maybe it's time constraints on providing adequate accessibility, as to why employers tend not to hire someone with a disability? This would be a viable reason, but like I said, all buildings (excluding listed buildings) should have basic accessibility as standard.

Chapter 10
The Care Sector's Point of View

As this book is more of a generalised view of disability through the eyes of society, I thought it necessary to also ask people who work in the care profession, their views on the treatment of carers, support workers and care companies, to cover all aspects of the subject of disability.

Many 'disabled' people rely on carers, support workers and care companies to help them to live their life to the fullest in many ways.

These people in a care profession have an amazing career really, as carers and support workers enhance a 'disabled' person's life. This should be cause for satisfaction to people who work in the care profession. The knowledge alone of positively impacting the life of a person with a disability should be an incredible feeling, yet humbling.

"Helping those in need is not charity, it's humanity." – [Abhijit Naskar]

The reality is extremely different from how it was years ago. *"Adult social care funding has been under pressure for several years." – [House of Commons Library, 'Adult Social Care Funding (England)']*

It's no secret that this is the reality of the care profession today, not just for adult social care, but also other areas within the sector. I want to delve deeper into why exactly this is. What went wrong, why, and can the care sector be salvaged and returned back to bygone days where the care profession wasn't under so much pressure?

"Local authorities have had their funding cut by central Government, leading to underfunded care packages, and a rising gap between fees paid and the cost of care caused by inflation." – ['Government Underfunding Social Care', Care Management Matters]

With constraints such as funding, overcrowding, lack of staff, inflation, and most recently, the COVID-19 pandemic, it's no wonder why the healthcare sector has been feeling abandoned in many ways.

The Care Sector's Point of View

It is more than just hospitals though, carers and support workers are often left to fend for themselves. I know this first hand, because of mum.

When I'm at home, mum is my main carer, yes I have Judi, but she only comes once a week to take me out, so mum is my main carer. She is absolutely incredible with what she does to help me everyday. Yes, I am mostly independent, but I need mum's help with certain things during the day, (mainly personal care). I maybe biased here because she's my mum, but it's true, she does everything in her power to help me when I need it, and in my personal opinion, deserves better treatment and support from the people who are supposed to help and support carers and support workers.

Mum won't mind me saying, but she's in her sixties now (as of writing this) and receives her pension. Years ago though, mum had a weekly Carer's Allowance which she had because of me. When mum reached pension age, her Carer's Allowance was automatically taken from her.

"You cannot get the full amount of both Carer's Allowance and your State Pension at the same time. If your pension is £76.75 a week or more, you will not get a Carer's Allowance payment. If your pension is less than £76.75 a week, you'll get a Carer's Allowance payment to make up the difference." – [Gov.UK]

I do find it utterly disgusting that if you're a carer, especially if you care for a family member, and you receive Carer's Allowance, why it should be then just taken when the carer reaches pension age, (if the amount is above the amount stated in the quote above)? It doesn't make any logical sense and completely baffles me if I'm honest.

Carer's Allowance is:

"If you spend at least 35 hours a week caring for someone with an illness or disability, you may be eligible for extra money called Carer's Allowance. It is paid at a rate of £76.75 per week (2023/24)." – [Carers UK]

A State Pension is:

"A regular payment made by the state to people of or above the official retirement age

The Care Sector's Point of View

*and to some widows and disabled people." –
[OED]*

It's not fair that carers who reach pension age are denied Carer's Allowance payment. Really, Carer's Allowance is basically for carers to spend that money on the person that they care for. State Pension is for a carer to have a means to live after a lifetime of working hard. It really doesn't make any sense that carers, who's pension is above the stated above, are then penalised just for a well-deserved reward. A pension isn't designed to be spent on the person being cared for, this is exactly why Carer's Allowance was introduced.

There's a danger that could potentially affect 'disabled' people because of this, carers may choose to leave the profession just because of something that could be reversed. 'Disabled' people will end up losing out as a direct result of the complete and utter disregard for human rights.

Nobody wants that, especially UK Government, as this would just create more strain on an ever decreasing healthcare system. Jeff Dawson, Managing Director of *1st Enable Ltd.*, explained to me that the care sector are basically already on their knees in terms of hiring the right staff for the job. So many of these care companies are turning to anyone who applies, hiring them on the spot, just as a means of keeping the company open. This is wrong because there is then a danger of hiring the wrong people, putting the person needing care at more risk. This is the harsh reality of the care sector in the twenty-first century.

"Almost all (99 per cent) of healthcare leaders agreed that there is currently a social care workforce crisis in their area. Almost all further agreed that the crisis is worse than it was 12 months ago (94 per cent) and expected it to deteriorate even more as we move towards winter (92 per cent)." – ['System on a cliff edge: addressing challenges in social care capacity', 28th July 2022, NHS Confederation]

UK Government should really look into this and try to rectify the situation. If this continues, then there **is a real danger** of putting those in need of care at real risk. Hiring anyone in the care profession isn't good enough. It's not ideal, nor is it responsible. This is only happening because the

The Care Sector's Point of View

care sector has no means of providing the resources and services to a high standard, because of either lack of funding, staffing shortages or just too much work for the amount of staff. I'm not saying this to shock you or cause any angst. It's the truth. It's basically on the news every single day and night. It's nothing new, but still nothing is happening to try and change this.

Deborah Bayley really gave me a harrowing account of the healthcare system from her point of view, both with having Ashley and her mum, Jean, on the state of support she's received from the healthcare system.

Ashley

QUESTIONS

"Did you receive any help from social services when Ashley was younger? If so, explain how easy/difficult was it to receive help?"

"Not when he was very young (Primary School age) but I wasn't asking for help in anyway. I was unaware of what was available in the form of physical help/funding/equipment. It was only chatting with other parents of children with

special needs that I began to find out what help etc. was possible." – [Deborah Bayley, social media participant, mum and daughter]

"Do you think social services could improve their support services? Why?"

"During Ashley's lifetime up to now, I don't think we could count on 2 hands how many social workers we have seen. Some have only been assigned to him for a very short time which is very frustrating because Ashley got to know them then he had to get used to someone new. Plus, it means I've had to explain Ashley's condition and needs, time and time again." – [Deborah Bayley, social media participant, mum and daughter]

This was indeed the overriding issue. UK Government lacked the obvious need for telling 'disabled' people and/or their families their entitlements. I personally went through the same issues when I was younger. It was really only through hearsay how 'disabled' people and/or their families received the entitlements/help. How was this fair? The Internet wasn't as prominent as it is today, people couldn't research these things, like they can today. I don't know if UK Government has changed their approach, I mean the Internet is a God send today for researching important issues such as entitlements and help for disability, so I'm guessing that knowledge of these things is far better than it once was, but UK Government should really have stepped up and provided information about entitlements and help that was out there for disability in the past, maybe through a pamphlet or a booklet that was distributed out by local councils who housed a 'disabled' person? It's not difficult.

Deborah's analysis of the improvements to social services also says a lot. Again, I've been through exactly the same. Social workers seem to come and go, and for me, it is frustrating but I can deal with it, however for someone like Ashley who has complex needs, understanding isn't an option. The issue of there being a turnstile of sorts when it comes to social workers, having to explain yet again your, or your loved ones needs is absolutely frustrating, pathetic and just generally a waste of time. As no sooner you've explained the condition, that support worker has suddenly left and another social worker has come to replace the previous one. It's tedious. You would think that the healthcare system would have your needs on file today? This would make the most logical sense after all. It would save a lot of time and money in the long run if they did exactly this. Time and money that could be better spent improving waiting times within the *NHS*? This is just a suggestion. People often talk about the current state of the healthcare system, not wasting time and money constantly having to replace social workers would significantly help, alongside having a person's condition on record, so that the person doesn't have to constantly repeat themselves, over and over, would be beneficial. I really don't know why this isn't logical to Government? I have a degree, in graphic design, but I've just come up with a couple of realistic ideas that would ultimately be beneficial to free up time and money to be better spent on sorting out the crisis the healthcare system constantly finds itself.

UK Government and local authorities have a duty of care. The problem is that the Government have no ideas for how to manage everything effectively and efficiently. I don't have a degree in healthcare, but even I can give suggestions, and that **is** saying something. The *NHS* is our most proudest and prominent achievement that the UK has produced. Yet, Government are just sitting idly by, watching our greatest achievement suffer. Government   need to realise this and make changes to their approach. They need to understand that disabilities require different types of care. Some, like with Ashley, need to keep to a routine, and some don't have to. I understand that funding can be an issue, but others may not, others only see their routine disrupted and this causes upset and frustration to the 'severely disabled' person. UK Government, and by extension, local authorities don't understand this, because simply, they don't understand disability. If Government acknowledged and prioritised disability as they like to claim they do, none of these things would be an issue. My need for writing would be redundant.

Jean

QUESTIONS

"What support have you received for your mum?"

"Offered a possible place in a home for a few days/nights for respite but I didn't ask for it and my mum didn't want to go." – [Deborah Bayley, social media participant, mum and daughter]

"Has that support been positive or negative in your own opinion? Why?"

"Negative. It scared my mum into thinking she was being put in a home. A few day visits would have been better but that wasn't possible." – [Deborah Bayley, social media participant, mum and daughter]

This is what needs to be recognised by Government. Good intentions are redundant when they put the person in the centre of it all under unnecessary pressure. People with illnesses such as dementia find it really hard to accept change. It can be anxiety inducing to the person with dementia, they don't understand why, they feel as if they are being bullied, forced into something that they don't want to do. Imagine if you had a very independent life, you were social and active, then you develop something as hard hitting to accept as dementia. You are then labelled as 'vulnerable' and 'unfit to look after

The Care Sector's Point of View

yourself'. All of a sudden you are catapulted into a life of confusion, angst, and frustration. The local authority suggests that moving to a care home would be the best option for you, leaving behind your life. You don't know why you are being forced into this. All you want is the life you once had, but local authorities have suddenly arrived to disrupt that life. How would you feel if this happened to you? Dementia patients cannot comprehend the world around them, they take each day at face value. They don't realise that they have a choice as more often than not, this isn't explained to them. Government should rethink their approach towards dealing with dementia patients. The anxiety of it all just causes unnecessary stress to both the person and by extension, their families. Offering something that isn't at all beneficial to a person who has an illness such as dementia, only creates more harm than good. Government desperately needs to change their approach to dementia patients. The current system, it seems, isn't working if Jean has had a negative experience.

1st Enable Ltd. have a wonderful and refreshing attitude to the care they provide. I know, because

The Care Sector's Point of View

I've seen it first hand from the events I have been lucky enough to attend, that has been organised by the company. First of all, they actually put their clients and staff first, I know that sounds obvious on the surface, but honestly and shockingly, few other care companies have this attitude. The staff at *1st Enable Ltd.* are careful to hire the right people for the job. I must say that from what I've personally witnessed, and I'm not just saying this out of pleasantries, I genuinely mean that each individual staff member hired at *1st Enable Ltd.* are so caring and friendly to the clients and also the public. Nothing's too much trouble. They listen to both clients and their families about how best to care for them. They do things with the clients, goals that they want to achieve, and they help the clients to achieve those desired goals. They have residential care where clients live in their own small communities and are able to live somewhat of an independent life. They listen to each individual client's needs and adapts accommodation to suit those needs. They hold events for clients and staff on a regular basis. They give out awards to staff members. The company is truly astonishing. *1st Enable Ltd.* truly deserves to have the recognition for the incredible work they do. What I'm saying just doesn't do the company justice but I hope that I've given you at least a sense of how fantastic they are? It's the little things that have the greatest impact in the long run.

This is exactly why other care companies should follow the example that 1st *Enable Ltd.* have created. If other care companies had the same level of determination to succeed, then I believe that the issues the Government have with social care would greatly lessen. However, this isn't a dream, this is the reality. The harsh reality of a sector basically exhausted from the constant demands from UK Government. A Government who finds it easy to ignore the issues. Not rewarding the healthcare system properly for their dedication, time and effort. If this continues, then I do highly believe that the healthcare system as a whole will unfortunately disappear. The high Street is experiencing the exact same issue with retailers replacing healthcare. Numerous stores have entered administration or filed for bankruptcy because they have no money or backing from UK Government to ensure that actual stores, physical stores survive. The rise of social media is one factor in this decline, but also the total ignorance of Government. Ignoring an issue, burying your head in the sand isn't going to rectify an issue. You are only making it worse. I wholeheartedly believe that if the healthcare system continues to have the same lack of attention from Government, then it'll only be a matter of time until the healthcare profession as a whole will face the same fate as retail.

"...I feel the staffing crisis has been ongoing for a long period of time and central government have not invested in social care." – [Cara White, Registered Manager, 1st Enable Ltd.]

The care profession **deserves** better. The care profession **deserves** more support. If the care profession receives the support they deserve, then there wouldn't be any hypothetical issues to any 'disabled' clients.

The National Bobath Cerebral Palsy Centre in London said:

"There are 130,000 people in the UK, living with cerebral palsy, of which 30,000 are children. We believe each one of those people

should have the opportunity to reach their full potential. We believe that true EDI in society for disabled people comes with a cost that our Government should meet. It requires appropriate health care services, bespoke educational provision, therapy services and equipment and an understanding that having a disability has added unseen costs that the Government should support." – [Lorraine Kirby, Marketing and Communications Manager, The National Bobath Cerebral Palsy Centre, London]

By rights, UK Government should be more financially supportive of disability and by extension, the care sector as a whole. By not providing this financial support, UK Government is putting into jeopardy people's potential, as the care sector doesn't really have the means themselves to provide adequate resources needed to ensure that people do reach their full potential. It's unfair on the person and the care sector. I can imagine that it's quite frustrating to the care sector, not being able to provide adequate resources.

If you've read *CP Isn't Me*, then you'll know how much *The Bobath Centre* means to me. I attended their Cardiff branch, (now *Cerebral Palsy Cymru*) three times as a child for a fortnight block of physiotherapy.

I am so pleased to say that *Cerebral Palsy Cymru* have also contributed to this book.

"At Cerebral Palsy Cymru, our mission is to improve the quality of life of all children in Wales living with cerebral palsy. Equality is a basic human right and should be available to all. We need to embrace this globally to ensure everyone can participate fully in society. This includes ensuring individuals and families have access to the resources and help they need to fully participate. We work closely with our families to ensure that they feel supported and empowered to help their child in the best way possible and we will continue to collaborate with families, supporters, funders and policy makers to achieve equality, and the best possible outcomes, for children and families living with cerebral palsy across Wales." –

The Care Sector's Point of View

[Jenny Carroll, Cerebral Palsy Cymru Centre Director & Consultant Physiotherapist]

This is what *Cerebral Palsy Cymru* do, and they do it so well. Their dedication to ensure that children with CP and their families have the best support to live as independently as possible is incredible. I saw it through those three times that I attended the Centre when it was still under the name *The Bobath Centre*. Their ethos hasn't changed. Their name may have changed over the years, but their selflessness hasn't. They go above and beyond to ensure that children and their families who attend receive the best possible chance of a 'normal' life. I remember when I attended for the last time at the age of sixteen, I stood up and took a few steps unaided, to the astonishment of my family, and to me. I will always have a special place in my heart for *Cerebral Palsy Cymru*. I just want to take this opportunity to thank you ever so much for your support and guidance. Without your input, I wouldn't have developed the motor skills I have to live as independently as I do. Thank you.

For context, I asked the main London Centre to also describe what they do.

"The National Bobath Cerebral Palsy Centre provides treatment and therapy for people of all ages living with the condition cerebral palsy. It is also a National Training Centre, educating health care professionals, care-workers and families in all aspects of the Bobath Approach, either in person at our purpose-fitted facility in Watford, online or remotely at external premises. We see children from just a few weeks old, right through their teens and into adulthood. We provide families with information and advice, and our therapy is family-oriented. After a block of therapy, for example, families can continue at home using instructions from our Bobath therapists. We are also, informally, a hub for families to make contact with each other through services such as BoBaby!, our weekly online and in-person sessions for children under 2.5." – [Lorraine Kirby, Marketing and Communications Manager, The National Bobath Cerebral Palsy Centre, London]

Not funding this type of treatment and support is baffling to me. Why wouldn't Government provide adequate funding for charities and organisations to continue to provide this level of support to those who need it? Government are really just shooting themselves in the foot by not supporting those who provide support to those who need support. *The Bobath Centre, London* and *Cerebral Palsy Cymru* in LLanishen, Cardiff, alongside the other branches across the UK do phenomenal work to ensure that their clients have the best possible chance of independence. I know first-hand.

"The National Bobath Cerebral Palsy Centre is a centre of excellence offering trauma-led, multi-disciplinary, holistic treatment, therapy, advice and information all in one place. Finding out that a child has a disability can be a challenging and emotional time for families. The standard healthcare pathways and provisions can't always meet their needs. We treat the individual and families are a vital part of the programme." – [Lorraine Kirby, Marketing and Communications Manager, The National Bobath Cerebral Palsy Centre, London]

Government should help the care sector with funding. These organisations such as *The Bobath*

The Care Sector's Point of View

Cerebral Palsy Centre, Cerebral Palsy Cymru, and *1st Enable Ltd.* do what they can to keep their services going, by holding events etc., but this isn't acceptable. The care sector has enough to do without having to constantly think about how to fund their services. Government should help in some way. I know Government have a lot of decisions to make that require funding to continue. I also realise that asking Government to help financially support the care sector more, would undoubtedly mean a knock-on effect on society in terms of cost, but surely there's a way to help the care sector a little more without it impacting greatly on society as a whole?

Going back to Jeff Dawson, and the harsh reality that care companies are hiring anyone regardless if they are qualified and suitable for a moment, I recently attended the *1st Enable Ltd.* PBS conference, and it was clear that their approach to providing care to their clients is profoundly better in terms of client needs and the ways in which they are dedicated to providing care. Staff are meticulously hired on qualifications and personality. Just because you may have a disability, doesn't mean you don't have a

The Care Sector's Point of View

personality. *1st Enable Ltd.* understands this, and goes above and beyond to make sure that the right level of care is provided to each individual. Every disability is different, so every need is different. The company does absolutely everything in their power to make sure that their clients are properly cared for and as independent as possible regardless of ability. This is the standard that all care companies should follow. I've personally told them this myself. The level of detail that goes into making sure that the company doesn't fall victim to the other care companies is incredible. They go above and beyond. *1st Enable Ltd.* should by rights have some recognition for the amazing work they do. It's honestly astonishing how much they do to ensure staff and clients alike are both happy and catered for. I've personally never come across a care company like it before, and sadly, I doubt I will ever see another equal or greater to *1st Enable Ltd.* Saying that though, *1st Enable Ltd.* aren't immune to staff shortages due to competitive game playing.

"...I think the margins for things such as staff uplifts is minimal which then directly affects

staff retention. We have competitors such as the council who are offering substantial staff perks and higher rates of pay. We have lost several members of staff due to this reasoning." – [Cara White, Registered Manager, 1st Enable Ltd.]

Cara is speaking from experience. It's incredibly bewildering to me that local councils are in effect, enticing people who work in the care sector with bribes, in order to gain more staff for other companies in need. That behaviour basically can be compared to a villain of a film. The only reason why these companies are in need in the first place is due to the incompetence of both local councils and UK Government alike. If they managed to do something productive about the situation rather than bribing others, ultimately affecting the abandoned care companies to pick up the pieces and go through the painstaking work of hiring another employee with the same qualities as the previous staff member, then far less stress would fall on the healthcare system as a whole, in my own personal opinion anyway.

The Care Sector's Point of View

Personally, I also feel quality of support is implicated due to financial reasoning. The sad reality is that other care companies are unfortunately falling victim to this dog eat dog scenario that the healthcare system is finding itself. Hiring individuals with little to no experience just to keep up with the pressures of the job, but that hiring becoming a regular occurrence as the staff may get bored, or find a better job that may pays significantly more than what they were making working for a care company.

"I think the system is very complex and is a bottomless money pit, I think the government is trying to destroy everything to make it private. I don't think the current government will ever fund it properly. However, I do think people abuse the system and money is wasted in a lot of areas." – [Hayley Harrison, healthcare support worker]

This comes directly from someone who is working in the *NHS*. Having this information is a real eye-opener. You hear it on the news constantly nowadays about the continuous battles the healthcare system is undergoing, especially since the recent COVID-19 pandemic, but somehow, unless we know someone who works in the care profession, we somehow distance ourselves from the reality in a way. We know about the issues of course, but unless you either work within the profession yourself, or know someone who does, we don't tend to concern ourselves with the difficulties. The **only time** we tend to really care about the state of the *NHS* is when it impacts our own lives.

Hayley Harrison is my cousin, Paul's wife, so she is family, she very kindly offered to participate in this chapter by giving her own thoughts on the state of the *NHS*. Hayley's answers were very direct, (as you can see), she didn't sugar-coat anything, of which I appreciate. It's brutal, but her answers are honest, which again, I personally appreciate. Honesty is vital in the fight for equality in **all areas of life**. We won't really learn anything if we still insist on not knowing the realities. The **real realities**. The **truthful and honest accounts**. It maybe hard to hear, but in order to give an opportunity for equality, we need to hear every single difficulty. Only then, by learning the true reality, we can have a choice to change it.

The Care Sector's Point of View

"I think central government does fund the care sector adequately, however, the delegated authority to councils and the NHS almost always means the sector never sees its genuine intentions of funding it properly – it gets swallowed up by the 'system', before we really see any of this investment for us to be able to set to work and innovate..." – [Jeff Dawson, Managing Director of 1st Enable Ltd.]

Jeff's analysis here is quite interesting, as he suggests that it's the delegated authorities who are actually responsible for this very deep decline of the care sector. That the actual finger of blame is to be pointed directly at the individual councils instead of main Government. He suggests that any money delegated, automatically goes straight to the main system before the other parts of the system can see any of the money. Jeff's analysis is that, Government delegates money to individual councils, and those individual councils decide who is in more need. Basically if true, (and I'm not by any means saying this is, - I'm just going by Jeff Dawson here), but if this is true, local councils are playing God in a way, deciding who needs money more. This is baffling, terrifying and just generally awful.

The PBS conference I attended with *1st Enable Ltd.*, had speakers who were a mixture of clients, employees, and client family members where they shared their own personal stories and experiences. I'm not going to divulge any of the individual's names who shared their stories out of respect, but what I will say is that I realised that the healthcare sector continues to struggle to not only survive, but a lot of care companies struggle to meet the needs of clients. It does seem to me that the healthcare profession just label people without actually putting in the effort to cater the care to individuals. It is down to the pressures that UK Government unfortunately put on the healthcare system, such as time constraints and the inevitable stresses they bring, but pressurising anyone in an impossible situation to deliver on unrealistic demands is enough to cause stress to anyone. I'm not naming names out of privacy, but the majority of the stories in the PBS conference, I personally feel needs to be highlighted to show the reality of the healthcare system.

The Care Sector's Point of View

One speaker spoke about an ordeal that they faced where they were constantly being moved into different mental health facilities, this one person has personality disorder and basically was really forced into the mental health facility without actually having an opportunity to find out about the person. They said in the conference that their constant argument with the healthcare sector was *"I'm sad, not mad"*, this absolutely speaks volumes. This speaker was forced into a facility with other, more severe individuals, (mental health wise) where there was constant violence towards staff members and in turn other patients.

Restraining patients in mental health facilities and using punishments us sadly a common occurrence of hospitals that are designed to assist people with mental health issues. Restraining patients especially in the twenty-first century is an absolute barbaric way to defuse any situation, especially if the situation isn't considered serious. It's something that belongs in asylums of the past, not today. I mean the act of restraining patients really is for the safety of others. Restraining is designed to defuse individuals who present a danger to others, not to be used as a means to harm those who don't present as a threat. However, it is safe to say that restraining is unfortunately used as a method of coping with the pressures advertently put on the healthcare system. This one speaker self harmed, and as punishment, they were restrained, which is an horrific ordeal in itself, but also they said as an added punishment, their possessions were taken away every time they self harmed. How is this plausible? Why did the hospital in question feel that this was the best method to use to encourage patients not to self harm? It had the opposite effect unsurprisingly. The speaker said as a result, they would still self harm, but do it secretly as to not have their possessions taken from them. This doesn't help individuals to overcome any issues, mentally or otherwise. The speaker said that self harm, was for them, a way to punish themselves, but the facility only added to that by inflicting punishments. Really, the speaker said that they were being punished for punishing themselves. This, to me at least, doesn't provide any logical sense. It's in fact ironically disgraceful. Facilities such as a mental health facility, should provide the care and the support that is needed to help those who need help the most, not just add to the torment.

Restraining and punishing those who are severely 'disabled' is sadly yet another reality. Other speakers, (family members of clients of *1st Enable Ltd.*) horrifyingly spoke about their past experiences with having their 'disabled' family members restrained in places which were supposed to care for them, where they sustained abhorrent injuries. (Side note, all of the negativity experienced from family members and the clients themselves happened **before** they joined *1st Enable Ltd.*) Again it's something that you would expect from the nineteenth century. Severely 'disabled' people by rule are defenceless and innocent. To restrain a severely 'disabled' person in this day and age is inconceivable to me personally. I cannot actually see a viable reason for it to occur. Maybe stress, especially if said client is being a bit uncooperative? This however is just a theory, (and not a very good reason in my own personal opinion).

A lot of this form of abuse, (because at the end of the day, that is what it is, abuse, whether the healthcare system, local councils and UK Government would like to admit it or not), is a frequent feature on TV, on the news, and even documentaries. This is the reality, I'm not saying anything new or controversial, the reality of the constraints and as a direct result, the risk to patients and clients on these facilities are clear to see.

I get that local councils have a difficult decision to make every time any money is delegated. It's quite overwhelming I can imagine. It's quite a difficult thing to manage in a way, if you really think about it. Basically I'm torn. If Jeff is right in his suggestion, it is important that money is delegated first to the main system (hospitals etc.), and any money left would trickle through the rest of the system. Prioritising the main system does make sense. That shouldn't be called into question, however, because of how much decline the main system is in reality currently, the majority of the money is really just swallowed up and really the rest of the care sector just gets the tiny leftovers, the scraps.

The Care Sector's Point of View

This decline is blamed largely on the COVID-19 pandemic, which again, makes a lot of sense on the surface, but if you actually look into the issues, you will realise that these problems stretch further back before the pandemic. The pandemic of course hasn't helped matters, but this **definitely** isn't the start of the decline. Government cannot just solely blame one thing for how many issues there are. Realistically, (and obviously), for the amount of issues currently, the care profession was in serious trouble years before the pandemic. I said that I'm torn, I'm torn about who deserves the money more. This **shouldn't** have to be a problem. This is sadly the world we live in today. We have to try to make difficult, (and often dangerous) decisions for extremely important topics. It's absolutely terrifying.

"Out of day-to-day revenue spending for 2021/22: £71.5bn (37%) was spent on NHS provider staff costs. £32.1bn (17%) was spent on procurement. £14.9bn (8%) was spent on primary care." - [Health funding data analysis, BMA]

PROCUREMENT DEFINITION:

*"the   action   of   obtaining
or procuring something.*

*"financial assistance for the procurement of
legal advice" – [OED]*

This is fascinating to actually find out. It's there in
black and white. Knowing now how the money
was spent in the years twenty-twenty-one/twenty-
twenty-two speaks volumes and answers a lot of
questions as to why the *NHS* is in the situation it
finds itself. It's no wonder why the care branch of
the healthcare system suffers so much. Only **eight
percent** was delegated in those years to the care
profession. This is abhorrent. You could point that
famous finger of blame solely on the *NHS*, as this
would be the most logical place. However, as
going by Jeff Dawson, UK Government delegates
funds to the *NHS*, who then are responsible for
delegating money to the local councils, who then
themselves provide what's left onto the care
profession, which by this point is usually minimal
at best. It is the job of Government to ensure that
there is enough money for institutions such as the
whole healthcare system, not just pick and choose
and play God in a way. Prioritising sectors within

The Care Sector's Point of View

the healthcare system should never happen or be an option. The healthcare system as a whole should be the priority. Absolutely no section should be favoured, it should be prioritised as a collective, not individual. I shouldn't have to say this, it's obvious how much danger this would ultimately cause, and unfortunately does cause, just because of the lack of organisation and actual respect by Government. Pre-planning and organisation should always be a part of the funding plan.

"The NHS and social care help bring people into the world, are often there at the end of our lives, and we want to make sure people receive the best possible care whenever they need it. That means having a general practice (GP) appointment or being diagnosed in a timely manner, receiving treatment quickly when required and being cared for in your own home when living with a disability. We can help people to be better informed about how to prevent the need for healthcare in the first place and how to readily access healthcare through various pathways, and equip them to make informed choices with an expectation of

the service that will be provided to them." - *['Our Plan To Patients', 22 September 2022, Policy Paper, GOV.UK]*

This would of course be ideal, but the way the healthcare system is currently, struggling with staffing, mental health deterioration, overworking etc., this plan, delivered in twenty-twenty-two unfortunately isn't viable, reasonable nor realistic. Government cannot just expect the healthcare system to deliver on these promises at a drop of a hat, without proper support or planning anyway, and even if Government does pre-plan and support, this still doesn't mean that all of those promises would be delivered. Some maybe at a push, but not all. Although people working within the healthcare system are considered to be 'superheroes' especially during the pandemic (of which they wholeheartedly deserve that title for all of the selflessness they showed during the difficult time), in reality, these people are only human and can only do so much before reaching breaking point. We went on our doorsteps every single Thursday to applaud and show gratitude to the hardworking *NHS* workers during the pandemic, which was lovely and it showed that society appreciated the sacrifices made by healthcare workers in providing the best possible care to the most sickest of patients at the time, but is that enough? Showing gratitude for selflessness is great, but the healthcare profession needed more help and leadership from UK Government, in the form of resources, proper PIP equipment, and above all the money to be able to continue to provide the best care and save lives. I don't think it helped, actually I know it didn't help the dire situation with UK Government continuously going back and forth on COVID-19 procedures/ restrictions that the population should follow. This only caused more confusion and chaos to what was an already overstretched *National Health Service* at the time. Really, UK Government made everything worse in terms of creating additional pressures. Applause wasn't enough, applause wasn't helping solve the problem, action would've been the only logical way to help, and of course, not causing confusion to already an anxiety induced society.

The amount of strikes that have been undertaken since writing this second book especially, just proves that the healthcare system deserves more. The *NHS* as a whole, was celebrated when the idea was conceived in nineteen-forty-eight:

"The National Health Service began on 5 July 1948. Already the NHS, which Bevan described as "a great and novel undertaking", is the stuff of history. Few people now working in it had been born when it began. Those with clear memories of the early days grow fewer, and this book is in part a tribute to their work. It is the story of the NHS, how it was set up, what happened next, and why. It aims to give the reader, whether professionally involved in the NHS or not, a chronological framework of the main clinical and organisational events." - ['The history of the NHS', Nuffield Trust]

To go from an *NHS* which was set up to provide adequate care to all corners of society, and it being celebrated for being a free service after WWII to get Britain through the aftermath of war, to now the service, and everyone who works in it, feeling the undeniable pressures and stresses if what is now, in many ways, a shadow of it's former self, is utterly heart-breaking, and quite frankly, UK

The Care Sector's Point of View

Government should feel ashamed that they allowed the service to get into the state it has. Action to relieve the *NHS* by UK Government should be a top priority. Instead we live in a reality where infighting from Government is a regular occurrence. The blame game is in full swing every single day. How is this going to help anyone rectify the issues society face? There needs to be a clear, achievable plan, an objective to repair what's left of the *NHS*. Current healthcare shouldn't have to ever suffer because of indecisiveness. In my opinion, instead of the constant infighting, the blame games towards the opposition, the childish way politicians are dealing with each other. Instead of all of that, in my own personal opinion, every single political party should work together to ensure that the healthcare system is totally secure and that they constantly get the resources needed to ensure safety to clients and patients regardless of party politics.

The *NHS* is a gem, and we should be doing everything in our power to resolve any further damage. We owe it to the *NHS* and the healthcare profession and even ourselves to look into resolving issues, not creating more. We only have one *NHS*, it doesn't deserve this mistreatment. It deserves respect, and dignity.

I have a plea to UK Government, I'm not sure if they will ever read this, or any of my books, but it's worth a shot. Please, for the sake of humanity, the people who work in the healthcare system, the doctors, the nurses, the carers, the support workers, even the patients and clients, please look into helping an overstretched healthcare system by providing the resources and support needed to carry on treating, caring for, and saving the lives of countless anonymous individuals every single day without any hesitation. You owe them that much. Going from a thing of celebration to a worn out, shadow of it's former self, who are crying out for help with the continuous increase and demand, is a sad and inconceivable thing. If you respect the healthcare system, as you say you do in media, then show it. Again, actions speak louder than words. The time of childish behaviour is over. Please help and support a system that Jeff Dawson honestly says that is *"on it's knees"*. If this carries on the way it's going, there won't be such thing as a healthcare system. We need to act now,

The Care Sector's Point of View

and Government needs to take responsibility, show some initiative to take the lead on this action.

Chapter 11
Summing Up / Conclusion

Admittedly, when I was coming up with ideas for a second book, I really struggled. I wanted to write a second book because on subjects such as disability, I know that you have to keep the conversation going for it to have any credibility. One book of one person's experience sadly isn't going to be enough to have the desired impact to ultimately change perceptions. I did toy with the idea of continuing my story, but then I thought it would be a short book as I wrote the majority of my life within the first book. I was really struggling with ideas.

Then it hit me.

A book focused on society. Their viewpoint on disability, from the general public to the higher ups in society. I didn't know if I could actually achieve it, get people on board to be honest, alongside having input from people of high standing involved. I didn't know if anyone would agree. I had to give it a shot though.

Conclusion

I was absolutely amazed by the positive response from the general public and the people of high standing who were willing to contribute to this second book. I am still stunned by the eagerness of society, but I'm ever so grateful to each and every single person who has contributed to this second book. Without your input, a second book wouldn't exist. Thank you.

So,

What's the take away after all of that? Simple. We have come a long way, but so much more needs to be done to achieve full equality for all, regardless of ability.

Society, Government, and local authorities alike need to realise this, and take responsibility for making it happen. It can't just be left up to 'disabled' people and the care sector to try to change perceptions. It just can't. There needs to be proper support from the whole world really, and not support in a 'vulnerable' sense, but support in the sense of understanding, respect, adequate funding for resources, and equal opportunities for all. Enough with this Dickensian viewpoint on disability, it's getting boring. At the end of the day, everyone has an ability to do something. We need to stop labelling with those negative prefixes, and start understanding the reality of disability.

There could potentially be some light at the end of the tunnel, with the 'Disability Action Plan' on the horizon by UK Government. I do hope something has come of it though for society's sake more than anything else. By the time this book is published, a change for the better should be at least in the works, if not already achieved.

Disability isn't life limiting, it's society that actually limits our lives by denying us life. The proper ups and downs of life. People wrap us up, protect us, treat us like children. Society supervises our every move. It needs to stop, and stop now for good.

The question of ability should never have to be a part of any conversation. That question is redundant. As mentioned, everyone has abilities, some abilities are stronger than others in certain areas yes, but abilities are individual. We shouldn't be judged on our abilities. If you are going by this logic, then nobody on the planet has the ability to

Conclusion

do anything. What's the quote from Albert Einstein?

"Everybody is a genius. But if you judge a fish by its ability to climb a tree, it will live its whole life believing that it is stupid. " - [Albert Einstein]

Judging ultimately leads to self-sabotage, as mentioned. Society judges, which leads to people with disabilities feeling insignificant, which in turn, may lead to potential mental health issues. This should never be acceptable.

"No-one is good at everything, but everyone is good at something." – [Unknown]

It took me a long time to get to where I am today. It wasn't easy, but I got there. It was a combination of love and support from family, self determination, medication and having people believe in me.

One day, I just thought enough was enough, I just wanted it all to stop, and I came to the realisation that the only thing stopping me really, was me. Of course, there were factors that initially contributed to the deterioration of my mental health, high school, workplaces, and general discrimination was the main focus of my deterioration. I blamed everything and everyone else for the mental health issues, but really, the only thing, (and person) that was making me feel worthless, was in fact me. I kept living in the past, all of the negative experiences I had in my life, I kept replaying them constantly in my mind, I just couldn't help it, of course, I desperately wanted to, but I just couldn't. My thoughts consumed me, I just couldn't function, and that; only leads to one thing, mental health issues.

Dealing with things over a long period of time by yourself can be detrimental to your mental health, especially if the cause of the stress is down to other people.

"Oh yes, the past can hurt, but you can either run from it, or learn from it." – [Rafiki, 'The Lion King', 1994]

If you find yourself in that horrible situation, you owe it to yourself to voice whatever it is openly. Bottling things up just creates more angst and turmoil within your own mind, and as a direct result, you may turn that anger you feel to the

Conclusion

wrong person or people, more than likely loved ones. It isn't fair on them or on you. Instead, if you can, try to tell those who caused you to feel insignificant.

I'm doing it with my books, although indirectly, not naming names, but I'm telling the truth of the situation, getting it all out to clear my own mind, to save me from a life of constant self-sabotage, depression, anxiety, OCD, whatever, I'm helping myself. I'm more content, happy and back in control. I'm more confident, and more importantly, I really don't care about what others think of me by finally letting everyone know what has been festering in my mind for so many years. I'm not apologising. Why should I? Those people who caused me distress never apologised. I refuse to be put upon any longer, and if that makes anyone uncomfortable, then that's their problem, I'm done worrying, it's time to start living.

Judging ultimately leads to self-sabotage, as mentioned. Society judges, which leads to people with disabilities feeling insignificant, which in turn, may lead to potential mental health issues. This should never be acceptable.

Conclusion

"No-one is good at everything, but everyone is good at something." – [Unknown]

It took me a long time to get to where I am today. It wasn't easy, but I got there. It was a combination of love and support from family, self determination, medication and having people believe in me.

One day, I just thought enough was enough, I just wanted it all to stop, and I came to the realisation that the only thing stopping me really, was me. Of course, there were factors that initially contributed to the deterioration of my mental health, high school, workplaces, and general discrimination was the main focus of my deterioration. I blamed everything and everyone else for the mental health issues, but really, the only thing, (and person) that was making me feel worthless, was in fact me. I kept living in the past, all of the negative experiences I had in my life, I kept replaying them constantly in my mind, I just couldn't help it, of course, I desperately wanted to, but I just couldn't. My thoughts consumed me, I just couldn't function, and that; only leads to one thing, mental health issues.

Conclusion

Dealing with things over a long period of time by yourself can be detrimental to your mental health, especially if the cause of the stress is down to other people.

"Oh yes, the past can hurt, but you can either run from it, or learn from it." – [Rafiki, 'The Lion King', 1994]

If you find yourself in that horrible situation, you owe it to yourself to voice whatever it is openly. Bottling things up just creates more angst and turmoil within your own mind, and as a direct result, you may turn that anger you feel to the wrong person or people, more than likely loved ones. It isn't fair on them or on you. Instead, if you can, try to tell those who caused you to feel insignificant.

I'm doing it with my books, although indirectly, not naming names, but I'm telling the truth of the situation, getting it all out to clear my own mind, to save me from a life of constant self-sabotage, depression, anxiety, OCD, whatever, I'm helping myself. I'm more content, happy and back in control. I'm more confident, and more importantly, I really don't care about what others think of me by finally letting everyone know what has been festering in my mind for so many years. I'm not apologising. Why should I? Those people who caused me distress never apologised. I refuse to be put upon any longer, and if that makes anyone uncomfortable, then that's their problem, I'm done worrying, it's time to start living.

Family Photos

Someone said to me whilst I was writing this book, that adding a few photos of myself would be a nice thing. I did think that myself, but I thought where could I put any? This book wasn't really about me or my life. I was nearly going to scrap the photo idea altogether, but then it dawned on me. This book is all about trying to change perceptions on disability, what better way to do that than to show past photos of myself with my family living a life as independently as possible?

All of these photos are of either myself growing up, or my immediate family, (mum, dad, Ian, Ceri, Rosie, Tommy, my late nan, Mary and my late dog, Bubbles), of without whom, I really don't think I'd be who I am today. So, to reiterate, I want to do this to let the world know that despite having a disability, you can live a life that is considered 'normal'. My family did this in abundance, as you can see.

"If you enter this world knowing you are loved, and you leave this world knowing the same, then everything that happens in between can be dealt with." – [Michael Jackson]

Thank you so much to my family for always making me feel loved and apart of society. All of you have always made me feel that I can do anything that I set my mind to. Everything that I have achieved is because of your love, support and encouragement.

For standing by me when times were tough, and not giving up on me. I will never forget your determination to help me through. I got there because of you. I love you all so very much, and I always will. I hope I've made you all proud.

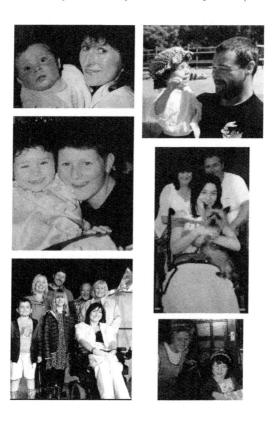

Acknowledgements

I would like to now personally thank the people and places who have kindly contributed to this book, of without whom, this book wouldn't be possible.

Publisher/Editor

J. Allan Longshadow

Book Cover Artwork

Samantha Maxwell, Original artwork concept

Martin Maxwell, book cover artwork artist

Clair Girvan, original book cover sketch artist, www.etsy.com/uk/shop/NeurospicyArtist

Research – Contributors

Lesley Griffiths, Member of the Senedd for Wrexham

All anonymous survey participants

Senedd Commission employee, The Senedd, Cardiff

Kerry Evans, Disability Liaison Officer at Wrexham AFC

Ciara Lawrence, ambassador, MENCAP

Jenny Carroll, Cerebral Palsy Cymru Centre Director & Consultant Physiotherapist, Llanishen, Cardiff

Lorraine Kirby, Marketing and Communications Manager, The National Bobath Cerebral Palsy Centre, London

Giovanni Cinque, Marketing & Campaigns Manager, Colostomy UK

Richard Luke, Specialist Information Officer and Programme Lead, Scope

Jeff Dawson, Managing Director of 1st Enable Ltd.

Cara White, Registered Manager of 1st Enable Ltd.

Darren Franks, Fire Safety Management and Evacuation Solutions, Globex Evacuation Solutions

Kandi Pickard, NDSS President and CEO (National Downs Syndrome Society)

Robin Tuffley, Closomat Ltd.

Jennifer Bergmann, actor, writer, and aspiring director, adayinthelifeofapwd.weebly.com/

Aideen Blackborough, disability trainer, speaker and author

Kim Kelly, author, 'FIGHT LIKE HELL: The Untold History of American Labor'

Michael M. Chemers, author

Jill Clark, campaigner, *Changing Places UK'* and blogger

Clair Girvan, disabled artist and social worker

Dr. Sally Witcher, former CEO of Inclusion Scotland

Dr. John Woolf, Labour Councillor, author and historian

Stephen Naysmith, Social Affairs Correspondent, The Herald

Brian Abram (Grandad Wheels), author

Keiligh Baker, broadcast journalist, BBC News

Helen Carroll, journalist

Natasha Ishak, freelance journalist

Kirsty Taylor, disabled model and Co Support Leader

Paul Wild, actor

Jacqueline Whelan, barrister

Mark Desa and Krystal Schulze, co-hosts of M4G Advocacy Media

Tanya Charteris-Black, Independent Cinema Office, (ICO)

David Parker, Windmill Barns Holiday Lets, Coughton, Warwickshire

Mark Masters, Community Leader, 'You Are The Media'

Hayley Harrison, healthcare support worker

Hayley Murphy, email participant

Social media participants, anonymous

Karen Wright, Wrexham University support worker

Judi Copnall, support worker, Bevris Support Ltd.

Natalie Copnall-Aspin, social media participant

Debbie Davies Bellis, support worker and social media participant

Elika Carrol, social media participant

Sarah Smith, social media participant

Hari Candlin, social media participant

Maja Tompkins, social media participant

Alice Trevor, singer/songwriter and social media participant

Brian Maddocks, social media participant

Anonymous, social media participant,

Lynne Davies Coulson, social media participant

Hayley Wellerd, Occupational Therapist and mum of a 'disabled' daughter

Margaret Foster, email participant

Maddy C, social media participant

Elle Williams, social media participant

Linda Smith, social media participant

Deborah Bayley, social media participant

Research - Companies and Organisations

House of Commons, London

The Senedd, Cardiff, South Wales

BBC

BBC News

UK Equality and Human Rights Commission

Australian Human Rights Commission

Scouts UK

Wrexham AFC

Liverpool FC

Wales Millennium Centre, Cardiff

Cerebral Palsy Cymru, Llanishen, Cardiff

The National Bobath Cerebral Palsy Centre, London

Eagle Passenger Lifters, Haycomp Pty Ltd.

Changing Places UK

MENCAP

Closomat Ltd.

Globex Evacuation Solutions

Scope

The Sequal Trust

Nuffield Trust

1st Enable Ltd.

Empeiria Training

Colostomy UK

The Lynchburg Museum System,
www.lynchburgmuseum.org

MDM Designs Ltd.

National Downs Syndrome Society (NDSS)

M4G Advocacy Media, Texas, USA

Independent Cinema Office (ICO)

Windmill Barns Holiday Lets, Coughton, Warwickshire

A Special Thank You:

Family

Mum

Dad

Ian

Ceri

Rosie

Tommy

My dear late Nan, Mary

My late little pumpkin, Bubbles

Friends

Rebecca

Stacey

Lucy

Shannon

Emily

Jasmine

Elika

Printed in Great Britain
by Amazon

40828405R00334